Westminster Cathedral
An Illustrated History

Patrick Rogers

First published 2012 by Oremus - The Magazine of Westminster Cathedral

© 2012 Westminster Cathedral
42 Francis Street, London SW1P 1QW
www.westminstercathedral.org.uk

British Library Cataloguing in Publication Data

A catalogue record for this book is available from the British Library

ISBN 978-0-9560211-2-0

Design and Art Direction: Julian Game
Printed in England by 4-Print

Previous page: The Great Rood standing in the Cathedral nave after being painted by William Christian Symons. Autumn 1903.

Contents

FOREWORD BY THE ARCHBISHOP OF WESTMINSTER

Westminster Cathedral was designed and built in the closing years of Victorian England. Discrimination against Catholics was largely a thing of the past, and they had become increasingly assertive and influential in the life of the nation. Westminster Cathedral, with its striking appearance, impressive size and imposing campanile, was both an assertion of this newfound confidence and a practical response to the need for a great national church in the centre of London to cater for the growing number of Catholics in the capital and elsewhere.

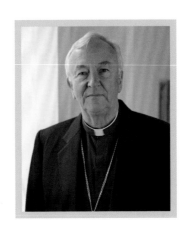

The Most Reverend Vincent Nichols, Eleventh Archbishop of Westminster.

Patrick Rogers takes us back in time to when the Cathedral site was a marshland called Bulinga Fen. He then describes the activities which took place there when it had become known as Tothill Fields, and then the prison or 'House of Correction' which was built on the site. Finally he discusses the reasons why the early Byzantine style of building was adopted as most appropriate for the Cathedral. There follows an account of the construction, the first parish, the formation of the Choir and Choir School and the development of the liturgy and music. Then the author turns to particular features - St Edward's Tower, the Great Rood, the baldacchino, the Stations of the Cross and so on, before proceeding to the Cathedral decoration, particularly the marbles and mosaics which are described in detail.

Patrick Rogers has spent the last twenty years studying the Cathedral, and this book, his fourth on the subject, is the result of considerable research both in this country and overseas. He has also interviewed many of those involved in the events he describes, or their descendants - Gilbert Pownall's daughter, Eric Gill's nephew, and the artist and mosaicist Aelred Bartlett, for example - in order to establish just what really happened. In particular he has tried to answer the questions for which there seemed to be no adequate explanation. He contacted Count Benckendorff's family members to find out why he, a Russian, had been buried in the Cathedral crypt, and he has sifted through newspapers of the 1940s to discover why a monkey, included in the carved altarpiece of St George's Chapel, was subsequently removed.

Westminster Cathedral has been described as one of the finest buildings in London and as the last great example of building in brick. But of course the Cathedral is also the centre of Catholic worship in England and a building of faith and prayer. For all who admire and appreciate the Cathedral - as parishioners, visitors, for its architecture or simply because of its sense of tranquillity and peace - this book is a treasure-trove of information and wonder.

I am most grateful to its author, Patrick Rogers, for his devotion to the Cathedral, for his painstaking work and for giving us such an authoritative and beautiful history and guide.

+ *Vincent Nichols*

The Most Reverend Vincent Nichols
Archbishop of Westminster

INTRODUCTION

I first came to Westminster Cathedral at the age of seven on my first visit to London, accompanied by a kindly maiden aunt. In contrast to the other places we went to, such as Buckingham Palace, the Tower of London, Madame Tussaud's, London Zoo, Hamley's Toy Shop, Lyons Corner House and the Charing Cross Hotel (where we stayed), I remember the Cathedral as a vast, dark, cavernous building, but I never forgot my first visit. After university I worked for the government, analysing and assessing information on political, economic, military and security developments overseas. While working in Whitehall I returned to the Cathedral to attend Mass and my retirement in late 1991 coincided with the formation of the Guild of Volunteers by the then Cathedral Administrator, Mgr Pat O'Donoghue. I was his second recruit.

While serving on the Cathedral Information Desk and as a tour guide, and subsequently as Visits Officer and Tours Director, it became clear that many of the questions asked by visitors went unanswered, (or indeed were answered incorrectly), examples being: When was the first Mass?; Who uses the little alcoves in the apse?; Where does all the marble come from?; What happened in the War? It seemed logical to use my previous experience to try to answer such questions. This resulted in thousands of hours spent in the Cathedral archives, in libraries, museums and archives elsewhere and in interviews with those who still remembered what had happened. It also resulted in me being bitten by a gypsy dog at a marble quarry in County Cork, suffering a serious fall on Mount Pentelicon near Athens, being pickpocketed on a bus in Sicily and getting trapped at night at the Imperial Porphyry quarries in the mountains of Gebel Dokhan in the Egyptian Eastern Desert. It was all huge fun and resulted in a series of articles and three books on the history and decoration of the Cathedral, its marbles and mosaics. I was then asked to bring together all the information I had collected on the Cathedral over the previous twenty years into one single volume, with plenty of pictures and an index. This book is the result.

The sources for the book are referred to in individual chapters and are also listed in Part VIII. However, I must thank a number of people, some of them now deceased, for their help, advice, encouragement and support: Mrs Pia Bruno Allasio of Moldovi in Italy, Aelred Bartlett, Paul Bentley of the British Association for Modern Mosaic, Walter Bernadin, Joan Bond of the Catholic National Library, Mrs Humphrey Brooke (granddaughter of Count Benckendorff), Evaline Brown, Jane Buxton (Gilbert Pownall's daughter), Stephen and Peter Cox, Gerald Culliford, Ivor Davies of Penarth in Wales, Alfredo Galasso of Rome, Tom Heldal of the Geological Survey of Norway in Trondheim, Peter Howell of the Victorian Society, Tessa Hunkin, Tanis Kent, Sheree Leeds of Surrey House, Norwich, Ian Macdonald, Christi Morgan, Alyson Price of the British Institute in Florence, Monica Price of the Oxford University Museum of Natural History, Birdie Scott and John Skelton (Eric Gill's nephew). Finally I must thank the Cathedral archivist Miriam Power, my *Oremus* colleagues Dylan Parry, Manel Silva and Julian Game, and most of all Elizabeth Benjamin and her son Paul, who painstakingly transcribed the text and whose constructive criticism and helpful suggestions were, as always, invaluable.

Patrick Rogers

PLAN OF WESTMINSTER CATHEDRAL

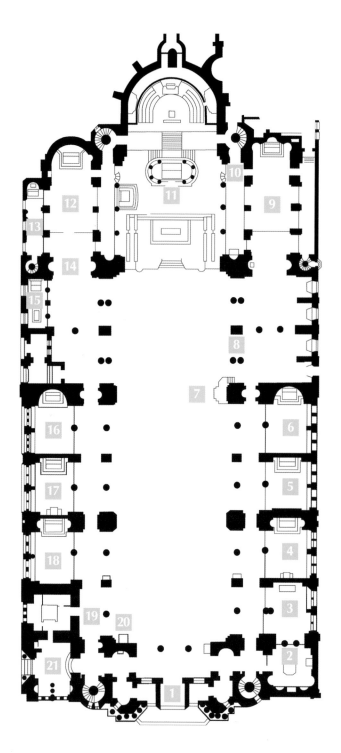

1. Main entrance

2. Baptistry

3. Chapel of St Gregory and St Augustine

4. Chapel of St Patrick

5. Chapel of St Andrew

6. Chapel of St Paul

7. Pulpit

8. Shrine of Our Lady of Westminster

9. Lady Chapel

10. Entrance to St Peter's Crypt

11. High Altar

12. Chapel of the Blessed Sacrament

13. Shrine of the Sacred Heart and St Michael

14. Peacock and phoenix mosaics

15. Chapel of St Thomas of Canterbury
    (Cardinal Vaughan Chantry)

16. Chapel of St Joseph

17. Chapel of St George and the English Martyrs

18. Chapel of the Holy Souls

19. Entrance to the campanile

20. Statue of St Peter

21. Gift Shop

Construction of the main gateway of Tothill Fields Prison on Francis Street. 7 July 1833.

1. Tothill Fields

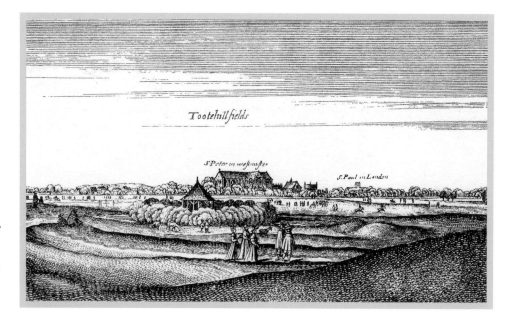

Tothill Fields in about 1640, showing the maze in the foreground with Westminster Abbey (St Peter's) and old St Paul's Cathedral behind.

In 1798 Jeremy Bentham wrote: 'If a place could be said that it was in no neighbourhood, that place would be Tothill Fields'. The area was originally marshland, regularly overflowed by the Thames and known as Bulinga Fen. It then became a largely uninhabited wasteland with scattered ponds and ditches and was used for military parades, sports and leisure activities, duels and burials. It appears to have been named from Toote Hill, or beacon hill, a raised vantage point or mound such as used to stand at Regency Place, where Maunsel Street joins Horseferry Road. Only slowly was Tothill Fields built on, as the land was drained and the population of Westminster expanded, the process finally being completed in the late nineteenth century.

The area was first described simply as the western boundary of Westminster extending to the Tye Bourne (Tyburn) brook, which now flows underground beside Vauxhall Bridge Road down to the Thames near Vauxhall Bridge. Beyond lay Pimlico, Chelsea Waterworks, the Grosvenor Canal bringing goods up from the Thames to Pimlico wharf, and oyster beds - an area now occupied by Victoria Station and its railway tracks. The other boundaries of Tothill Fields were Tothill Street to the north and its continuation westwards along Petty France and Castle Lane, the Thames at Millbank to the south, and St Peter's (Westminster Abbey) to the east. Westminster Cathedral lies close to the north western boundary.

Parades and Burials

Activities taking place on Tothill Fields featured a wrestling match between the young men of Westminster and those of the City of London in 1221 - which ended in a riot when the Westminster men, who had previously lost, armed themselves and attacked their opponents; a tournament in celebration of the coronation in 1236 of Eleanor, Henry III's Queen; and a weekly market and annual fair (St Magdalen's) introduced by the Abbot of Westminster in 1248. Military activities included a parade by the London contingent of 600 archers with longbows, 200 horsemen and 100 men-at-arms, before embarking for the war with France in 1346. This parade was held on 10 July - a significant date, for the battle of Crecy was fought and won six weeks later on 26 August, success resulting from the accuracy and rapidity of fire of the English longbowmen.

Three hundred years later, on 25 August 1651, 14,000 trained men from London and Westminster paraded on Tothill Fields before the Speaker and Members of Parliament, ready to defend London. Nine days afterwards Charles II's royalists were defeated by Cromwell in the Battle of Worcester and the surviving Scottish prisoners were 'driven like a herd of swine' through Westminster to the same fields. Some 1,200 of them were buried there at a cost of £1.10.0d for 67 loads of soil to cover their graves, and the rest were sold to merchants and sent to Barbados as slaves. The Scottish were not the last to be buried there. At about the same time a group of 'pest houses' for plague victims, known as the Five Houses or Seven Chimneys, was established beside the Thames, with another, for those who could pay for their treatment, set up by Lord Craven near the butts (now Artillery Place) in 1665. This was the time of the Great Plague during which many were buried on Tothill Fields because the churchyards could take no more.

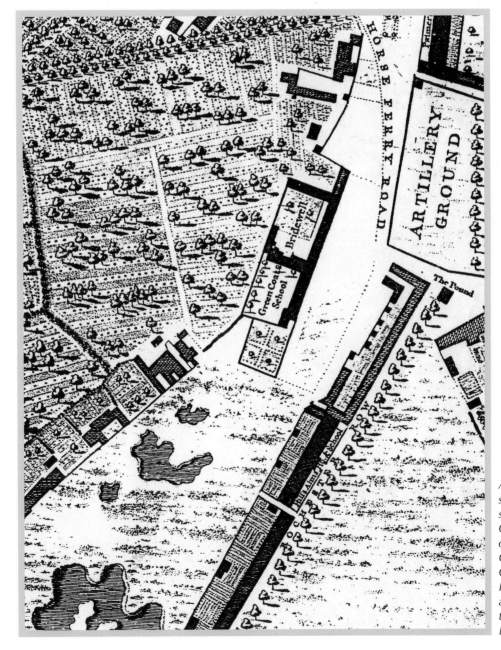

A map of 1745 showing the site which the Cathedral will occupy (far left), Grey Coat, Green Coat, and Emery Hill's almshouses and schools, and the Tothill Fields Bridewell.

But Tothill Fields was not just a place of military parades and burials. It was a pleasant locality to walk or ride in when the trees and wild flowers were in bloom, with ponds and streams for fishing and locally grown melons, watercress and parsley available. A maze was much frequented in the summer-time, horse-racing was organised, with bear and bull-baiting on the site of the present Vincent Square (enclosed for Westminster School as a sports field in 1810 to save it from development). Duels took place until 1711, and there was prize-fighting, dog-fighting, cock-fighting and cock-throwing!

There were areas, however, best to be avoided. As the population of Westminster expanded in the 18th and 19th centuries, the area west of Westminster Abbey became increasingly congested. Houses were divided and rented out as rooms by middlemen. Lanes became alleyways without proper sanitation, drainage, or clean water, and disease was rife. St Ann's Street was renowned for its brothels, Duck Lane (now St Matthew Street) for its thieves, and Strutton Ground (which possessed but a single shop in 1800) for its pubs. Further west there were breweries and a distillery, charity schools, almshouses and a prison, and further west still was the site on which Westminster Cathedral would be built.

Charity Schools and Almshouses

East of Artillery Row stood the old artillery ground, used for practice with longbows, crossbows, pistols and muskets (not cannon despite the miniature cannon over the entrance to Artillery House on Artillery Row), from Tudor until Victorian times. This was the area for charity schools for orphans and children whose parents were unable to look after them, and almshouses for the industrious poor. At the junction of Greencoat Place with Artillery Row stood St Margaret's, or Green Coat, Hospital school, founded by Charles I in 1633 for 25 boys of which six wore yellow caps and were maintained by the Duchess of Somerset. A public house, the 'Greencoat Boy', now marks the site. Opposite stands Grey Coat Hospital, the largest of the local charity schools, founded by local tradesmen in 1698 for 40 boys and 40 girls. A hospital or 'spital' signified a charitable institution for the poor, needy, aged or infirm, in other words almshouses, which often included a school.

A Blewcoat (Blue Coat) boy above the entrance to Blewcoat School.

On Caxton Street on the other side of Victoria Street stands the Blewcoat (Blue Coat) School, founded on Duck Lane in 1688, but built here in 1709 and now owned by the National Trust. There was also Emanuel (Brown Coat) School, founded in 1594 by Lady Dacre on Buckingham Gate, Palmer's (Black Coat) school founded in 1656, Butler's (1675) and Emery Hill's (1679) Schools, each for 20 children and now commemorated by Palmer Street and Butler Place across Victoria Street, and Emery Hill Street, off Rochester Row. These schools, whose pupils wore uniforms of the appropriate colour, were established to teach children Christian values, patriotism and diligence, for later employment from the age of 12 as watermen, tailors, seamstresses, domestic servants etc, to be arranged by the school.

So what happened to the Westminster charity schools and to the almshouses customarily established with them by the benefactors? In 1873-74 the boys of Greencoat and Greycoat Hospital Schools were transferred to Emanuel School on Buckingham Gate, which in turn moved to new premises as a boarding school on Wandsworth Common in 1883 and stands there today - one of the United Westminster Schools. Palmer's, Emery Hill's, and St. Margaret's Schools were amalgamated as the Westminster City School for dayboys, erected on the gardens of Emanuel School and opening onto Palace Street. Similarly in 1874 the girls were transferred to Grey Coat Hospital which is now a large and successful girls' comprehensive school. The almshouses were separated from the charity schools and also amalgamated in 1880-82. Three of them can be found on the west side of Rochester Row. United Westminster Almshouses there consists of Butler's on the left, Palmer's in the centre and Emery Hill's on the right (its original site). Nearby Emery Hill Street leads on to Westminster Cathedral.

Tothill Fields Bridewell in 1796, showing the inmates begging from visitors.

Tothill Fields Bridewell

And so to Tothill Fields Bridewell, which stood to the north of Geencoat School and west of Artillery Row, on land now occupied by shops and offices. Built in 1618, expanded in 1655, and closing in 1836, above its gateway was inscribed: 'Here are several Sorts of Work for the Poor of this Parish of St Margaret, Westminster, as also the County according to Law, and for such as will Beg and Live Idle in this City and Liberty of Westminster. Anno 1655'. The gateway is now at the back of the Supreme Court which opens onto Parliament Square. The Bridewell was established for indolent paupers, vagrants and beggars, but other short-term prisoners were admitted from the beginning of the eighteenth century during the reign of Queen Anne. It appears in a picture of 1796 with only the iron spikes on the walls and awnings showing its true purpose. A couple are clearly visiting, and the inmates, of course, are begging.

2. The House of Correction

"That land is for sale, I wish you to buy it for me." Cardinal Manning was addressing his solicitor, Alfred Blount, in November 1882. What both men were looking at, from the Cardinal's residence at the bottom of Carlisle Place, was Tothill Fields Prison. Blount formed a company and bought the site in 1884. The western half was immediately sold to the Cardinal at cost, the remainder to a property developer. On the land sold to the Cardinal now stands Westminster Cathedral.

Tothill Fields Prison was officially entitled the Middlesex (Westminster) House of Correction. Established by Act of Parliament in 1826, it opened in 1834. It was designed on enlightened, Benthamite principles and built on an eight-acre site of open ground, now enclosed by Morpeth Terrace to the west, Francis Street to the south and east, and Ashley Place and Howick Place to the north. From 1618 a much smaller prison, Tothill Fields Bridewell, had stood immediately north of Greencoat School (now a pub) and west of Artillery Row. It was knocked down in 1836, two years after the new prison opened, and the site is now occupied by shops and offices.

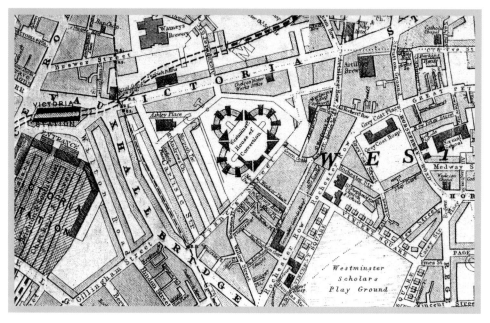

A map of the area in 1883 showing Tothill Fields Prison (Westminster House of Correction) in the centre.

'Vast, airy, light and inexorably safe'

The Tothill Fields Prison of 1834 was built in the form of a shamrock or ace of clubs, each 'leaf' effectively forming a separate prison, with a planted courtyard in the centre and exercise yards beside each brick-built cell block. The main entrance, of massive granite blocks with iron gates, opened onto Francis Street. North of the planted courtyard was the prison governor's house surmounted by a chapel. 'Vast, airy, light and inexorably safe', only one inmate escaped from the prison, when the door-keeper absentmindedly laid down his key.

Initially for both men and women with sentences less severe than transportation, from 1850 it was restricted to convicted female prisoners and males below 17 years. Each of the three prison 'leaves' contained about 300 prisoners, the one on the left for the boys and the other two for women. Westminster Cathedral, Clergy House and the Choir School now stand on the site of the boys' wing and a part of one of those occupied by the women. The rest of the prison complex now lies beneath Ambrosden Avenue, Ashley Gardens and Thirleby Road.

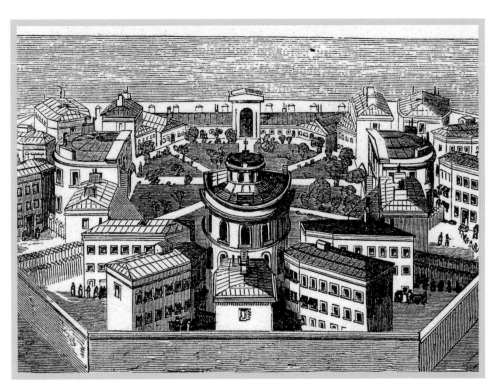

*Birds-eye view of
Tothill Fields Prison
(seen from the back).*

We know much about the prison from Henry Mayhew's *Criminal Prisons of London*, written after a visit there in 1861. It operated on the 'silent associated' system in which inmates mixed but were not allowed to talk among themselves. Of course they did and it is significant that by far the main punishment was restriction of diet (usually for talking). Nevertheless, only 3.5% of the boys were punished each year and the most serious punishment, whipping, had only been inflicted twice in the five years 1851-55, considerably less than elsewhere. Mayhew wrote that the staff of the boys' prison were entitled to the highest praise for enforcing strict discipline with a minimum of physical coercion.

Three piece suit without pockets

The oldest boy in 1861 was 18, having lied about his age to get in and avoid Coldbath Fields Prison. A number were aged six and one as young as five, having stolen 5/9d from a till (his second offence). But the great majority were aged 14-16 years. Almost all had no trade or occupation and most could not read or write. On arrival the boys were given a bath and a meal and issued with the prison uniform of a tricolour striped woollen cap with earflaps (used as a night-cap in the unheated cells), an iron grey (prison blue for minor offenders) three-piece suit without pockets, check shirt, stock, boots and a small red cotton handkerchief to be tied to a buttonhole. They were given a foot-bath twice a week and a warm bath once a month.

The boys were identified by numbers on the left arm. A yellow number 1 identified the 1st-class – sentenced to more than three months, a 2 denoted a sentence of between 14 days and three months (2nd-class), while 3rd-class inmates (14 days or less) bore no number. A badge was worn for a sentence of two years or more, a yellow ring around the arm denoted penal servitude and a yellow waistcoat collar committal for larceny or felony. Also worn, often proudly, was a red number revealing how many times they had been imprisoned before, one 14 year-old as many as 17 times.

The boys were awakened by a gun at 6.25am. Then followed a communal wash in cold water, Chapel and breakfast of oatmeal gruel (porridge), bread and water, the basic diet at all three meals. Most worked at oakum picking (unravelling old rope for use in caulking the seams of vessels) for six hours a day. Other work consisted of mending clothes and shoes, carpentry and gardening. An hour was spent in exercise and another in the schoolroom. At dinner at 2pm the 2nd-class prisoners received tinned cold meat (beef or mutton) with potatoes twice a week and oxhead, barley and vegetable soup twice a week, while the 1st-class received this superior diet (and cocoa at breakfast) six days out of the seven. Supper was at 5.30 and lock-up at 6pm.

Boys exercising at Tothill Fields Prison.

"I seem to like thieving"

Most were in for theft, over a third for picking pockets. As one boy put it "I seem to like thieving". But others were there for throwing stones, ringing and knocking at doors and then running away; an eight year-old had been sentenced to 14 days and a flogging for taking some half-dozen plums from an orchard; and boys aged ten and eleven were there for spinning a top! Nearly half were recommittals (against 25 per cent nationally). One youth was suspected of throwing stones at a street lamp just to get a month's shelter. Many were fending for themselves on the streets of London. They looked on the prison as a place where they would at least be given shelter, food and warm clothing. Indeed Mayhew was prevented from using a drawing of the boys at breakfast as it would have made the place seem far too comfortable!

Mayhew described the part of the prison occupied by the women in less detail. They wore close white caps with deep frills and loose blue and white spotted dresses. They wore the same identifying numbers as the boys and, like them, longer-term prisoners received the better diet. Over half were recommittals, many for non-payment of fines and for offences such as prostitution. One girl of eight had been sentenced to three months for stealing a pair of boots. When asked why she replied "cause I hadn't got none of my own". Besides oakum picking, there was straw plaiting, knitting and laundry work. There were two schoolrooms, one of them for girls of up to 16, and a nursery where those with young children could look after them when not working. The other main difference from the boys was the number of punishments – 38.5% of the women were punished each year.

So why did Tothill Fields Prison, well-built and well-run, close after less than 50 years? Two reasons, I think. Firstly, it was not an effective deterrent. Recommittals were twice the number elsewhere and some seemed happy to return. The regime was strict rather than harsh and those released often went out into a harsher and less secure world. The prison was enlightened and enlightenment can be expensive. The cost per prisoner at Tothill was a third more than at Middlesex (Coldbath Fields) House of Correction for adult males at Clerkenwell. But if the prison had not been built where and when it was, or if, perhaps, its regime had been harsher and more cost effective, Westminster Cathedral would not stand where it does today.

Mothers, with their children, exercising at Tothill Fields Prison.

3. We might have been Gothic!

Westminster Cathedral is built in the Byzantine style, modelled on the brick-built churches of Constantinople, Ravenna and Venice. But almost to the last, the plans were for a Gothic-style building built of stone, similar to almost all the other cathedrals in Britain. So what would our Cathedral have looked like if the last minute change of plans had not occurred?

In 1850 the Roman Catholic hierarchy returned to England and Wales from Rome and Cardinal Wiseman became the first Archbishop of Westminster. There being no suitable cathedral in central London, Wiseman used St Mary Moorfields, then London's major Catholic church, as his pro-cathedral. Soon after his arrival support started to grow for a great Catholic cathedral to be built, but Wiseman's priorities lay elsewhere. His immediate problems were a lack of priests, schools and parish churches, exacerbated by the huge influx of Irish Catholic immigrants who flooded into England as a result of the potato famine in Ireland in the 1840s.

Cardinal Manning buys a site

Cardinal Wiseman died in 1865 and his friends and supporters resolved to build a metropolitan cathedral in his memory. Wiseman's successor, Archbishop (Cardinal from 1875) Manning supported the venture but, like his predecessor, he believed that the provision of schools and orphanages for the 20,000 abandoned or neglected children of London must take precedence. Nevertheless fund-raising for the new cathedral went ahead and in September 1867 Manning bought the freehold for a long strip of land, 488ft long by 85ft wide, on the west side of Carlisle Street (now Carlisle Place), between the Convent of the Sisters of Charity near the north end and the large detached building (then used as an officers' club by the Brigade of Guards) at the south end. The cost was £16,500.

Henry Clutton, the architect who produced a series of designs for a Gothic cathedral for Cardinal Manning.

Manning commissioned the architect Henry Clutton to prepare designs for a Gothic cathedral of great length but without transepts and only 70 feet wide on this site. Clutton, who converted to Catholicism in 1857, was related to Manning and his appointment provoked a good deal of criticism and accusations in *The Tablet* of favouritism and nepotism. In fact Clutton spent six years of his life working on designs for Westminster Cathedral but only charged £250 towards expenses such as his clerk's salary. A year later, in August 1868, Manning bought the vacant freehold land on the other side of Carlisle Street, 430ft long by 108ft wide, for a further £20,000. Since the road between the two sites had never been made public and so could be used for building purposes, this provided Manning with an area of two and a third acres on which he could build his new cathedral.

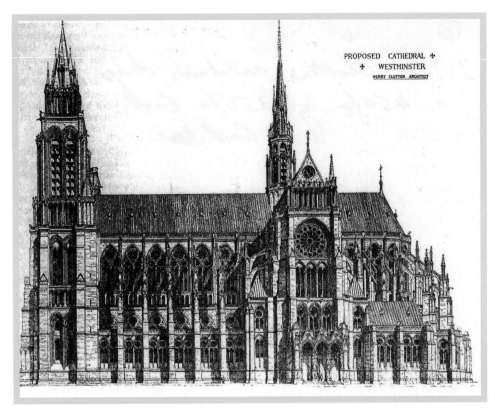

Clutton's ambitious design for a 450ft by 250ft Gothic cathedral.

Once again Henry Clutton returned to the drawing board to produce plans for a Gothic cathedral either occupying the entire site, or just the second site if it was decided that the first site should be sold. But no final decision was taken, perhaps because of the irregularity of the total area, the first site being 90ft longer than the second site at one end and about 130ft shorter than it at the other end. This was improved in 1872 when Manning bought the Guards club building at the south end of the first site which subsequently became Archbishop's House, his residence. For the fourth time Henry Clutton produced designs for a cathedral, this time on a far grander scale. It was to be in the Early English Pointed style and was compared by Manning to Cologne Cathedral. Its external measurements would be 450ft in length and 250ft in width across the transepts. Internally it would be 412ft by 140ft and 130ft. high.

Enter Sykes of Sledmere

The latest plans produced by Henry Clutton for Manning (now a cardinal), were for a huge building, much larger than any other English cathedral and quite beyond the resources of the diocese for the foreseeable future. So there the matter rested until 1882 when Sir Tatton Sykes of Sledmere, a wealthy Yorkshire landowner, came on the scene. Manning was informed that he was considering converting to Catholicism and was willing to pay £25,000 a year for 15 years, or £295,000 in the event of his death, to fund the new cathedral. Encouraged by this unexpected generosity, Manning decided to sell the (less than satisfactory) land he had acquired at Carlisle Street and buy the eight acre Middlesex County Prison site known as Tothill Fields Prison (where Westminster Cathedral stands today), which had just come onto the market. It was bought for £115,000 in February 1884, the Carlisle Street site was sold in 1885 and the eastern half of the prison site (now occupied by the buildings beyond Ambrosden Avenue) was sold the same year,

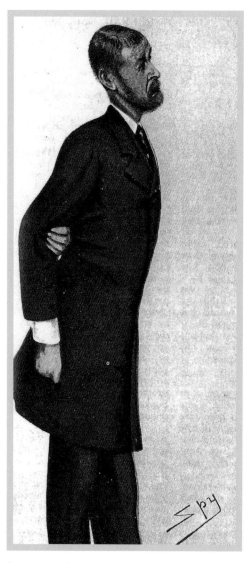

Sir Tatton Sykes, as seen by the caricaturist 'Spy'. Vanity Fair 1879.

But then the indecisive Sir Tatton Sykes began to get cold feet about the cost of the project, at a time of poor harvests and agricultural depression, and the likely reaction of his relatives and the largely non-Catholic population of Sledmere. A celebrated but reclusive traveller, he was obsessed with his own health and digestion and travelled accompanied by his own special cook who prepared his daily diet of milk puddings. He wore a series of overcoats, sometimes as many as six at a time, which he discarded as he grew warmer. He disliked the cottagers on the Sledmere estate using their front doors, and the sight of their children playing and running about in the street. He also had an obsessive hatred of flowers as 'nasty, untidy things', uprooting those in the gardens of his own great house and doing his best to destroy those in the cottage gardens of Sledmere, which he slashed at with his walking stick as he passed by on his regular inspections.

In 1874 Sir Tatton Sykes had married an eighteen-year-old girl thirty years his junior. The marriage was arranged by his determined and manipulative future mother-in-law, Prudence Penelope Cavendish-Bentinck, popularly known as 'Britannia'. Meeting him by chance in Bavaria and discovering that he possessed an estate of 36,000 acres, she contrived to bring about a situation in which her daughter, Jessica, became separated from her and had to turn to him for help overnight. She then feigned outrage, forced him to propose to avoid a scandal, arranged for a lavish wedding at Westminster Abbey and drove him there in her own carriage. It was the start of a disastrous marriage during which Jessica converted to Catholicism in 1882 and became obsessively determined that her husband should pay for Westminster Cathedral. There seems little doubt that it was Jessica who was behind the offer to Cardinal Manning.

In offering to pay for the cathedral Sir Tatton Sykes had insisted that Baron Heinrich von Ferstel, who was architect to the Emperor of Austria, should design it. Von Ferstel had designed the Votivkirche in Vienna which had much impressed Sir Tatton who wanted this to be the model for Westminster Cathedral. With complete disregard for national sentiment and for the feelings of Clutton, Manning accepted. In the event von Ferstel died in 1883 (though his son offered to take over the project) and Sir Tatton Sykes failed to convert. Despite all the efforts of his wife and of both Cardinals Manning and Vaughan, the money he had offered was never forthcoming.

Cardinal Vaughan chooses Byzantine

Cardinal Manning died in 1892 and Herbert Vaughan succeeded him as third Archbishop of Westminster. He believed he had only ten years to live (he died in June 1903) and was determined to see Westminster Cathedral built. Both Clutton's and von Ferstel's Gothic designs were available and Vaughan received more from a friend, Archibald Dunn of Newcastle, in 1893. But he knew that construction of a Gothic cathedral could take decades and easily cost

Baron von Ferstel's design for Westminster Cathedral modelled on the Votivkirche in Vienna.

£500,000. His own preference was for a basilica modelled on Constantine's ancient Church of St Peter in Rome. In appointing John Francis Bentley as the new Cathedral architect he is said to have been quite taken by the latter's plan 'to go and study the basilica in its own native haunts', which he did from November 1894 to March 1895. Bentley had worked in Henry Clutton's office from 1857-60 and at first his own preference was for Gothic. But he subsequently agreed with Vaughan's choice of the early Byzantine style.

Archibald Dunn's design for a Gothic Westminster Cathedral produced for Cardinal Vaughan.

So what were the arguments for a basilican cathedral built in the early Christian style? In appealing to his friends for funds, Cardinal Vaughan laid them out. Firstly, a church of this type, with a wide nave and a view of the sanctuary unimpeded by columns or screen, was best suited to the needs of a metropolitan cathedral in providing the congregation with both sight and sound of the liturgies. Secondly, the early Christian basilican style allowed the whole building to be erected quickly and economically since its decoration and ornamentation did not form part of its structure.

Thirdly, it would be impossible to build a new Gothic cathedral worthy of comparison with Westminster Abbey, close by, without imprudent and excessive expenditure; it would be wiser not to try.

4. But Is It Byzantine?

By 1895 Cardinal Vaughan, founder of Westminster Cathedral, had decided against the popular Gothic style for his new building and had chosen the early Byzantine. His architect, John Francis Bentley, agreed with him. So how far is Westminster Cathedral based on early Byzantine architecture?

The ruins of the church of St John of Stoudios, Istanbul, showing the nave, aisles, galleries and semi-circular apse.

Roman Basilicas

When Christianity was officially recognised in the Roman Empire in 313, Christians looked for a building in which they could congregate. Roman temples were too closely associated with paganism so they chose instead the basilica, used by Romans as a meeting house for centuries. Christian basilicas were longitudinal, rectangular buildings with an open timber roof or flat ceiling, side aisles sometimes separated from the central area by columns, and usually a semi-circular apse at the far end. Examples of basilican churches in Rome are St John Lateran which the first Christian Roman Emperor, Constantine, began in 313, St Paul's Outside the Walls (385) and St Mary Major (432). However fire, reconstruction and Baroque embellishment have much altered these buildings over the years and none of them now has much in common with brick-built Westminster Cathedral.

Cardinal Vaughan favoured a basilica of the Italian type (which Bentley disliked) and expressed the view that Westminster Cathedral should be based on Constantine's Basilica of St Peter in Rome, dating from about 333 and entirely replaced by the present Baroque church. Constantine's unusual basilica was a martyrium, a pilgrim shrine over St Peter's tomb. The colonnaded nave and aisles served as an enclosed graveyard for the burial of Christians, and also as a funerary banqueting hall. At the far end of the nave was a broad, lateral transept where thousands of pilgrims could congregate to venerate the tomb of St Peter. The building was thus in the form of a T, timber-roofed, without domes, galleries, sanctuary, choir or side chapels. Its focus was the shrine of St Peter. It was very different from Westminster Cathedral.

In looking for a model we therefore have to leave Rome for Byzantium - Constantinople when Constantine made it his capital and founded the Byzantine Empire in 330, and now called Istanbul. Many of the old Christian churches built by Constantine and his successors have not survived, destroyed in the Nika riots of 532, despoiled at the hands of the Fourth Crusaders in 1204 or suffering in the Turkish conquest of 1453 when many became mosques. The oldest church in Istanbul, and the only one to survive from the period between Constantine and Justinian, is that of St John the Baptist of Stoudios, now called Imrahor Ilyas Bey Camii. A basilica founded in 463, roofless, ruinous and difficult to access, it stands near the sea just inside the city walls. But we can still recognise the style in the atrium (courtyard), narthex, wide nave, aisles, galleries, sanctuary and semi-circular apse, while the columns dividing the nave from the aisles are of the same Verde Antico marble that we see in Westminster Cathedral.

The church of Haghia Eirene, Istanbul, from the north-east, showing the main dome, apse and northern transept partly concealed by trees.

The Byzantine Style

The destruction of so much of Constantinople in the riots of 532 heralded the introduction of the style known as Byzantine. Already Emperor Justinian had moved away from the pure basilican form of St John of Stoudios and experimented with a domed plan. His earliest such church was dedicated to the two saints Sergius and Bacchus and is also known as Kucuk Haghia Sophia (little Haghia Sophia). It is now a mosque. It was built in 527, the year Justinian came to power, and consists of an octagon in a square, with a projecting apse and a large central dome supported by eight piers joined by arches. Between the piers are pairs of columns, the lower ones supporting a spacious upper viewing gallery and the upper ones a triple arcade beneath the dome. Sergius and Bacchus was one of a pair of adjoining churches. The other, of which nothing now remains, was built as a basilica. So the two styles coexisted side by side.

In Haghia Eirene, the Church of Divine Peace, the two styles have been combined. The church was rebuilt by Justinian from 532 after the riots and is now an exhibition and concert hall. A glance down the wide, empty nave from the western entrance suggests that we are in a basilica. It is only when standing under the dome at the other end of the nave that the form of the building is revealed, with barrel vaults opening out to left

Haghia Sophia, dominating Istanbul, showing the central dome, semi-domes and massive buttresses.

and right and another above the chancel. Like Westminster Cathedral what appears at first sight to be a transeptless basilica, is in fact cruciform. Other similarities are the galleries which run the length of the nave to the chancel, above the aisles with their columns and arcades, penetrating the supporting piers; and the semi-circular apse itself which contains elevated seats for the clergy, rising up above an enclosed ambulatory.

The most famous of Justinian's churches is, of course, Haghia Sophia (Santa Sophia), the Church of Divine Wisdom. Like Haghia Eirene it replaced an earlier church destroyed in the riots, but Justinian's replacement was in the radically new Byzantine style. Built in 532-37 it consists of a huge rectangle enclosing a central square space defined by four piers which carry a shallow dome 107ft in diameter and 180ft high. Rather than squaring the circle, Justinian's two mathematician-architects circled the square, using pendentives rising from the piers. The space beneath the dome could thus be opened out into semi-domes to east and west, and into two-storeyed screens of marble columns carrying arches and fronting aisles and extensive upper viewing galleries to north and south, a feature replicated either side of the sanctuary in Westminster Cathedral.

Far from Istanbul

Byzantine churches were built throughout the Byzantine Empire, notably in Ravenna in northern Italy in the sixth century, but these were for the most part based on models developed in Rome and Istanbul. San Vitale, for example, is a development of its near contemporary in Istanbul, Sergius and Bacchus. The churches of Ravenna are best known for their mosaics which, as a result of iconoclasm and invasion, have largely been destroyed in Istanbul. St Mark's Basilica in Venice is another example of a meeting between East and West. Partly based on Justinian's church of the Holy Apostles in Istanbul (destroyed in 1469), it is cruciform in plan with open transepts, side chapels and five large domes - one over each square main bay with another (the Ascension dome) at the central crossing. Encrusted with mosaic and marble (much of it looted from Constantinople in 1204), it was built not only for the glory of God, but perhaps even more, for the glory of Venice.

So how far is Westminster Cathedral based on Byzantine models and how far on other factors? Liturgical and congregational requirements demanded a spacious, elevated sanctuary and choir with a long, wide nave providing an uninterrupted view. Aisles needed to be wide enough for ceremonial processions and able to provide access to side chapels. A bell tower was required and a crypt for the interment of past Archbishops of Westminster. It was Cardinal Vaughan who chose saucer domes rather than a vaulted roof, and Bentley who opted to run viewing galleries above the nave aisles, across the transepts to the apse, thus concentrating all eyes on the sanctuary, baldacchino and altar.

Bentley described Westminster Cathedral as 'an example of what might have been unfolded had not the decadence of the Roman Empire terminated the growth of congregational requirements in the East'. It has features to be found in the ancient basilica of St John of Stoudios; in domed Haghia Sophia with its two-storeyed screens of marble columns and arches fronting aisles and galleries; in Haghia Eirene with its stubby transepts concealed behind galleries and arcades; and in St Mark's, Venice, with its series of square bays, each surmounted by a shallow dome. In reconciling liturgical and congregational requirements with the early Byzantine architectural style, Bentley may be said to have succeeded, admirably.

The interior of St Mark's, Venice, from the museum above the narthex, showing the mosaic-decorated vaults, domes, open transepts and apse.

5. Beginnings

John Francis Bentley, the architect chosen by Cardinal Vaughan to design Westminster Cathedral, returned from his tour of European basilicas in March 1895 without notes but with his mind largely made up, and immediately started work on the designs. On 4 May 1895 *The Tablet* announced that he had submitted two preliminary ground plans for the Cathedral.

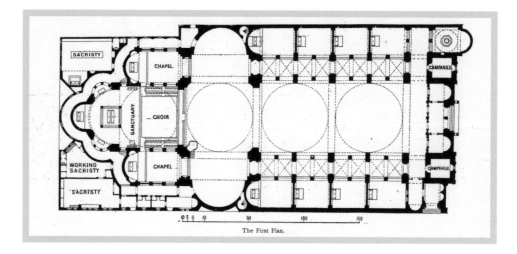

The First Plan.

Bentley's first ground plan for Westminster Cathedral, May 1895.

Bentley's Three Plans

Bentley's (undated) first plan provides for two campanili (bell towers), one either side of the main entrance at the western end of the Cathedral, a projecting baptistry at the south-west corner, a narthex running the full width of the Cathedral, aisles dividing the side chapels from the nave, and prominent, open transepts (which Cardinal Vaughan favoured), each terminating in the form of a curved apse. At the eastern end the high altar appears under a square, four-columned baldacchino similar to that which Bentley had seen and admired in the church of Sant' Ambrogio in Milan. It appears not under the fourth dome of the Cathedral as it does today, but in a triple-apse at the eastern end. Around the apse runs an ambulatory connecting with two sacristies and two large chapels, one each side of the choir which is placed in front of the sanctuary.

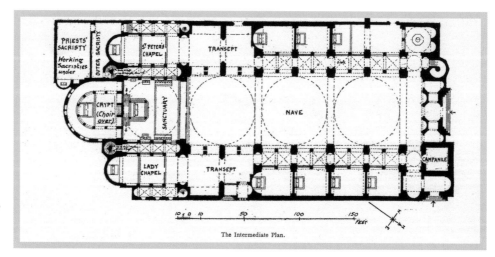

The Intermediate Plan.

Bentley's second ground plan for the Cathedral, dated June 1895.

The second plan is dated June 1895, though it presumably was submitted earlier, and is much closer to the cathedral of today. At the request of Cardinal Vaughan there is only one, somewhat larger, campanile; the narthex terminates at the baptistry, which is now recessed, on one side and a lobby (now the Gift Shop) on the other; the transepts have lost their apsidal ends and are no longer open, the galleries and arcading being carried in front of them to the sanctuary, rendering them far less prominent and directing all eyes towards the sanctuary and high altar, as Bentley intended. The altar under its square, four-columned baldacchino has been brought forward to its present position in the sanctuary while the apse is now single, rather than triple, has lost its ambulatory and has been elevated to form a retro-choir, providing space for the interment of deceased archbishops in the crypt below.

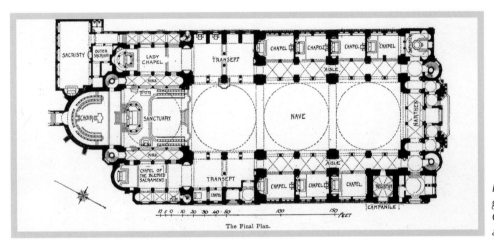

Bentley's third ground plan for the Cathedral, signed and dated 1895.

Bentley's third and final plan was also completed in 1895, when it was signed and dated. It shows the cathedral that, in all essentials, we see today - a brick-built, 360ft long by 156ft wide, shallow-domed basilica, terminating in a raised sanctuary and apse. In a radical departure, the baldacchino over the high altar is now shown with eight, rather than four, columns. The transepts are truncated and inconspicuous and a single bell tower stands at the north-west corner. By now construction was underway. The foundation stone, a block of Cornish granite from Penryn quarries, was laid on 29 June 1895 by Cardinal Vaughan in front of almost 10,000 people from Britain and overseas. The stone, inscribed in gold, can be seen today on the left side of the sanctuary, behind the lectern and seats for the clergy.

Foundations and Brickwork

In July 1895 Mowlem & Co of Westminster started work on excavating the area and building the new foundations. It was immediately found that a 9ft plateau of hard and solid concrete from the foundations of Tothill Fields Prison underlay more than half the site. This extends under the northern half of the Cathedral and the whole of Archbishop's House. To this 6,000 tons of new concrete was added, consisting of Thames ballast, and 'Goliath' brand Portland cement. Perry & Co of Bow then took over in January 1896, laying over two million hand-made bricks to bring the concrete foundations up to ground level. Blue Staffordshire damp-proof, vitrified bricks were used for the outside facings of the underground basements and damp courses, Fletton wire-cut for the large piers and walls, and Poole wire-cut for the smaller piers and abutments. All three types were first rigorously tested, the Staffordshire blues, for example, resisting a pressure of 700 tons per square foot.

Despite a strike by the site labourers for an extra 1/2d an hour in May, the foundations were finished up to ground level by October 1896. The contract for continuing up to the level of the domes and vaulting was then signed with Shillitoe & Sons of Bury St Edmunds in November. Bentley decided on a combination of Bracknell red-facings ('Bracknell thins') together with courses of white Portland stone for the exterior, similar in appearance to neighbouring, older buildings. He chose Faversham stocks for the interior brickwork. Originally this was said to be honey-coloured but more than a century of dirt, dust and candle-smoke has by now rendered it a uniform grey to black. In all 12,454,474 bricks were laid to build the Cathedral. Freeman & Sons of Penryn, who had previously presented the foundation stone, provided the grey granite for the Cathedral entrances and steps. The work was directed and coordinated by C H Mullis, the Clerk of Works, assisted by Percy A Lamb.

Preparing the Cathedral foundations, 10 October 1895.

Circling the Squares

A new contract, for the domes and vaulting, was agreed with Shillitoe & Sons in May 1899 and Cardinal Vaughan was optimistic that the building might be opened in 1900 - 50 years after the return of the Catholic hierarchy from Rome. But this proved unrealistic. In June 1899 the brick and stonework had reached their full height (except in the case of the tower) and the Cathedral began to be filled with avenues of timber designed to carry the centering for the domes. Bentley distrusted the use of iron and had resolved that the domes should consist of concrete made up of one part of Portland cement which had been seasoned on site for at least 13 weeks, mixed with four parts of broken brick and a minimum of water. The assistant Clerk of Works, Percy Lamb, was recalled from other work and instructed that the dome concreting 'required carefully and constantly watching'. The eastern dome of the nave was constructed first, followed by that above the sanctuary, then the middle dome and finally the westernmost. External surfaces were clad with artificial stone slabs.

The domes were completed during 1900 after 14 months work. The galleries, tribunes and organ loft were then constructed, requiring 27 marble columns to support them. By Christmas Day 1900 all were in position. It was now possible to climb internally up to the level of the domes and the small balconies immediately below them, to look down on the work taking place in the sanctuary and chapels and watch the little steam engine used to hoist materials up the unfinished bell tower. Thirty feet wide at its base, the tower now rises to a height of 284ft of which the last 11 consist of the bronze metropolitan cross at the summit. By December 1900 the tower had reached a height of 182ft. When Bentley last visited it on 1 March 1902, the day before his death, it had risen a further 40ft. But it was not finally finished until January 1903 and will be described in greater detail in a later chapter.

6. A Cathedral in Miniature

While Westminster Cathedral was being built of brick, stone and concrete beside Victoria Street during the closing years of the 19th century, another, somewhat smaller, cathedral was being built of wood across the Thames beside Westminster Bridge Road.

It was a 1/48th scale model of Westminster Cathedral measuring 8ft by 4ft with the tower rising 6ft. The model was first mentioned in a letter of 16 January 1899 from J F Bentley, the Cathedral architect, to a friend and fellow architect, Charles Hadfield, regretting that he had not been available to show the model to him during Hadfield's recent visit to the Cathedral. It was then described in the *Westminster Cathedral Record* of February 1899 and again, with an illustration, in June. It was said to have been made by Farmer & Brindley. A longer description appeared in the *Westminster Cathedral Chronicle* of October 1919 stating that it had taken about 15 months to make. This may have been an under-estimate since a letter of October 1921 from the makers, Farmer & Brindley, recalled that it had taken them about two years to execute and was finished early in 1899. So work on the model must have started by early 1897.

A photograph of the model which appeared in the Westminster Cathedral Record in June 1899.

'A most exceptional model'

In their letter of October 1921, Farmer & Brindley described the wooden model as 'a most exceptional model, being complete as to interior as well as to exterior, taking apart showing each chapel complete in itself'. They added that the drawings used to make it were most intricate and that Bentley had constantly called on them during the carving process. Bentley was fascinated by models. When he was 14 and growing up in Doncaster, his local Anglican parish church burned down and he constructed a cardboard scale model of it from memory, complete in every detail. At his father's wish the model was exhibited and sold for five guineas to a local man who illuminated the interior with candles. Predictably, and perhaps appropriately, the model burned down. So Bentley built another which was kept in the family.

Bentley started to design Westminster Cathedral in March 1895, on his return from a six month tour of European Byzantine and Romanesque churches. By early 1896 his building plans were complete and a special set was submitted to Pope Leo XIII in April of that year. It must have been these early plans which were used to design the model. The firm chosen to construct it, Farmer & Brindley of 63 Westminster Bridge Road, were a well-established company of decorative stone and marble merchants, sculptors and wood-carvers. William Brindley, the firm's co-founder and owner, carved the capitals and other stonework for the Albert Memorial and was described by George Gilbert Scott in 1873 as 'the best carver I have met with and the one who best understands my needs'. Farmer & Brindley were subsequently responsible for the majority of the early marblework in Westminster Cathedral before ceasing trading in 1929.

A section of the model showing the main entrance to the Cathedral.

Francis Child, wood-carver

At the end of the 19th century the principal wood-carver at Farmer & Brindley was Francis Child, who lived with his unmarried daughter, Kate, a savings bank clerk, at 40 West Square, Southwark. He was born in Birmingham and Kate in Gloucester so he probably worked for several firms before joining Farmer & Brindley, which was formed in 1868. The absence of any mention of a wife in the census records suggests that Francis Child was a widower. In 1897, when work on the model got underway, he would have been 65 and Kate 25. It can be safely assumed that he was responsible for carving the model though, in view of its complexity, he would have had assistants. Fortunately he lived fairly close to his workplace, a journey on foot from his house at 40 West Square to Farmer & Brindley's works at 63 Westminster Bridge Road (now a block of flats) takes just six minutes.

The model cost over £750 (£50,000 today) to make, though not all of this was charged. It was made of Kauri Pine, a softwood which grows in Australasia, South-East Asia and the Pacific. But other woods, including mahogany and pearwood, have been incorporated. Damage unfortunately occurred when the model was moved (which it frequently was) - initially

A close-up of the baldacchino and sanctuary arcades showing the detail of the carving.

to the Clerk of Work's office in the Cathedral grounds where it would have been used to explain to contractors what was required of them, and shown to visitors such as Charles Hadfield; then to Archbishop's House to be used to help the fundraising in which Cardinal Vaughan was directly involved; to the premises of the Architectural Association in Tufton Street where John Marshall (Bentley's successor) used it to illustrate a presentation on the Cathedral in 1907; to the Cathedral Hall for displays and exhibitions; back to its normal position in the Cathedral south gallery and Architect's Room; to St Joseph's Chapel in 2010 for extensive renovation and restoration by George Rome Innes, and finally to the north gallery below the tower for inclusion in the present 'Treasures of the Cathedral' exhibition.

It is fascinating to compare the model with the Westminster Cathedral we see today. Many of the side walls of the model can be removed to see the delicate features which reveal Bentley's initial ideas. The main structure is the same but the details – the mouldings above the great west doors, the carved eagles on the tower, the finials on the turrets, the windows and decoration of the chapels, and many other features - have been developed and modified during the century and more since Bentley first returned from his tour of European cities and set down his plans to build a cathedral.

The model under restoration by George Rome Innes in St Joseph's Chapel in March 2010.

PART II

LITURGY AND
MUSIC

His Holiness Pope Benedict XVI celebrating Mass in Westminster Cathedral. 18 September 2010. Photo: L'Osservatore Romano.

1. The Choir That Never Was

Cardinal Herbert Vaughan, founder of Westminster Cathedral, came from a Catholic recusant family and had a strong sense of history. Right from the first he saw his new cathedral as a means of providing the daily Divine Office in its entirety, a practice long since abandoned as part of public worship in this country. The body he chose to carry this out were English Benedictine monks, expelled from Westminster Abbey at the Reformation. For besides their return to Westminster appealing to his sense of history, he believed that no other body of men could present the Divine Liturgy so reverently and so effectively.

The Benedictine Mission

Thus it was that when John Francis Bentley, the Cathedral architect, started work on the new Cathedral on his return to England in March 1895, his plans included a monks' choir, a large chapel and a monastery for the exclusive use of Benedictine monks. Meanwhile, as the first step in bringing the monks back to Westminster, in May 1896 Vaughan contacted the Benedictines at Downside Abbey and offered them a mission in the prosperous, middle-class London suburb of Ealing, from which they could easily commute to Westminster for choral duties in the Cathedral.

Cardinal Herbert Vaughan, third Archbishop of Westminster 1892-1903.

A 1902 advertisement for the Cathedral Choir School.

Vaughan's intention was that the Benedictines at Ealing would provide a community of monks on which the Cathedral could draw for its liturgical needs. The aim of the Benedictines, however, was to establish a monastery and secondary school (which Cardinal Vaughan opposed) in London, rather than existing purely to serve the needs of Westminster Cathedral. Secondly, Fr Richard O'Halloran, the Catholic priest then in charge of the Ealing mission, had trained for the priesthood at Mill Hill Missionary College, which was founded by Cardinal Vaughan, but had then refused to take the missionary oath and had crossed swords with Vaughan on several occasions. He refused to vacate his mission in favour of the Benedictines and continued to minister to a small but loyal congregation in Ealing until his death in 1925.

The Cathedral Hall, where the Divine Office was first sung in 1902.

The French Connection

Nevertheless Downside Abbey accepted Cardinal Vaughan's proposals. The Benedictines moved to Ealing in 1897 and a church (St Benedict's) was opened two years later. But then Vaughan began to have second thoughts. English Benedictines were unusual in that they did not live a truly monastic life but at that time were bound by a missionary oath to work in a pastoral capacity in their missions or parishes. There was a real risk of rivalry and resentment between them and the secular clergy at the Cathedral. Were there any other Benedictines who could sing the Divine Office without being bound by a missionary commitment? Thus it was that in 1899 Cardinal Vaughan took the surprising step of offering a position already offered to English Benedictines to the French Benedictines of Solesmes Abbey, who were truly monastic and renowned for their plainsong.

The response of Solesmes was favourable. They envisaged a French-controlled monastery at Westminster with rooms for 30 monks. But for the first year of a three-year trial period they could supply only about 15, not all with good voices. Could the English Benedictines help by bringing the number up to 20? Thus in late 1900 Vaughan was forced to write to Downside Abbey to ask them to assist in the establishment of a French Benedictine community at Westminster Cathedral. The proposal was regarded as a public insult. In February 1901 Abbot (later Cardinal) Aidan Gasquet, President of the English Benedictine Congregation, wrote to Vaughan refusing to countenance foreign Benedictines at Westminster. Without such agreement Vaughan knew that he could not proceed and regretfully wrote to the French accordingly.

In an attempt to defuse the ill-feeling which the issue had by now engendered both between the English and French Benedictines and between them and the secular clergy (and no doubt also to relieve the Ealing monks of their Cathedral responsibilities), Abbot Gasquet suggested that secular priests should be responsible for the liturgy at the Cathedral and that a choir school should be formed. And so, with a mixture of regret and relief, Vaughan abandoned his plan for a return of Benedictine monks to Westminster and turned to the secular clergy. At the Westminster Diocesan Synod in the spring of 1901 he announced the change of plan and called on them to provide the high standard of church music required. At the same time the formation of a choir school was announced. The response was enthusiastic, and on 5 October 1901 Vaughan was able to welcome the first eleven boy choristers with the words "You are the foundation-stones". The Cathedral Choir was instituted and formed three months later, in January 1902.

The Cathedral Choir in 1905 with Sir Richard Terry in the centre.

The New Choir

On the Feast of the Ascension 1902, Cardinal Vaughan got his wish. The Divine Office was chanted for the first time within the precincts of Westminster Cathedral, and the first Solemn High Mass sung by the Cathedral Choir consisting of 25 boy trebles and 15 men singers directed by Richard Terry (Sir Richard Terry from 1922), the Choirmaster and Director of Music. As the Cathedral was unfinished, it took place in the Chapter Hall (now the Cathedral Hall), which was arranged like the Sistine Chapel in Rome. The First Vespers of the Feast, followed by Compline, were solemnly chanted on the eve of the festival. The following morning the Hours of Prime and Terce were recited, a solemn High Mass was sung to the five-part setting by the great 16th century Catholic composer William Byrd, with the motet *Tu es Petrus* by Palestrina, followed by the offices of Sext and None. In the afternoon the Second Vespers of the Feast, followed by Compline, were solemnly sung. Cardinal Vaughan presided at all services.

So what became of Vaughan's romantic dream of bringing about the return of the Benedictines to London? Like Vaughan the Benedictines got what they wanted, but without having to serve in the Cathedral. Ealing Abbey became a priory in 1916, an independent priory in 1947 and an abbey in 1955, and serves a large parish. A school, started in 1902, caters for 750 senior pupils, 270 juniors and 30 infants. In Westminster Cathedral it is to Vaughan's plan for a Benedictine choir that we owe the excellent acoustics from the raised, six-windowed retro-choir behind the high altar, designed to provide the space and light needed for the monks to sing the Divine Office. At the back, and still in use, are twin oak doors for the monks to process across a bridge, along the cloisters (now Long Corridor) to the monastery, currently occupied by the Cathedral Choir School with its renowned boys' choir.

And finally to the two alcoves, with their balconies, twin marble columns and glittering mosaics, which look down from the apse of Westminster Cathedral. Attractive in themselves, they provide a perfect view of the choir while allowing occupants to remain unseen from public gaze. That on the right is a one minute walk from Archbishop's House, via the Library and Long Corridor. I suggest that it was intended for Cardinal Vaughan, who was devoted to the Divine Office but would have been loath to cause distraction by appearing in public. The one opposite provides symmetry and would have been available for important visitors. Support for this theory is provided by Vaughan's occupation of a similar private oratory when attending Divine Office in the Cathedral Hall. This was located on the upper gallery at the back, access being through the private library in Archbishop's House.

Ealing Abbey and school.

2. The First Cathedral Parish

At 8.30am on the Feast of St Joseph, 19 March 1903, the first High Mass was held in Westminster Cathedral, the event being described in *The Tablet* two days later and recorded both in *The Universe* and *The Catholic Herald*. It was celebrated not, as might have been expected, on the main sanctuary but in what was to become the Lady Chapel of the Cathedral. Neither did the congregation consist of the great and the good, as also might have been expected. It was made up instead of those at the other end of the social scale who inhabited the rookeries, tenements and slum dwellings of old Westminster, then being rapidly demolished, in the area known as Tothill Fields between Victoria Station and Westminster Abbey in the north, and the Thames Embankment between Claverton Street and Westminster Bridge in the south and east.

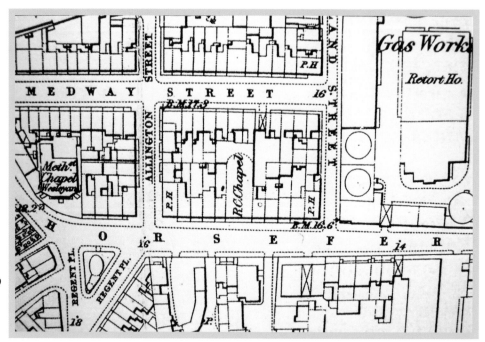

A map of Westminster in 1869 showing St Mary's Chapel (centre) on Horseferry Road.

St Mary's, Horseferry Road

Those attending the Mass in the Lady Chapel were from St Mary's, the old mission chapel at 94A Horseferry Road, founded in 1813 by a French refugee, Fr Charles Adrien Lengrenay of Vauville in Normandy. In 1850 it was adopted by the Jesuits as one of the conditions under which their Farm Street church in Mayfair was licensed. At that time there were 5,000 Catholics in the area administered by St Mary's, many of them Irish, often unable to read or write and working at the local gasworks (the world's first). Policemen patrolled only in pairs and at night it was essential to be armed with a stout stick. The Jesuits established free schools for boys, girls and infants in cottages at 28-30 Medway Street, backing onto St Mary's. They also provided chaplains for the 240-270 Catholic men and 30-40 women in Millbank Penitentiary, and the Catholic women and boys in Tothill Fields Prison. But in 1900 responsibility was transferred from the Jesuits to the new Cathedral and the mission was administered from Archbishop's House.

It seems clear that, realising the vastness of the Cathedral and the lack of Catholics living in the immediate vicinity, Cardinal Vaughan feared that the new building might not attract a sufficient congregation. He therefore resolved to close neighbouring churches which might compete, such as St Mary's, Horseferry Road. Writing to a close friend, Lady Herbert of Lea, on 3 January 1903, he explained that St Mary's mission

*The garden at 94A
Horseferry Road,
where St Mary's
Chapel once stood.*

chapel was going to be sold. He wanted to introduce its congregation to the Cathedral before the solemn opening and the arrival of others, and make them feel at home there 'with all their devotions, and even benches and furniture from Horseferry Road'.

Alerted to the danger by their parish priest, Fr Eric Green, who was told of the plan by Cardinal Vaughan in January, the congregation of St Mary's (numbering 1,200 according to the *Daily News*) held a public meeting in Westminster Town Hall on 8 February 'with the full sympathy of the clergy'. They petitioned Vaughan to keep their church open, even offering to guarantee the rent for three years. But Vaughan was determined that St Mary's should provide a ready-made parish for the Cathedral. In a letter of 15 March to Fr Green and his parish, published in *The Catholic Herald* on 27 March, he explained that he understood the reluctance of the congregation to move but he wanted them to 'have the preference' in the Cathedral before the public opening and the arrival of others. He added that 'I have fixed the Feast of the Glorious St Joseph as the day for the removal from the chapel to the Cathedral and I commit the whole congregation, with all its interests and hopes, to the care of this our blessed and most powerful Father'.

The closing services at St Mary's took place on Sunday, 15 March, to the surprise of many of the congregation. The Mass was celebrated by Revd Charles Brown, soon to be appointed Rector of the College of Chaplains, Prefect of the Choir and Precentor at Westminster Cathedral. He described it as an awful ordeal: 'The place was filled, mostly with poor people, many of them in tears, and all sad and dejected; for, naturally it was to them a hallowed spot and was linked up in their lives with many sacred associations. Many of them had been baptised there, many also had been married there, and all had performed their religious duties there for several generations'. Afterwards the congregation gathered in small groups outside to reminisce, reluctant to leave the chapel for the last time. Parish officials, now without a role, lingered as if they had been evicted from their own homes. The legless-cripple, a familiar figure, received his last alms just within the entrance before giving the chapel one last, wistful glance and shuffling off to find another pitch.

The Parish Chapel

The new parish chapel (the Cathedral Lady Chapel) was opened with High Mass at 8.30am on 19 March 1903, the Feast of St Joseph, as directed by Cardinal Vaughan. The chapel had been partitioned and curtained off from the rest of the Cathedral which was still in the hands of the builders. Access was by a side door of the west front. The new congregation brought their own choir and organ and had tested the excellent acoustic properties of the chapel after Mass on the previous Sunday. The Stations of the Cross, the mission crucifix and pulpit, the statues and benches were all carried over from St Mary's on Horseferry Road and these, together with a number of temporary confessionals, provided the chapel with a degree of warmth and habitation lacking in the bare brick walls.

Mr M H O'Connor, schoolmaster, choirmaster and organist at St Mary's Chapel from 1889.

Numbers attending the new parish chapel services rapidly increased. On Palm Sunday 1903, 900 attended Mass and 1,100 were present at the renewal of Baptismal vows on Easter Sunday. On Whit Sunday on 31 May the first 200 candidates received the Sacrament of Confirmation in the chapel - the first Confirmations in the Cathedral. Nor were the traditions of St Mary's abandoned. The annual procession in honour of St Aloysius, long an established custom there, took place on 12 July with Catholics coming forth from the tenements of Westminster and assembling in front of the Cathedral. Accompanied by priests, they then carried the processional cross, statues of saints, torches, emblems, flowers and fluttering banners through Victoria Street, Artillery Row, Great Peter Street, Marsham Street, Millbank, Vauxhall Bridge Road and back to the Cathedral.

The procession on the Feast of St Aloysius had been delayed by the death of Cardinal Vaughan on 19 June 1903. In his letter of 15 March to the congregation of St Mary's, he had expressed his regret that he was not well enough to celebrate St Joseph's Feast Day with them in the Lady Chapel of the new Cathedral. He was devoted to St Joseph, naming the missionary college which he founded at Mill Hill 'St Joseph's College', and writing in a letter to Lady Herbert of Lea on 22 March 'I received the Last Sacraments on the 19th and thought St Joseph would have come for me; but he saw I was not ready then. Perhaps I may be on the 25th - perhaps later'.

The Wrong Date

So why, when the first Mass in the Cathedral clearly took place on St Joseph's Feast Day, 19 March 1903, in accordance with Cardinal Vaughan's express instructions, was the date recorded by the Cathedral as Lady Day (25 March) for almost a century? For an answer we have to go back to the Cathedral records. There was no Cathedral magazine between June 1902 and January 1907 when the *Westminster Cathedral Chronicle* appeared. In its second issue in February, there was a history of the Cathedral by William Johnson, Bishop of Arindela and Auxiliary Bishop of Westminster. In it he writes that 'On Lady Day 1903 one of the Chapels of the Cathedral was screened off to be used temporarily as a parochial or mission Chapel'.

Bishop Johnson's history of the Cathedral was reproduced for the Eucharistic Congress of 1908 and for the Consecration of the Cathedral in 1910. The reference to Lady Day 1903 subsequently appears as the date of the first Cathedral Mass in Winefride de l'Hôpital's *Westminster Cathedral and its Architect*, published in 1919 and generally regarded as the most authoritative source on the early years of the Cathedral. This date is repeated in subsequent books and guidebooks. It was not until early 2003, when the centenary of the first Mass was approaching, that the true date was revealed. So why was the mistake made, only four years after the event, and why did it go unchallenged? Most probably Bishop Johnson simply made a mistake. He was not present at the Mass in the Lady Chapel in 1903, and published his history of the Cathedral in 1907, the year of his death, aged 75. As to the absence of any challenge, he was, after all, a bishop.

The Cathedral Parish Chapel (later the Lady Chapel) in 1903.

3. Death of a Cardinal

By April 1903 the parishioners of St Mary's Chapel, now standing empty on Horseferry Road, were becoming accustomed to their new surroundings in the Lady Chapel of Westminster Cathedral. All the services were crowded and all available standing room taken up. Meanwhile in Chapter Hall (Cathedral Hall) the daily services which had started on Ascension Day in May 1902 had continued, accompanied by the Cathedral Choir, though numbers attending were far smaller than in the Lady Chapel. So what was happening in the main body of the Cathedral?

Music and Oranges

Decoration there continued throughout 1902, with first J Whitehead & Sons' marbleworkers and then George Bridge's mosaicists engaged in both the Holy Souls Chapel and that of St Gregory and St Augustine opposite. The bronze statue of St Peter, the Archbishop's throne, the pulpit and the baptismal font arrived from Rome one by one in packing cases to await assembly and installation. On 3 May 1902 a concert of Catholic choirs was held for a visit of the Catholic Association and on 11 June a grand recital of sacred music was organised to test the acoustics and raise money for the Choir School. The music was provided by an orchestra of a hundred and a choir of two hundred, including the Cathedral Choir directed by Richard (later Sir Richard) Terry. The programme consisted of Wagner's *Holy Supper of the Apostles*, Purcell's *Te Deum in D*, Beethoven's *Symphony in C Minor*, Palestrina's *Surge illuminare* and motets by Byrd, Tallis, Blow and Wingham. Cardinal Vaughan and an audience of 3,000 attended and the acoustics proved to be excellent.

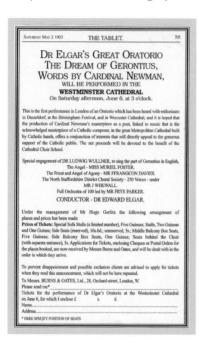

Announcement of The Dream of Gerontius.

During the summer months of 1902 free organ recitals were given on Saturday afternoons to attract visitors to the Cathedral and interest them in its music. But it was not until 26 April 1903 that the first truly religious ceremony occurred in the main body of the Cathedral. Good Shepherd Sunday was celebrated there by Bishop Algernon Stanley who was standing in for Cardinal Vaughan during his absence through ill-health. Some 1,100 children representing 30,000 from 267 elementary schools in the archdiocese presented their annual contributions for the welfare of less fortunate Catholic children. During Lent and afterwards they had saved up their pocket money, raising a total of £520, which they now presented to Bishop Stanley, seated in the centre of the sanctuary. Meanwhile the Cathedral was filled with priests, teachers and parents - 5,000 of them according *The Catholic Herald*. Afterwards the children were given sweets and oranges - Ambrosden Avenue, beside the Cathedral, bearing ample evidence of this for some time afterwards.

A year later, on 6 June 1903, Cardinal John Henry Newman's 1865 poem *The Dream of Gerontius*, an old man's dying vision of the journey of his soul, set to music composed by Sir Edward Elgar, was performed in The Cathedral. It was its first performance in London. The composer himself conducted an orchestra of a hundred musicians from the Symphonic Orchestra of Amsterdam with Richard Terry at the organ. The chorus was provided by the North Staffordshire Choral Society, numbering two hundred and fifty voices. The performance aroused great interest in the musical world and the audience packed the floor, tribunes and galleries of the Cathedral. The net proceeds went to support the Cathedral Choir School. Once again, Cardinal Vaughan was unable to be present. He was lying close to death in St Joseph's Missionary College which he had founded at Mill Hill in north London.

The Founder's Requiem

A fortnight later, on a misty Sunday night in June, the first solemn religious ceremony to be performed in the Cathedral took place. The body of Cardinal Vaughan, the Cathedral's founder, was carried through the great west doors to lie in state on a black-draped catafalque positioned where the nave meets the sanctuary at the crossing of the Cathedral. There it was surrounded by six huge candles. The Cardinal had passed away just before midnight on Friday, 19 June at St Joseph's College, and his body was brought to the Cathedral two days later. Through Sunday, Monday, Tuesday and Wednesday nights the vigil around his body continued, kept by members of the Franciscan, Dominican, Carmelite and Servite orders and by nuns from the Sisters of Nazareth and the Sisters of Charity. The Cathedral clergy themselves kept the watches of the deeper night.

Cardinal Vaughan's body lying in state in the Cathedral. June 1903.

Each morning a series of Low Masses were said from 6am until 9am at a temporary altar erected at the foot of the sanctuary steps, after which a solemn High Mass of Requiem was celebrated. Throughout the day on Monday and Tuesday the Cathedral was open to the public, allowing those who so wished to pay their last respects to their cardinal. On Tuesday alone 27,000 people were counted as they filed past the catafalque. At nightfall Vespers and Matins of the dead were sung by the clergy and choir, after which the Cathedral closed and the vigil continued. On Wednesday the Cathedral was closed all day after the High Mass until the solemn dirge (Matins and Lauds of the Dead) at 6pm, in order to prepare for the funeral on the following day, Thursday 25 June.

The Requiem Mass was a simple one, as requested by Cardinal Vaughan. The sanctuary was draped in black, the coffin covered by a black velvet pall embroidered with a gold cross, with the Cardinal's red hat at the foot. Crowded into the sanctuary, transepts, nave, chapels and galleries were the Cathedral clergy and other representatives of the Catholic Church. Members of the public were given 1,000 seats. The Mass was celebrated by Algernon Stanley, Bishop of Emmaus and Bishop-assistant to the Cardinal, and the absolutions given by four bishops including Cardinal Logue, Archbishop of Armagh. The music was provided by the Cathedral Choir and another made up of priests from the dioceses of Westminster, Southwark and Portsmouth. The following day, after a last night of vigil, Cardinal Vaughan's body was removed to St Joseph's Missionary College where he had asked to be interred. It was reinterred in the Cathedral on 14 March 2005, when the college faced closure.

Christmas Eve Midnight Mass, 1903.

The Doors Open

The next major event in the Cathedral was its long awaited opening on Christmas Eve 1903. Cardinal Vaughan had hoped to open it in 1900, and again in 1902, but the architect's death and the absence of the planned marble baldacchino over the high altar prevented this. Of course the Cathedral had been open before, but only for specific events such as *The Dream of Gerontius,* Good Shepherd Sunday, Cardinal Vaughan's lying in state and his Requiem Mass. Meanwhile Mass had been regularly celebrated in the Lady Chapel since 19 March 1903. But these were essentially private events and the Christmas Eve celebrations were public. They started with the First Vespers of Christmas, followed by Midnight Mass - the first public Mass to take place in the Cathedral. With more than 2,000 in the congregation, it was celebrated by Provost (later Bishop) William Johnson, accompanied by the Cathedral Choir.

From now on the Divine Office, which had been sung in the Chapter Hall since May 1902, would be in the Cathedral, with Matins and Lauds at 9.45am, Prime and Terce at 10.30am, High Mass at 10.45am and None and Vespers at 3.15pm. Sung Mass at 11.30am on Sunday in the parish chapel (Lady Chapel) would now be replaced by High Mass on the Cathedral sanctuary at 11.00am, but the parish children's Mass at 9.30am and the Low Mass with music at 12noon would continue to take place in the Lady Chapel. In this manner the reluctant parishioners from St Mary's, Horseferry Road, who had petitioned Cardinal Vaughan earlier in the year to remain there, became integrated into the new Cathedral.

The enthronement of Francis Bourne as fourth Archbishop of Westminster.
29 December 1903.

Celebrating Mass and the Divine Office had at first been undertaken by clergy from neighbouring parishes, assisted by Cathedral staff. But of course they had their own parish duties. So Vaughan had arranged for Cathedral chaplains to move into Archbishop's House, taking over the residential accommodation previously occupied by the Choir School, which moved to Pimlico. But the Cathedral was now responsible not only for the area administered by St Mary's, Horseferry Road, but also for the whole of the Pimlico District which had come under St Mary's, Cadogan Street, Chelsea. Its parish thus consisted of the semi-circle formed by the Thames from Chelsea Bridge to Westminster Bridge, with the Cathedral at the centre. After the opening of the Cathedral, the number of chaplains was therefore increased from twelve to eighteen and the whole area was divided into districts, each with two priests who alternated between parochial duties and celebrating Mass and the Divine Office at the Cathedral.

Cardinal Vaughan's successor, the newly appointed Archbishop Francis Bourne, had taken formal possession of the Cathedral on 25 September 1903 when he met the Cathedral Chapter and presented them with his Brief of Appointment. The date chosen for his enthronement was 29 December, the feast of St Thomas Becket, the martyred Archbishop of Canterbury. On that day, returning from Rome with the Pallium, Bourne was solemnly installed as the fourth Archbishop of Westminster. Both the ceremony itself and the antiphons sung by the Cathedral Choir were the same as those used when the Archbishops of Canterbury returned from Rome with the Pallium before the Reformation. The enthronement was followed by High Mass and the Papal Blessing. For this, the first great ceremony in the newly opened cathedral, the public was allowed in without a ticket.

Consecration

The final act in the establishment of Westminster Cathedral was its consecration which took place on 28 June 1910. The ceremonies began the previous evening in the Cathedral Hall, with the exposition of the relics of the saints which were to be deposited in each of the altars in the Cathedral. Those for the high altar were relics of four English saints - St Boniface of Fulda, St Thomas and St Edmund of Canterbury and St William of York - and also of St Francis de Sales who was the patron saint of Archbishop Bourne. The ceremony was accompanied by music by William Byrd, sung by the Cathedral choir, and was followed by Matins and Lauds. Early next morning the ancient consecration ceremonies began, with Archbishop Bourne making three circuits around the outside of the Cathedral while sprinkling the walls and ground with holy water - symbolic of baptism and triple immersion in its saving waters - before entering the empty building.

The Cathedral nave had been previously painted with two broad diagonal white lines, intersecting in the form of a cross, with little mounds of ashes, each marked with a letter of the Greek or Latin alphabet, placed at regular intervals. During the Rite of Consecration the Archbishop traced first the Greek alphabet, and then the Latin, along the two intersecting lines, thus symbolising the instruction of the newly baptised in the elements of Faith and of Christian doctrine. There followed a procession three times around the interior to bless the walls and floor of the Cathedral from within. Afterwards all the altars in the Cathedral were simultaneously consecrated by the Archbishop and thirteen other bishops, and the holy relics deposited. The Mass of Dedication was then celebrated to 16th century music by Orlando di Lasso and Peter Philips, sung by the Cathedral Choir. At the Elevation of the Host, the great bell 'Edward' in the Cathedral tower was heard for the first time.

Archbishop Bourne tracing the letters of the alphabet during the Rite of Consecration. 28 June 1910.

4. A Sequence of Organs

During the lifetime of the Cathedral several different organs have been brought into service, culminating in the present T C Lewis organ in the apse and Henry Willis III grand organ at the west end of the Cathedral. This is their story.

The First Organs

The first in the series was a small three manual organ by Waddington with tracker action and about ten speaking stops with the usual couplers. Presented by a donor, in 1902 it was placed on the raised stage in the apse of the Cathedral Hall (then called the Chapter Hall) and curtained off behind the altar. It never seems to have been used, being voiced as a chamber organ and described as hopelessly defective and out of tune. It was later dismantled, the pipes sold and the action and console thrown away.

To accompany the Divine Office which started in May 1902 in the Cathedral Hall, a Positive organ, a one manual instrument built by the Positive Organ Company of Mornington Crescent, London, stood on the left below the altar platform. The firm was

The Positive organ above the Vaughan Chantry, where it still stands.

founded in 1887 by J Mewburn Levien and Thomas Casson (Managing Director) and the organ is sometimes referred to as the Casson organ. The organist was usually Richard (later Sir Richard) Terry, the Director of Music, who also conducted the Cathedral Choir. When the services were moved to the main body of the Cathedral at the end of 1903, the organ was mounted on a trolley so that it could be moved to wherever it was needed. For quite some time it was wheeled between the Blessed Sacrament Chapel, where it was used for evening services, and the Lady Chapel when the Cathedral Choir sang the Divine Office there. Eventually it was realised that the frequent moving was bad for the organ and it was transferred to the tribune above the Vaughan Chantry, where it is today, fitted with an electric blower. It was used as recently as 1994 to accompany the liturgy in the Blessed Sacrament Chapel while the Lady Chapel was being renovated.

The next organ arrived with the congregation from St Mary's, Horseferry Road. As instructed by Cardinal Vaughan, they reluctantly moved to the Lady Chapel of the Cathedral and held their first service there on 19 March 1903. Among the items they brought with them was a two manual organ with tracker action which was set up in the niche where the mosaic-surrounded confessional now stands. While the Lady Chapel served as their parish chapel during the remainder of 1903, the organ accompanied the choir and congregation with Mr O'Connor, the St Mary's schoolmaster, acting as the organist. Even after the Cathedral was opened, the organ was still played on Sundays in the chapel at the children's Mass and midday Mass. But before long the independence of St Mary's came to an end and the organ was first moved to a tribune above the entrance to the Blessed Sacrament Chapel and then sold.

The Apse Organs

The next organ was a giant. It was a three manual instrument built by Norman & Beard of Chalk Farm, London, with an electric action on the Hope-Jones system. It was hired from the builders at £100 a year, installed in 1902 and played at the performance of *The Dream of Gerontius* on 6 June 1903. The detached console stood in the apse and was connected to the organ by a long, flexible cable. The organ itself was mounted in two parts in the tribune above the Archbishop's throne on the left of the sanctuary. Between the two parts was the blowing apparatus consisting of three feeders and a wind-chest powered by an electric motor. Unfortunately the fuse of the motor occasionally blew requiring it to be replaced by one of

The Norman & Beard organ in the tribune above the sanctuary in 1902.

the choristers (Blackwell by name), or the belt connecting the motor to the flywheel slipped off. Norman & Beard had men in the tribune ready to remedy such problems on important occasions, but by 1907 the organ had been returned to the firm permanently.

The new organ console installed in the apse in 1926.

The organ which replaced the Norman & Beard was a small two manual instrument built in about 1906 by Thomas (T C) Lewis & Co of Ferndale Road, Brixton, founded in 1854. Initially hired, but subsequently purchased, by early 1907 the organ was in regular use to accompany the Cathedral Choir. It appears in front of the central doors at the back of the apse in pictures of the 1910 consecration of the Cathedral. In 1923 the instrument was divided into two sections containing the swell and great organs and positioned either side of the apse doors, allowing them to be used. The organs were encased in oak in 1925. The following year Henry Willis & Sons, founded in 1845, which had amalgamated with Lewis & Co in 1919, provided a large new four manual console at the extreme east end of the apse. This controlled both the apse organ and the newly installed grand organ at the west end of the Cathedral by means of electric cables running the length of the building, thus allowing one organist to play both instruments. The apse console was subsequently rebuilt by the firm of Harrison & Harrison of Durham in 1984 as a two manual, controlling the whole of the apse organ and part of the grand organ, and moved to its present position on the right of the apse.

The Grand Organ

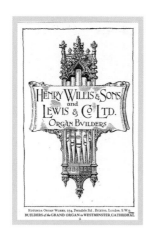

A 1924 advertisement for Henry Willis & Sons and Lewis & Co of Brixton.

Soon after the Cathedral was opened in 1903, a specification for a grand organ was obtained from Harrison & Harrison. It would have been a huge instrument and would have cost £18,000 at a time when the Cathedral was in substantial debt. Nevertheless, soon after it was started in January 1907, the monthly *Westminster Cathedral Chronicle* was appealing for funds for an organ for the proper accompaniment of congregational singing, adding that the existing apse organ 'can only be regarded as a temporary expedient'. Cardinal Bourne had realised the inadequacy of the apse organ to accompany the Cathedral congregation. In 1909 a 'Westminster Cathedral Organ Account' was opened and the following year, in the *Book of the Consecration of Westminster Cathedral*, Richard Terry also appealed for funds. He estimated the total cost of a grand organ, which could be installed in sections, to be £10,000.

But it was not until Christmas Eve 1920 that the first contract for the grand organ was signed. It was John Courage of the brewing family who advised Cardinal Bourne that the commission should be entrusted to Henry Willis & Sons and Lewis & Co. The requirement was for a four manual instrument of 67 speaking stops, complete with console, to be installed in the gallery above the narthex at the west end of the Cathedral. The first stage was blessed by Cardinal Bourne on 14 June 1922 and inaugurated on 2 July when Marcel Dupré played at a Mass to commemorate the Battle of Verdun. At that time it was estimated that the total cost would be £16,000. Construction work then continued for a further ten years. The marble and oak organ screen was completed in 1924 and the two gilt bronze angel trumpet players added in 1926. As described above, in the same year a large console was installed in the apse to control both the grand and apse organs. By the time that the, now dual control, grand organ was finally completed in 1932, an event fittingly celebrated with recitals by Marcel Dupré on 1 and 2 March, the number of its speaking stops had grown to 78 and the number of its pipes to 4,398. The grand organ was completely overhauled and restored by Harrison & Harrison in 1984. This included conversion of the pneumatic actions to an electro-pneumatic system.

David Chapman, of Harrison & Harrison, tuning the Grand Organ during one of his regular maintenance checks between 1984 and 2000.

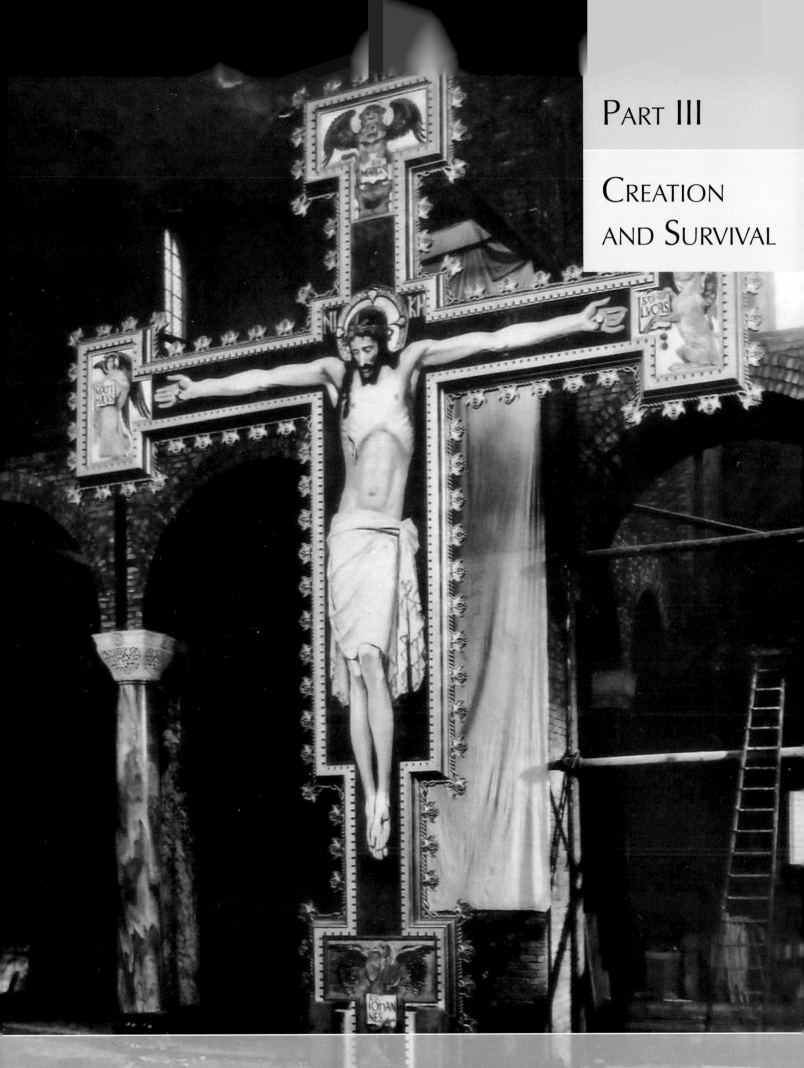

The Great Rood standing in the Cathedral nave after being painted by William Christian Symons. Autumn 1903.

1. St Edward's Tower

The most well-known feature of Westminster Cathedral must be its bell tower or 'campanile'. Standing prominently on the London skyline for the last one hundred years and more, it reaches a height of over 284 feet if the cross on the summit is included, and provides spectacular views over London. Understandably, if a little unkindly, it was initially known by many as 'The Roman Candle'.

Initial Designs

The tower is clearly influenced by the campanili of Italian churches, particularly those of Lombardy and Venetia. J F Bentley, the Cathedral architect, spent four months, from November 1894 to March 1895, studying early church architecture in Italy before starting to build the Cathedral in June. The many campanili he saw in the places he visited such as Milan, Ravenna and Venice - where that of St Mark's Basilica, for example, is such a prominent feature, formed the basis for our campanile.

In fact Bentley initially planned twin towers at the west end, one on the outer side of each of the two small entrance lobbies, in the positions now occupied by spiral staircases, and thus directly in line with the nave aisles. Bentley's second plan, dated June 1895, shows a single larger tower projecting from, and forming part of, the western façade. Only in the third plan, published in the *Westminster Cathedral Chronicle* of January 1896, is the campanile shown in its present position, set back from the west front with its base between the Cathedral Gift Shop and the Chapel of the Holy Souls beside Ambrosden Avenue.

Construction and Prayers

The excavations for the foundations of the tower were 17 feet deep and 46 feet square. Into this were poured hundreds of tons of concrete, consisting of 'Goliath' brand Portland cement mixed with Thames ballast, the work being completed by Mowlems of Westminster in late 1895. Then, in early 1896, came the brickwork foundations up

A view of the Cathedral from Ambrosden Avenue, showing the unfinished tower surrounded by scaffolding. Summer 1902.

to ground level, consisting of hand-made blue Staffordshire bricks, impervious to moisture and laid in cement by Perrys of Bow. Finally the tower proper was built, faced with 3ft courses of thin red Bracknell bricks alternating with 12 inch bands of Portland stone, the work being undertaken by Shillitoe & Sons of Bury St Edmunds.

The tower was erected using internal scaffolding only, with the building materials being taken up in baskets by a hoist powered by a small steam-engine in the nave. No external scaffolding was thus required until the cupola came to be built. The contract with Shillitoes was placed in November 1896 and by March 1902 the tower was 220 feet in height. On 2 January 1903 the great wrought bronze metropolitan cross, made by Elsley & Co. and containing a relic of the True Cross in a small silver tube, was put in place. The cross had been privately blessed by Cardinal Vaughan on New Year's Day.

Thirty feet square at the base and tapering by seven inches, the tower remains on a level with the rest of the building before rising clear at the fourth floor. At 185 feet the eighth floor has four twin balconies which form the present public viewing platform. At 218 feet the ninth floor is surrounded by more arched balconies with buttress-like projections capped by turrets. This was the upper viewing platform, reached by a narrow spiral staircase and closed now to the public. At 225 feet the campanile changes from a square to a polygon, then to a drum surrounded by 12 carved stone eagles, and finally to a teak-framed, lead-covered cupola surmounted by the bronze, metropolitan cross. In all there are ten floors, the top of the cupola rising to 273ft 3in with the cross increasing this to 284ft 6in.

Miss M E Stephens ('The Speaker') with the 23 stonemasons and bricklayers who built the tower.

Shillitoes employed fourteen stonemasons and bricklayers to build the tower with nine more (including a 'mess room man') at ground level to prepare the materials and run the steam-driven donkey engine. A regular event at the top of the structure was a religious service organised by two sisters, Miss M E Stephens and Mrs L N Knott. Each week at noon they were hoisted to the top of the tower in baskets to conduct a short service of prayer, bible reading and hymn singing, and all the men were invited to their home in Beckenham when Miss Stephens (referred to by the men as 'The Speaker') was married.

A Bell, a Lift and a Foreign Correspondent

St Edward the Confessor was chosen as the tower's patron saint at the time of King Edward VII's Coronation in August 1902, when a crown of light shone from the top of the tower in celebration. The blessing and dedication of the tower took place two months later on 13 October, the Feast of St Edward the Confessor. After High Mass in the Chapter Hall (Cathedral Hall) and the parish chapel (the Cathedral Lady Chapel), at successive heights of the tower the Cathedral Choir, conducted by Richard Terry, sang first *Veritas Mea*, the offertorium for the Feast of the Confessor, to a setting by Francesco Foggia; secondly the hymn *Iste Confessor,* with the antiphon, versicle and prayer of St Edward; and thirdly, at the summit, *Tu es Petrus*, which was followed by the *Domine Salvum Fac Regem Nostrum Eduardum* and the prayer for the reigning sovereign. The singing could be heard as far as the Army & Navy Stores.

The top of the tower showing the metropolitan cross.

The interior of the drum and cupola at the top of the tower.

The belfry possesses a single bell weighing 52cwt 10lbs and known as 'Edward'. Given by the Duchess of Norfolk and cast by Mears & Stainbank of Whitechapel in April 1910, it was to have been consecrated in May of that year, but the death of King Edward VII resulted in an indefinite postponement. The bell is one of the 50 notable bells in the British Isles. It is inscribed in Latin 'Pray for Gwendolen, Duchess of Norfolk, who has given this bell to the Glory of God and in honour of St Edward the Confessor in the year 1910. Whilst the sound of the bell travels through the clouds, may the bands of angels pray for those assembled in thy Church. St Edward pray for England'.

The Cathedral was finally opened to the public on Christmas Eve 1903, and once the tower flooring and staircases were completed the tower was also opened. Providing an unrivalled view of up to twenty miles over London and the surrounding countryside, it was an immediate success. In the five days over Easter 1919, for example, it was recorded that over 1,100 climbed the 374 steps to the top (though few did it a second time). In 1929 a contract was signed with Marryat & Scott for an electric lift. Carrying ten people and travelling at 350 feet a minute, it rose 185ft to the lower viewing platform, previously the belfry. In consequence 'Edward' was moved 15ft further up to its present position above the lift shaft (accounting for its muffled tones) and visitors climbed the stone spiral staircase surrounding it to reach the upper viewing platform. The new lift was said to be the highest to be found in any building in Europe.

Five years before the lift was installed, in February 1924, a woman and her two young children tragically fell from the tower, resulting in the fitting of iron grilles across the viewing balconies in 1924-25, with an additional grille in 1931. Hollywood, however, was undeterred. In Alfred Hitchcock's film 'Foreign Correspondent' of 1940, an American reporter (Joel McCrea) is sent to Europe to cover the impending war. His bodyguard (Edmund Gwenn) is really an enemy agent with instructions to kill him. Lured to the top of the Cathedral tower, McCrea suddenly realises Gwenn's real intention and steps aside as the agent rushes towards him only to plunge over the balcony to the ground far below. Fortunately the 'fall' had no lasting effect on Gwenn's career. Seven years later he won an Oscar for his portrayal of Santa Claus in 'Miracle on 34th Street'.

2. Let There Be Light

Providing appropriate lighting in a neo-Byzantine building the size of Westminster Cathedral posed very real problems both for the architect, John Francis Bentley, and for his successor, John Marshall. Whether or not they succeeded is a matter which only those using the Cathedral can judge.

Natural Light

Internally the Cathedral is 342ft long by 148ft wide and is surmounted by four shallow domes rising to 112ft, the last of these, above the sanctuary, being somewhat lower. Bentley's objective was to provide sufficient daylight without putting in long rows of identical windows which could have made the building look like a factory. So he decided to use two very different styles of windows, generally placed high up in the building in the Byzantine fashion, not always arranged in the same way and with a series of different patterns for the tracery and glazing. He chose a greenish glass, conscious that future decoration with mosaic and coloured marble would make anything approaching stained glass both unnecessary and inappropriate. But he had to override the objections of Cardinal Vaughan who wanted something warmer in effect.

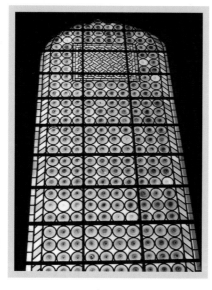

A round-headed, vertical window in the nave, composed of Venetian roundels.

Looking first above the main entrance doors, the head (tympanum) of the arch here is filled with a great horizontal semi-circle of terracotta tracery, tailor-made by the firm of Doulton & Co of Lambeth. Enclosed within this framework are leaded glass panels of tinted glass, arranged to resemble flowers. Below this great window Bentley inserted three contrasting vertical windows, round-headed and filled with serried ranks of lead-framed Venetian roundels or 'bull's-eyes'. Though there are variations, including a few small, round windows, these are essentially the two styles chosen by Bentley for the main windows of the Cathedral.

Bentley wanted to break up the featureless expanse of the great arches on each side of the nave, which are essential to support the domes. So he built a pair of smaller, coupled arches into each one. Into the head of all but one of these new arches went a semicircular window of terracotta, of alternating pattern, with the enclosed glass panels forming fleur-de-lys and other flowers. Below it went a pair of vertical round-headed windows with 'bull's-eye' glass, each containing a decorated panel different from its neighbour. Only below the third dome, where the nave meets the transepts, is this scheme varied. Here the semicircular terracotta window is absent and there is a triangle of three vertical round-headed windows.

The sanctuary also has a semicircular window of terracotta at the head of the arch on either side, with a pair of vertical round-headed windows below. But the drum of the shallow dome above is itself pierced by a circle of 12 round-headed windows to provide additional light for this, the focal point of the Cathedral. Behind the sanctuary, the apse, which Bentley understood was to be used by Benedictine monks for the singing of the Divine Office, is amply provided with six round-headed windows facing east.

Finally twin recesses in the side chapels each enclose two or three windows containing leaded and patterned glass. Perhaps most attractive are the flower-like patterns in the Holy Souls Chapel, and St Andrew's Chapel, where the white cross of the saint appears on an azure blue ground.

One of twelve chandeliers which illuminate the nave.

Artificial Light

Bentley died in 1902, before the Cathedral was complete, and it fell to his successor, John Marshall, to design the artificial lighting. The 12 great electric light chandeliers in the nave were made by the firm of J W Singer & Co of Frome of wrought iron. Although put in place in early 1909, they were not used until 1912 when their cost of £2,005 (about £100,000 today) was finally met. They resemble descriptions of the circular chandeliers which carried oil lamps in Emperor Justinian's sixth-century Byzantine church of Haghia Sophia (Santa Sophia) in Constantinople. The top ring is 6ft in diameter and carries 15 lamps, the next bears ten and the lowest and smallest, three, the rings being independently controlled. The six chandeliers in the sanctuary follow a similar design but are considerably smaller and gilt.

The Byzantine-style lighting of the Lady Chapel consists of eight chandeliers of silvered copper suspended from bronze cantilevers. Each is in the form of a corona or crown, pierced and decorated, and suspended from a star. Below hang medallions pierced with fleur-de-lys and bearing four electric lamps, with a fifth in the centre attached to an oval medallion displaying Our Lady's monogram. Either side of the altar, graceful bronze pendants carry a single light. These are repeated on the other side of the Cathedral in the Blessed Sacrament Chapel but here there are also eight more pendants in the form of bronze gilt diamonds, pierced and enamelled with alpha and omega symbols and small, coloured diamonds. They carry five electric lights, the lowest attached to a cross. The three silver oil lamps suspended before the tabernacle are decorated with blue and green enamel and set with onyx and rock crystal.

A graceful bronze pendant bearing a single light in the Lady Chapel.

Next door, in the shrine of the Sacred Heart and St Michael, beams carry four silvered bronze pendants in the form of a cross, each bearing a single light. They resemble descriptions of ancient light crosses in Haghia Sophia. The oil lamp before the statue was designed by Osmund Bentley, the architect's son. At the other end of the Cathedral, the light pendants in the Chapel of St Gregory and St Augustine and the Chapel of the Holy Souls are virtually identical and have been compared to Byzantine jewellery. From six frames of burnished bronze hang shaded little lamps and droplets of semi-precious stone around blue enamelled medallions showing a dove. Though designed by Marshall, the Cathedral light pendants show marked similarities in style to those designed earlier by Bentley for the Church of the Holy Rood in Watford, demonstrating Marshall's faithfulness to Bentley's ideas.

But most Byzantine of all the lighting in Westminster Cathedral must be the simple, pierced bronze chandelier with an ostrich egg (symbol of rebirth and of God's love for mankind) clasped within its chain, which hangs from the vault in the Chapel of St Andrew. Designed by the Byzantine specialist Robert Weir Schultz for the Fourth Marquess of Bute and made by William Bainbridge Reynolds, with the clouds of heaven in gold mosaic glittering above, one only has to imagine olive oil and a burning taper in each of its nine glass beakers to be back in the age of Justinian.

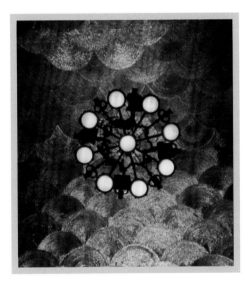

The Byzantine-style chandelier in St Andrew's Chapel with gold mosaic on the vault above.

Light and Shadow

In the *Westminster Cathedral Record* of 29 December 1900, Bentley wrote: 'The westernmost dome is in strong light, which streams through a large lunette window immediately on a line with the pendentives. The dome of the next bay is deeper in mysterious shadow; the third is still more so; while the sanctuary dome is brilliantly lighted by the twelve windows around its drum, so that our attention is led up to and powerfully focused upon the high altar beneath its marble baldacchino, necessary to give it emphasis and dignity'.

As for Marshall, he was determined that his designs should be both true to the Byzantine tradition and up to Bentley's standards. The twin lines of great, gaunt chandeliers which march up the nave to the brilliantly lit sanctuary, and the delicate enamelled pendants to be seen hanging in the side chapels, form the basis on which his work on the Cathedral lighting can be judged.

3. The Great Rood

Westminster Cathedral is also known as the Metropolitan Cathedral of the Precious Blood. Its full dedication (in translation from the original Latin) is: To Our Lord Jesus Christ who redeemed us by his Most Precious Blood, to the Most Blessed Virgin Mary his Immaculate Mother, and the Apostle Saint Peter his First Vicar, to Saint Joseph Patron of the Catholic Church and of the Interior Life, and, as secondary Patrons, to Saint Augustine Apostle of England and all Saints of Great Britain, and to Saint Patrick and the other Saints of Ireland.

SECTION ON LINE EE.

Bentley's drawing of the Great Rood dated 1896.

Origins

At the dedication of the Cathedral and laying of the foundation stone on 29 June 1895, a plain red wooden cross stood where the Cathedral high altar now stands, symbolising the dedication in chief to the Most Precious Blood of Our Lord Jesus Christ. A feast day in honour of the Most Precious Blood of Christ had been instituted by Pope Pius IX in 1849 and in choosing the dedication Cardinal Vaughan, the Cathedral's founder, is likely to have been influenced by this, and perhaps also by the original dedication of the Church of St John Lateran, Rome's first Cathedral, as the Basilica of the Saviour (Basilica Salvatoris), and Canterbury Cathedral as the Cathedral Church of Christ, or Christ Church. In Vaughan's own words: 'We want to announce the glad tidings of Redemption in our Saviour's Precious Blood'. Shortly before Westminster Cathedral was opened to the public in December 1903, a 30ft high, 23ft wide, red crucifix bearing a painting of the crucified Christ was raised up to hang at the junction between the nave, sanctuary and transepts and thus at the centre of the cross formed by the building itself. Except for an interlude of three years, it has hung there ever since.

Design

The crucifix or Great Rood (from the Old English 'rod' meaning cross), was designed by the Cathedral architect, J F Bentley, soon after starting work on the Cathedral in 1895. He refers to it in the first edition of the *Westminster Cathedral Record*, in January 1896. An architectural drawing (A-8) signed by him in 1896 shows it hanging in its present position between the nave and sanctuary. The scale below the drawing shows the rood dimensions (30ft by 23ft) to be the same as the rood of today, while the figure of Christ also seems identical. Differences now are the absence of the five great hanging lamps and in the end panel paintings. In the

The Great Rood being taken down from the wall in the north-west corner of the nave before being returned to its original (and present) position in February 1937.

drawing these show the dove of the Holy Spirit (above), the Lamb of God (below), and Our Lady and St John to left and right. Today they show the symbols of the four Evangelists who described the crucifixion - Matthew (a winged man), Mark (a lion), Luke (an ox) and John (an eagle).

Cardinal Vaughan played a direct part in designing the rood, writing to the artist William Christian Symons, who was to paint it, that the representation must be of 'the live Christ whose eyes may appear to rest on everyone as they move about the church'. There must be no pierced side. Vaughan's views also appeared in the last edition of the *Westminster Cathedral Record,* published as a supplement to *The Tablet* in June 1902. This confirms the height (30ft) of the rood and its position (to hang between the sanctuary and the nave), and refers to the paintings of the four Evangelists in the end panels and of Our Lady of Sorrows (Mater Dolorosa) on the reverse side.

Creation

By this time the rood was being carved by Charles Beyeart in Bruges from Bentley's designs. Canvas was then stretched over the teak and deal wooden frame and Symons painted it at floor level in the Cathedral nave in 1903, from sketches seen by Bentley shortly before his death in March 1902. In portraying the dead Christ, Symons remained faithful to Bentley's design, but the Evangelists and Our Lady of Sorrows were portrayed as the Cardinal wished. Vaughan also chose the quotations from the *Stabat Mater* for the end panels around Our Lady. These are taken from a late thirteenth century Latin hymn by a Franciscan, Jacopone di Todi. The English version of the hymn starts: 'At the cross her station keeping, stood the mournful mother weeping'. The words in the rood panels read: *Stabat Mater Dolorosa; Eia Mater Fons Amoris; Fac ut Ardeat Cor Meum; Juxta Crucem Tecum Stare.* They may be translated as: Stood the sorrowful mother; O Mother, fount of love; Make my heart to burn in me; Beside the cross to stand with Thee.

Once the painting was complete the two ton cross was hauled into position over a period of more than three hours on 16 December 1903. There it remained for thirty years while the liturgies, music and decoration of the Cathedral took place below. But a new Archbishop of Westminster, Francis Bourne, had succeeded Cardinal Vaughan in 1903 and in 1932-33 the arch, or tympanum, between the sanctuary and the apse, behind the rood, was decorated with a great blue mosaic of Christ in Majesty. Bourne found that the rood obscured the central figure in his new mosaic and, late in 1933, he had it removed to a position in the north west corner of the Cathedral nave - above the bronze plaques listing the Chief Pastors of the Church. The four steel girders which supported it can still be seen protruding from the wall.

A Question of Proportion

In his New Year message in the *Westminster Cathedral Chronicle* of January 1934, Cardinal Bourne justified his decision on the grounds that Bentley had originally planned a much smaller cross to hang over the baldacchino, that the Great Rood was an afterthought, miscalculated in preparation and out of proportion. In this he seems to have been echoing a comment about the rood by Winefride de l'Hôpital (Bentley's eldest daughter) in her 1919 book *Westminster Cathedral and its Architect* that: 'Thirty feet high and made of wood, it was made in Bruges to Bentley's designs, though, from some error in measurement afterwards impossible to rectify, its proportions are not exactly as he intended'. It is true that Bentley did briefly consider a smaller cross to hang over the baldacchino. He refers to this just once, in the *Westminster Cathedral Record* of January 1896. But the small hanging cross was clearly in addition to, rather than instead of, the 30ft high rood which he also refers to at the same time.

The reverse of the Great Rood showing Our Lady of Sorrows.

Bentley himself never saw the rood. He died before it was made and it did not arrive in the Cathedral until a year afterwards. But his drawings A-8 and F-84 (the rood frame) show that the dimensions of the present rood are approximately as he had planned. Both he and Cardinal Vaughan clearly gave it much thought and Bentley was meticulous in his drawings and instructions. The most likely explanation for the 'out of proportion' jibe seems to be contained in a letter from Revd Herbert Lucas SJ to W C Symons of 10 January 1904. He writes: 'By the way, Fr Jackman had a mistaken impression that I did not like the big cross. That is not true (as I complained to him), but Mrs B [Bentley's widow] told me that the proportions of the cross were not just what Bentley designed, and rightly or wrongly it did seem to me that the upright limb was rather broad (in proportion) and that it narrowed rather suddenly above the head. If the [upright] had been three inches narrower, and the [crossbar] three inches broader, perhaps it would have looked better. But I may have misunderstood Mrs B or *she* may have been mistaken'.

In Cardinal Bourne's 1934 New Year message he explained that the new mosaic of Christ in Majesty on the sanctuary arch was intended to recall the dedication of the Cathedral (to the Most Precious Blood) and was inspired by the church of which he was titular bishop, Santa Pudenziana in Rome. In this church a graceful, late fourth (or early fifth) century apse mosaic, the oldest in Rome, dominates the nave. Above the central figure of Christ enthroned appears a great jewelled mosaic cross, similar to that in the Blessed Sacrament Chapel of Westminster Cathedral. After this it must have been galling to Bourne to have his own sanctuary mosaic in the Cathedral obscured by a 30ft high painted rood, and he seems to have searched for a reason to have it removed.

The Rood Returns

Cardinal Bourne died in January 1935 and one of the first recommendations of the Cathedral Art Committee, set up by his successor, Archbishop Hinsley, in October 1936 was that the rood be restored to its original position. In February 1937 it was. The Great Rood has now hung undisturbed for seventy-five years while, once again, the liturgies, music and decoration of the Cathedral have proceeded below. Together with the high altar under its great marble baldacchino, the rood is the focal point of the Cathedral. Without it there would be a vacuum at the centre. In the last edition of the *Westminster Cathedral Record* in June 1902 (in effect the voice of Cardinal Vaughan), it was forecast that the Great Rood would 'dominate the whole Cathedral by its majestic presence, and it will be the first object to catch the eye on entering. This is as it should be - *Christus vivit, Christus regnat, Christus imperat'*.

The Great Rood hanging in position between the nave and sanctuary.

4. The Baldacchino

On Christmas Eve 1906 the baldacchino, the great marble canopy over the high altar in the Cathedral, was publicly revealed for the first time. It had been planned for ten years and argued over for the last five. But neither the architect who designed it nor the cardinal who authorised it ever saw it. Nor would they have been very happy if they had.

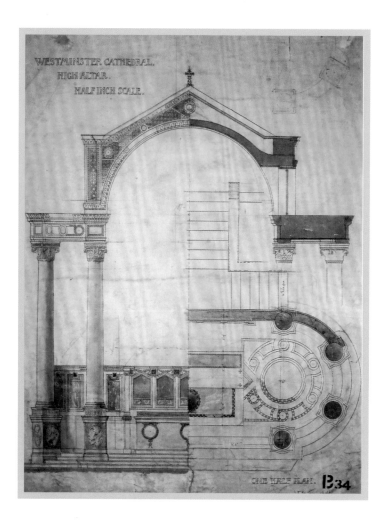

Bentley's design for the baldacchino complete with cross.

First Designs

When, in July 1894, J F Bentley was commissioned by Cardinal Vaughan to be the architect of Westminster Cathedral he resolved to study Romanesque and Byzantine churches before starting work on the Cathedral plans. Leaving London in November his first destination was Milan where he was struck by the appearance of the church of Sant' Ambrogio, particularly its very early baldacchino supported by four ancient purple porphyry columns. Returning from his travels in March 1895 he immediately set to work on designing the new Cathedral. By May two ground plans had been produced - the first showing a square baldacchino in the apse (now occupied by the choir) and the second showing it in its present position in the sanctuary. But it was Bentley's third and final plan, produced and approved by the Cardinal later that year, that was of most interest, for it showed the baldacchino as it is today, supported by a semi-circle of four columns on each side.

The baldacchino under construction in 1906.

By 1901 construction of the Cathedral had reached the point at which decoration of the sanctuary could start. Bentley was determined that the high altar and baldacchino 'should be the crown of his work, the ark within the Holy of Holies' as his daughter and biographer put it. He was bitterly disappointed when his design for an elaborate altar was rejected by Cardinal Vaughan in favour of a twelve ton block of unadorned Cornish granite, twelve feet long and four feet wide. But he was determined not to give way on the baldacchino. As he wrote in November 1901, 'At present I see no other way of doing the baldacchino than what I have shown, but I shall be glad of any suggestions. I know I spent a great deal of thought upon it, and I think it is the best thing about the Cathedral'. Bentley was determined to have eight columns of yellow Verona marble 15 feet high, and was ultimately triumphant over those (including the Cardinal) who argued for the more usual four columns which would, of course, have been cheaper.

The Cardinal wants Onyx

On his choice of yellow Verona, however, Bentley was opposed by the Cardinal. While in Rome after his appointment as Archbishop of Westminster in 1892, Vaughan had visited the Basilica of St Paul Outside the Walls and was much taken by the translucency and colour of the Egyptian onyx columns standing at the west end. But these columns consist of sections and Vaughan was determined on monoliths for the Cathedral at Westminster for 'all the columns are monoliths and the baldacchino ought to be reared on nothing inferior'. This was despite the view of the marble merchants of London, Belgium and Paris that onyx could not be obtained in lengths of more than five and a half feet whereas

The baldacchino unveiled. Midnight Mass, Christmas 1906.

15ft columns were needed for the baldacchino. As luck would have it, Vaughan had a friend in Marseilles, Marius Cantini, who had supplied the marbles for the new Byzantine cathedral there and owned onyx quarries in Algeria. Although it would require many months, Cantini believed he could supply onyx columns of that length.

The winter of 1901-02 passed without success but in May 1902 Cardinal Vaughan was able to write to Lady Herbert of Lea that, for the first time and to the surprise of the marble merchants, eight onyx columns 15ft long had been obtained. The following month this was announced in the *Westminster Cathedral Record*. Bentley never saw the columns, for he had died on 2 March 1902. After his death his assistant, John Marshall, took over. But against Bentley's express wish that the baldacchino should be produced by an English firm under the constant supervision of the Cathedral architect, Cardinal Vaughan asked Marius Cantini to submit an estimate for the whole baldacchino. This was to be made in Marseilles and delivered ready for assembly, as also occurred with the font, archbishop's throne and pulpit - all made in Rome to the dismay of Bentley. But when the eight onyx columns were unpacked in the Cathedral, three were found to be broken and a fourth badly cracked. So the idea of prefabrication in Marseilles was abandoned.

Downsizing

What then happened is unclear. Bentley had produced a number of drawings of the baldacchino prior to his death in 1902. In a very early one (B-22), he had drawn in pencil a decorative finial for the top of the baldacchino. Initially this consisted of a pineapple mounted on a globe, then on the same sheet it becomes a cross above a globe and in subsequent coloured working drawings (B-24, B-26 and B-34) just a gilt bronze cross 18 inches high and 12 inches wide. Two drawings of the baldacchino (B-23 and B-31) refer to a contract with the marble merchants Farmer & Brindley of 5 March 1903. In B-24, B-27 and B-33 the overall height, width and span above the altar have all been reduced by three feet and the columns are 14ft high rather than Bentley's

15ft; B-24 is also annotated 'old onyx reduced in length'. So Bentley's dimensions were reduced, perhaps to try to save the onyx columns by making them shorter or simply to save on cost. Marshall was completely faithful to Bentley but Vaughan was much more interested in economy. Authority to alter Bentley's plans could only have come from him. This is supported by a letter from Revd Herbert Lucas SJ in *The Tablet* of 19 September 1903 (after Vaughan's death on 19 June) protesting against the 'clipping and paring of a great artist's careful and thoughtful work' - the baldacchino. The present structure is about 36ft high, 31ft wide and has a span above the altar of 15ft. It cost £7,500 (almost £400,000 today).

It was not until after Francis Bourne had taken over as Archbishop of Westminster at the end of 1903 that things moved on. A new contract was placed with Farmer & Brindley, eight columns of the yellow Verona on which Bentley had set his heart arrived in July 1905 and, after 17 months' work, the scaled-down baldacchino was unveiled on Christmas Eve 1906. So Vaughan never got to use his onyx columns. They stood in St George's Chapel for many years before being sold. In 1914 one was installed either side of Our Lady's Altar in Birmingham Oratory where they are listed, rather ironically, as Siberian onyx. The fate of the others is unknown. Bentley did finally get his yellow Verona columns, albeit posthumously, but they are 14ft long rather than the 15ft he had planned. And neither on the drawings of the scaled-down baldacchino sent to Farmer & Brindley in 1904-05, nor on the structure revealed in December 1906, was there any sign of the little bronze cross. Like Cardinal Vaughan, who referred approvingly to the cross in June 1902, Bourne had strong views on the Cathedral decoration. As far as the cross is concerned it rather looks as if he did not like it.

The baldacchino today.

5. A Tale of Five Pulpits

One of the most decorative features in the Cathedral, immediately seen by visitors on entering, stands two-thirds of the way down the nave on the right. Sadly, for such an attractive feature which was intended to be used several times a day, it is now largely redundant.

The first plans for the Cathedral, produced in 1895 by its architect, J F Bentley, show the pulpit on the left of the nave - first of all in the north-east corner, close to the lectern which is now used at Mass, and then against the pier at the north-west corner of the north transept, directly across the nave from the present pulpit. But in 1896 Bentley's drawings show that he had decided on a position on the right-hand side of the nave, where the present pulpit stands today.

The original, first, pulpit of 1903.

The First Pulpit

The first pulpit was ordered from Rome by Cardinal Vaughan, founder of the Cathedral, and was installed in the Cathedral in June 1903. It was designed by Cavaliere Aristide Leonori, an artist employed by the Vatican who had never seen Westminster Cathedral and admitted the unsuitability of his design when he eventually did. It was made by Ditta Paolo Medici & Figlio in Rome. Bentley had died in March 1902 and had nothing to do with the pulpit which was paid for by Ernest Kennedy, an important benefactor of the Cathedral. The pulpit was large enough to accommodate the Archbishop and two assistants and was one bay further forward than the present pulpit - near the Thirteenth Station of the Cross. It was 11 ft wide and 5ft deep and raised the speaker 4ft above floor level. It was made of marble inlaid with red and green porphyry and mosaic in the Cosmati style.

Marshall's 1905 design (H-37) for a replacement, second, pulpit.

Cardinal Vaughan was destined never to use the pulpit for he died the same month as it was installed. His successor, Archbishop Bourne, became increasingly critical of it, not so much because of its style, for the Cosmati style is closely related to the Byzantine one intended by Vaughan and Bentley for the Cathedral, but because of its position, inconvenient steps and small size (55 sq ft internally). It also had no sounding board or amplification, resulting in the speaker's voice being virtually inaudible at the back of the Cathedral. In July 1905 Bentley's successor, John Marshall, produced an alternative design (H-37) which improved the access and increased the size by replacing the lower panels with four colonettes to support the superstructure. It was to be positioned against one of the main nave piers with a carved and gilt wooden sounding board suspended above, thus improving both the visibility and audibility of the speaker.

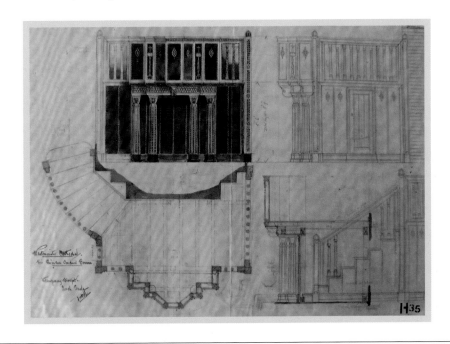

Marshall's (undated but probably 1913) design (H-35) for a temporary, third, pulpit.

A Visit to Sicily

In October 1905 Bourne visited Monreale Cathedral and the Palatine Chapel in Palermo in Sicily to study the medieval Norman-Byzantine mosaics there, with a view to adopting the same style in Westminster Cathedral. Some 700 years earlier the Cosmati craftsmen of Rome had also made the journey to Sicily and it was the style they observed there that they had adopted. So the style that Bourne so much admired in Sicily and resolved to employ in his Cathedral was very close to that of his existing pulpit. As a result Marshall's 1905 design for an eminently practical but decidedly un-Byzantine pulpit, which would have discarded much of the original Cosmati-style decoration, was rejected, and the original pulpit remained in use.

In September 1908 the Cardinal Legate gave the inaugural address at the opening of the Eucharistic Congress from the Cathedral pulpit. Because of its small size the canons and master of ceremonies had to remain at the foot of the steps. Bourne himself became a cardinal in December 1911 and, when preaching from the pulpit, should have been accompanied by his cross bearer, trainbearer and master of ceremonies but this also proved impractical. Once more John Marshall produced a design (H-35), this time for a larger, temporary pulpit which would have left the original one untouched. His design was both practical and attractive with a combination of dark red and green panels supported by four colonettes, with a store-cupboard underneath. But once again it was not in the Byzantine style so it was rejected. Instead, on Good Friday 1914, a much cheaper, severely practical, temporary pulpit of unpainted wood, polygonal in plan and 9ft in diameter, with no stylistic pretensions of any kind, was first used. It was erected one bay further back from the sanctuary and was thus where the present pulpit stands today. It provided an internal area of 64 sq ft and had a sounding board.

The wooden temporary, fourth, pulpit of 1914 seen in front of the original pulpit in 1930.

The present, fifth, pulpit of 1934 showing the decorated sounding board above.

A masterly example of recycling

Twenty years went by and in 1934 Cardinal Francis Bourne had served thirty years as Archbishop of Westminster and fifty as a priest. To commemorate both this and the restoration of the pilgrimage in honour of Our Lady of Walsingham in that year he commissioned a permanent new pulpit. The wooden one was taken down but rather than starting afresh Bourne instructed Lawrence Shattock, Marshall's successor, to reconstruct the first pulpit using as much as possible of its material. Its lower panels were brought up and eight new colonettes made to bear the weight of the structure. In August 1934, on the Feast of the Assumption, the new pulpit was inaugurated.

In this manner the attractive upper central panel of the Lamb of God, the figures of the Evangelists, and almost all the Roman Cosmati-style panels were retained from the original pulpit. Its lower central panel was replaced and an inscription recording the new dedication inserted and an *opus sectile* panel of painted glass on a slate backing by John Trinick, portraying Our Lady of Walsingham, was put in place to face the sanctuary. A highly decorated sounding board was suspended above the speaker, though this was discarded after amplifiers (first used in 1938) were introduced.

Even if, as Bourne himself admitted, it was not strictly in the Byzantine style, it was a masterly example of recycling; only the little spiral columns on the front of the first pulpit and a few of its minor marble panels were unused. The 1934 pulpit is 14ft wide and 7ft deep. It thus provides the speaker and his assistants with an area of 100 sq ft, almost twice the size of the original, and raises them 5ft 9ins above floor level.

Each of the eight colonettes supporting the pulpit is surmounted by an attractive carved marble capital. The last, that furthest from the sanctuary, bears the initials EK and FB - Ernest Kennedy and Francis Bourne who, though separated by three decade, together provided the pulpit. For more than 30 years it was in daily use. But with the changes brought about by the Second Vatican Council it is now employed only on great feast days and other special occasions, such as the annual Christmas Celebration.

6. Cathedral Bronzes

There are few bronzes in Westminster Cathedral, indeed there are few sculptures of any sort. The reason for this is that the Cathedral is in the Byzantine style and the Byzantines largely abandoned the sculpture so prevalent in Greek and Roman art, preferring to portray their Christian saints in mosaic, fresco and as painted wooden icons.

St Peter. The north-west corner of the nave.

The first bronze, that of St Peter, is also the largest and was the first to arrive. It is located in front of the north-west pier of the nave near the Gift Shop. It is a facsimile of the statue in St Peter's Basilica in Rome, though the one there has a (very worn) silver foot - the result of being touched by millions of pilgrims. This statue was thought to date from the fifth or sixth century but restoration in 1990 revealed it to be most probably the work of Arnolfo di Cambio in about 1296. The Westminster Cathedral statue was made by A Röhrich in Rome. It was blessed by Pope Leo XIII in February 1902 and arrived here in May before being placed on its marble plinth. Originally intended for St Peter's Crypt, it was found to be too large and was moved to the nave in February 1903. It was presented as a memorial to a selfless and dedicated ex-Anglican priest, writer and scholar, Revd Luke Rivington DD, by his friends after his death in 1899, and is inscribed with the words *'Tu es Petrus et super hanc petram aedificabo ecclesiam meam'* (You are Peter and upon this rock I will build my Church).

Cardinal Henry Edward Manning. St Edmund's Chapel in St Peter's Crypt.

The next bronze arrived in the Cathedral five years later, in 1908. It is an effigy of Cardinal Henry Edward Manning, second Archbishop of Westminster. It was Manning who bought the land (previously a prison) on which the Cathedral now stands. An Anglican priest and Archdeacon of Chichester who converted to Catholicism, Manning is widely remembered for his sympathy for the oppressed and disadvantaged in society and his support for Trades Unions against exploitation by employers. Great crowds lined the streets during his funeral procession in 1892 to Kensal Green Cemetery. In 1907 his body was reinterred in Westminster Cathedral where his tomb occupies a recess within St Edmund's Chapel in St Peter's Crypt, below the sanctuary and high altar. His effigy, based on a model by the well-known sculptor and friend of Manning, John Adams-Acton, was cast in bronze by Messrs J W Singer & Sons of Frome in Somerset.

Byzantine Style

Singers also made much of the later metalwork in the Cathedral. The architect, John Francis Bentley, died in March 1902 before the building was complete and his chief assistant, John Marshall, took over the running of the Bentley firm and as architect-in-charge of the Cathedral. Marshall had worked with Bentley for 25 years and brought to fruition many of his designs and concepts. Thus the bronze chandeliers in the nave and sanctuary are in the Byzantine style advocated by Bentley, while the lighting pendants in the Blessed Sacrament Chapel, that of St Gregory and St. Augustine and that of the Holy Souls, are in the same style as those in the Church of the Holy Rood, Watford, which Bentley designed. Other bronzes designed by Marshall include the gilt triptychs of St Joseph and St Paul which appear above the altars in St Joseph's and St Paul's Chapels and were installed during the 1914-18 War.

On the south and west walls of St Patrick's Chapel are sixteen gilt bronze plaques enclosing badges of the Irish regiments which fought in the British army during the 1914-18 War. There is an additional plaque, for the Royal Irish Constabulary, on the east wall. To the left of the altar is a cabinet containing the names of some 50,000 Irish soldiers who died in the War. With Irish independence in 1922 the Irish regiments of

Ste Thérèse of Lisieux.
The south transept.

the British army were largely disbanded or amalgamated. Designs for the decoration of St Patrick's Chapel were produced by John Marshall in 1919, the work being carried out in 1923-30. Marshall's last design was for the two gilt bronze angels with trumpets, which front the organ loft above the narthex. They were installed on 23 December 1926. A week later, aged 73, John Marshall died.

Vilnius (Vilna), now capital of Lithuania, is commemorated in the form of a gilt bronze medallion on the wall of the Lady Chapel. It was given in 1944 by 317 (City of Vilna) Polish Fighter Squadron, which flew with the Royal Air Force from 1941-47, destroying more than 50 German aircraft. Nearby on a wall in the south transept is a bronze of Ste Thérèse of Lisieux. Cardinal Griffin, sixth Archbishop of Westminster, was devoted to Ste Thérèse and arranged for a mosaic of the saint, designed by John Trinick, to be installed as a wall panel in 1950. But the mosaic was much criticised and was replaced in April 1958 by a low-relief bronze of the saint. This shows Ste Thérèse in a religious habit, carrying a bunch of roses and looking back over her shoulder as she hurries along. It was given by Janet Howard in memory of her sister, Alice, and cost about

£680. Designed by the Italian sculptor Giacomo Manzu, it was cast in Milan. Though a Marxist, Manzu was a friend of Pope John XXIII and designed several religious bronzes including the monumental 'Door of Death' for the left-hand main entrance door to St Peter's Basilica in Rome.

St Patrick. St Patrick's Chapel.

Austere and striking gilt bronze

Moving further up the south aisle we come back again to St Patrick's Chapel. For many years there was just a framed picture above the altar and by 1956 the Cathedral Art and Architecture Committee, which had been appointed by Cardinal Griffin in 1953, had decided that a bronze of St Patrick should replace it and the reredos behind it be remodelled. Between 1958 and 1960 six sculptors - Giacomo Manzu, Huw Lorimer, Elizabeth Frink, Oisin Kelly, Seamus Murphy and Arthur Pollen - were considered and, after considerable argument, models of St Patrick were prepared and submitted to Cardinal Godfrey (who had succeeded Griffin in 1956) for his decision. After much deliberation, in March 1960 he chose one of those submitted by Arthur Pollen, himself a member of the Art and Architecture Committee, who had also attempted to obtain

St Vincent de Paul.
The south transept.

Cathedral commissions on previous occasions, both for himself and for his two sons. In approving his model of St Patrick, Godfrey asked that in future Art and Architecture Committee members should not submit their own work or those of their family and Pollen resigned. His austere and striking gilt bronze of St Patrick cost around £1,500 and was unveiled on St Patrick's Day 1961, the 1,500th anniversary of the saint's death,

The last two bronzes are by the sculptor Bryan Kneale RA. After initially studying painting, in 1960 Kneale moved over to sculpture, becoming Head of Sculpture first at Hornsey College of Art and Design and then at the Royal College of Art in London. He was also Professor of Sculpture at the Royal Academy Schools. In 1998 he was commissioned to design a bronze relief of St Vincent de Paul, the 'Father of the Poor', for the south transept of the Cathedral. Kneale was selected by the Cathedral Art and Architecture Committee from a number of artists who had submitted proposals. The work was to be funded by the Society of St Vincent de Paul assisted by a grant for the casting of the bronze from the Royal Academy. After much research, particularly in the archives of the Daughters of Charity at Mill Hill, Kneale produced a plaster sculpture of the saint from which the bronze was cast. The features of St Vincent - his benevolence, compassion and enigmatic smile - are all shown in that remarkable face. The bronze was unveiled by Cardinal George Basil Hume on 27 September 1998, St Vincent's Feast Day.

'Father of Western Monasticism'

And so to the last Cathedral bronze, that of St Benedict of Nursia. Between this bronze and that of St Vincent is a war memorial made of nails in the form of a chi-rho (the first two letters of the Greek word for Christ). It was created by David ('Birdie') Partridge in 1972 to commemorate the 17,000 members of the Canadian Air Force who died in the 1939-45 War. To the left is the bronze of St Benedict, the 'Father of Western Monasticism' whose Rule envisages the monk not as a solitary ascetic but as a brother among a family of brothers, serving God together. The bronze, again produced by Bryan Kneale, is a tribute to our own Benedictine, Cardinal George Basil Hume, ninth Archbishop of Westminster, who died on 17 June 1999 shortly before it was unveiled on 10 July. Hume was insistent that St Benedict should be shown with the Rule which he himself followed from the age of eighteen. By the time he became Archbishop of Westminster in 1976 he had spent most of his life at Ampleforth, the Benedictine monastery in North Yorkshire, first as a schoolboy, then as a schoolmaster and monk and finally, from 1963, as Abbot. During the Cathedral's Centenary Celebrations of 1995, Cardinal Hume welcomed Her Majesty the Queen to Solemn Vespers on the Feast of St Andrew on 30 November. This was the first attendance of a reigning sovereign at a Roman Catholic liturgy since the Reformation. The bronze is a memorial both to St Benedict and to Cardinal Hume, whose body lies in the Chapel of St Gregory the Great and St Augustine, near the entrance to the Cathedral.

St Benedict of Nursia.
The south transept.

7. The Stations of the Cross

What type of Stations of the Cross do you have in a great cathedral built in the Byzantine style, when Byzantine churches have no Stations of the Cross and the cathedral architect has died without leaving clear instructions? That was the problem facing the Westminster Cathedral authorities when the building was finished in 1903. The decision finally reached was deeply controversial but thought today to have been inspired.

Devotion to the Passion of Christ only became widespread from the twelfth and thirteenth centuries, fostered both by Crusaders returning from the Holy Land and by Franciscans, who took over responsibility for the holy places there in 1342. It was in Franciscan churches that devotion to the Way of the Cross, made up of a series of contemplative halts or 'stations' first became commonplace, though the form of devotion could vary greatly and the number of halts could range from five to thirty or more. Only in 1731 did Pope Clement XII settle on the form of devotion to be followed and approve the custom of having fourteen Stations of the Cross.

Bentley and *Opus Sectile*

J F Bentley, the architect of Westminster Cathedral, died in March 1902 without leaving designs for the Stations of the Cross. But members of his family and colleagues at his firm were sure that he envisaged them in *opus sectile* - painted glass tiles, cut and assembled to form patterns or pictures. Examples of the technique in the Cathedral can be seen above the altar in the Chapel of the Holy Souls, and above the altar and either side of the entrance in the Chapel of St Gregory and St Augustine. Bentley also used *opus sectile* in many churches elsewhere - as on the main altar frontal in St James, Spanish Place. The only Stations of the Cross that Bentley is known to have designed are in the Church of the Sacred Heart in Wimbledon in 1900. But this is a Gothic-style church and Bentley's designs there were painted on canvas by the artist Innis Fripp between 1900 and 1903.

After Bentley's death his assistant, J A Marshall, took over as architect in charge of the Cathedral. Architectural drawings from this time show that *opus sectile* remained the plan for the Stations of the Cross. Similarly, when the *Westminster Cathedral Chronicle* of March 1909 appealed for donors, they were described as panels of *opus sectile* surrounded by white marble frames. By October all fourteen had been paid for, the cost of each ranging from £62 initially to £75.11s at the end. In this way some £1,000 was raised and it was stated that 'The work will be put in hand at once'. The marble frames were in place by March 1910 but they were to remain empty for four years and were then taken down.

Eric Gill's preliminary drawing of the First Station of the Cross. Dated Spring 1914.

Not until October 1913 did the *Westminster Cathedral Chronicle* return to the subject, recording that cartoons of the Stations of the

Cross, all but two by different artists, had been put up in the Cathedral for selection and approval which, 'with such a large number, should not be difficult'. One of the artists, George Daniels, produced several designs, five of which are still held. They show a marked resemblance to Bentley's designs in the Church of the Sacred Heart, Wimbledon, and in the case of the Fourteenth Station they are virtually identical. Clearly the intention at this time was to remain faithful to Bentley's vision. A subsequent letter to *The Observer* suggested that Robert Anning Bell, a Nonconformist whose blue mosaic altarpiece went up in the Lady Chapel in late 1912, was 'within an ace of obtaining the Stations'. However, Cardinal Bourne, though growing increasingly restive at the absence of the Stations of the Cross in his ten-year-old Cathedral, did not like the altarpiece and had concluded that only a Catholic artist could provide what was needed.

Enter Eric Gill

One of those asked to submit designs was Eric Gill. Only 31 and a sculptor for just three years, Gill was introduced to Marshall in 1913 and in August he was asked to produce preliminary drawings for fourteen square stone carvings for the Stations of the Cross. In April 1914 Gill produced a 9 inch square design for the Stations and the commission was approved by Cardinal Bourne in May. The fourteen panels, each 5ft 8ins square, were to be carved in low relief in Hopton Wood limestone from Derbyshire for the very low price of £765.

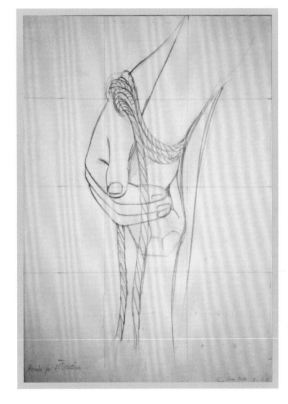

A drawing by Eric Gill of Christ's hands for the First Station of the Cross. March 1915.

At this time Gill was almost unknown as a sculptor and extremely anxious to get such an important commission - hence the price. Even before his designs were accepted he had produced at his own expense a sample 4ft 6in version of the Fifth Station (Christ with Simon of Cyrene) and put it up in the Cathedral. Once commissioned he set to work at once, producing the Tenth Station (Christ is stripped of his garments), for which he used himself as a model, and the Second (Christ receives the Cross) by November 1914. Then followed the Thirteenth (Christ is taken down from the Cross) and the First (Christ is condemned to death), the panels being carved in the studio with the final touches being added by Gill in the Cathedral.

First reactions were unfavourable. Gill himself was unhappy with the Tenth Station and Marshall's response to it was that it showed Gill's style was 'neither suitable for the peculiar light of the Cathedral nor the Catholic public' - to which Gill's advice to him was to cover it with a sheet and wait until at least three or four more of the panels were finished before taking any decision.

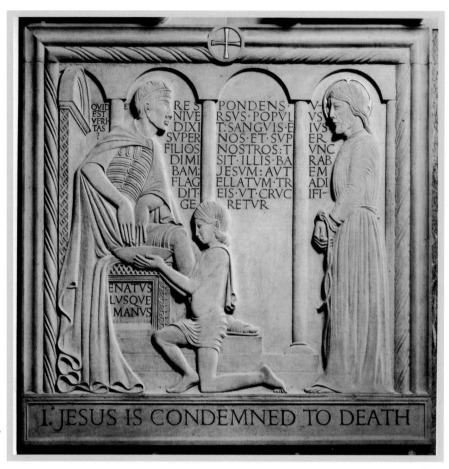

QVID
EST
VERH
TAS
?

RES PONDENS
NIVE RSVS·POPVL
DIXI T·SANGVIS·E
SVPER NOS·ET·SVP
FILIOS NOSTROS·T
DIMI SIT·ILLIS·BA
BAM; JESVM: AVT
FLAG ELLATVM·TR
DIT EIS·VT·CRVC
GE RETVR

V-
VS
IVS
ER
VNC
RAB
EM
ADI
IFI-

ENATVS
LVSQVE
MANVS

I. JESUS IS CONDEMNED TO DEATH

Eric Gill's First Station of the Cross. June 1915.

A Series of Critical Letters

The first four Stations of the Cross, including two of the best (the First and Thirteenth) were finished and on view in the Cathedral by June 1915. It was then that, first in *The Universe* and then in *The Observer*, there appeared a series of critical letters, many of them abusive. More reasoned was an article by P G Konody, *The Observer's* art critic. He accused Gill of assuming a 'child-like naïveté, a disguise of archaistic affectation' and of producing carvings utterly inexpressive of the sublime tragedy of which they profess to be an interpretation. He added that Gill's relief carving was out of place in a Byzantine church and was never intended by Bentley, whose intentions regarding *opus sectile* had been deliberately disregarded. On the one hand the Stations were variously described by writers as 'grotesque and undevotional', as 'cold as the mind that produced them', as hideous, primitive and pagan. On the other they were seen as 'dignified in conception, superb in outline and restrained in feeling' and as showing 'admirable breadth and simplicity of design'.

Gill was interviewed in *The Observer* in October 1915. On the question of style he responded that he was simply a stone carver. 'I can only work in one style and that is my own'. He accepted that Bentley's intention was for *opus sectile* but this 'is factory work and to any real craftsmanship it is death'. It had been decided that it was not suitable for the Stations of the Cross in the Cathedral and that they should be carved in low relief, which was the only form of carving used in a Byzantine building. As to the question why he had been given the commission he replied: 'I suppose that the architect approved of my work'.

In his autobiography Gill writes 'there were sufficient people to tell him (Cardinal Bourne) the things were good to outweigh those who said they were bad - especially when you take into account the infernal business of taking all the panels down again' - a pretty broad hint that Bourne himself was not over-keen on them. So he continued to carve. Completion of the first four Stations was followed by that of the Fifth, Third, Fourth and Sixth by the end of 1916, then the Eighth and Seventh in 1917 and finally the Fourteenth, Eleventh, Twelfth and Ninth in 1918. The Ninth Station was finished on 11 April 1918, after they were consecrated on Good Friday, 29 March. Gill's drawings show that he continued to use himself as a model - for the left-hand soldier in the Second and Christ's hands in the Third Station, while Our Lady's hands in the Fourth are those of his wife, Ethel Mary, and those of Christ in the First are Joseph Cribb's, an assistant.

'The boy for the job'

So why did Gill get the job? Firstly he had been received into the Catholic Church in February 1913, and Cardinal Bourne wanted a Catholic, threatening, according to Gill, to appoint the first one he met in the street. Secondly it seems to have been Marshall who decided on carved stone for the Stations of the Cross, and who chose Gill, who had the technical ability to carve them. Marshall was a Nonconformist and Gill's simple, restrained, unpretentious style may have appealed to him. It should also be said that the drawings presented by Gill in the spring of 1914, on the basis of which his commission was approved, are gentler and more expressive than the subsequent

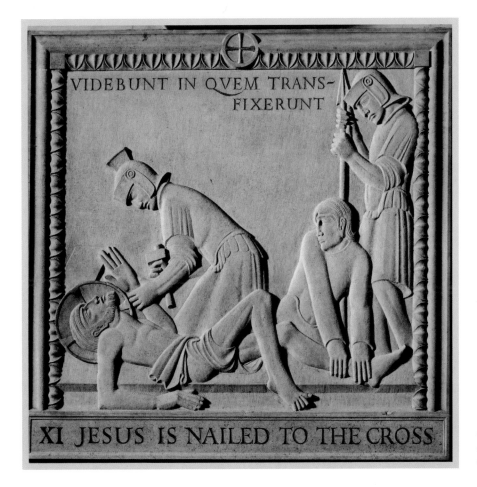

Eric Gill's Eleventh Station of the Cross. March 1918.

stone reliefs, which Gill seems to suggest in his autobiography would probably have been rejected by Cardinal Bourne had he known. Last, and by no means least, Gill's fee of £765 was considerably less than both the sum raised in 1909 and that asked for by other artists, and Gill relates that according to Marshall, 'had it not been that I was willing to do the job at a price no really 'posh' painter or sculptor would look at, I should certainly never have got it'.

Eric Gill's Fourteenth Station of the Cross. March 1918.

Gill's 1914 drawings show Latin biblical texts in three of the scenes. But Gill loved letters and finally included texts in nine of the Fourteen Stations - perhaps a pity as few now understand Latin and the decision after Gill's death in 1940 to colour the lettering red and black has made some scenes seem rather cluttered. Late in 1914 Gill also added touches of colour to the Tenth and Thirteenth Stations - blue, red and green to the edges of the soldiers' garments and the foliage - and he also coloured in some of the inscriptions and gilded the haloes. But he later removed all colouring, probably on the instructions of Marshall. Nevertheless, the series as a whole, designed to be seen with the figures thrown into relief by light coming in from the side, has many attractive and unusual features - the boys Alexander and Rufus following their father, Simon of Cyrene, in the Fifth, the dice used by the soldiers, with the 'two' and 'one' uppermost (the Holy Trinity?), in the Tenth, the wound left by the spear in Jesus's left side (by tradition and in Gill's 1914 drawings, on the right), and Jesus blessing even in death in the Twelfth and Fourteenth Stations.

Gill's retrospective view of the Stations of the Cross is characteristic. He wrote 'I really was the boy for the job, because I not only had a proper Christian enthusiasm but I had sufficient, if only just sufficient, technical ability combined with a complete and genuine ignorance of art-school anatomy and traditional academic style'. He had become a Catholic just six months before he was approached about the Stations of the Cross - indeed this was one of the reasons he got the job. For him they were both a statement of personal belief and church furniture produced for his fellow Catholics as a focus for prayer - 'a statement without adjectives'. The figures are impassive and are meant to be so, for we are the crowd on the Jerusalem road and the emotion must come from us.

8. The Russian in the Crypt

Westminster Cathedral is not renowned for its tombs. There are only ten, one of which (Cardinal Vaughan's) was, until recently, not a tomb at all but a monument with a sculpted effigy of the man. The founder of Westminster Cathedral wished to be buried in another of his great foundations, the Missionary College at Mill Hill, and his body was only transferred to the Cathedral in March 2005. Seven other Cardinal Archbishops of Westminster and the great Bishop Challoner, who led the Catholic Church in England for a large part of the eighteenth century, are also interred in the Cathedral. The tenth sepulchre is that of a layman who held no position whatsoever in the Diocese of Westminster. And thereby hangs a tale...

A 'SPY' cartoon of Count Benckendorff on his arrival in London in 1903.

The Russian Ambassador

Count Alexander Benckendorff was born on 1 August 1849 in Berlin, his father being the Tsar's roving ambassador for Europe, and he did not go to Russia until he was eighteen, two years before joining the Diplomatic Service. As a result of this, his Russian was always rather poor and his dispatches were written in French. Before becoming a diplomat he was educated in France and Germany, and then represented his country in Rome, Vienna and in Copenhagen. Finally, from 1903 until his death, he was Russian Ambassador to Great Britain. Regarded in Russia as a Liberal and in England as an Anglophile, in 1911 his only daughter, Natalie, married the second son of Viscount Ridley, the Hon Jasper Ridley. Count Benckendorff was instrumental in arranging the Anglo-Russian Agreement of 1907 which, together with France, resulted in the Triple Entente. He encouraged the teaching of Russian at British universities and was Honorary President of the newly formed Russo-British Chamber of Commerce. Unusually for a Russian, he was a Roman Catholic.

The Great War broke out in 1914 and Russia, allied with Britain and France, suffered a series of crushing defeats. By early 1917 war-weariness, antagonism towards the Tsar's family (the Tsarina in particular) and the allure of revolutionary socialism had brought Russia close to collapse. By March, Tsar Nicholas II had offered to abdicate, intending to spend the rest of the war abroad and then to settle quietly in the Crimea where he would devote his life to the education of Aleksei, his haemophiliac son. Instead he was placed under house arrest and in July 1918, on the orders of the Bolshevik Urals Soviet, he and his family were shot.

Meanwhile a severe influenza epidemic was sweeping across Europe. Count Benckendorff, the Tsar's ambassador to the Court of St James's, was one of the first to be struck down. On 8 January 1917 he took to his bed. Three days later the condition had congested his lungs and he died, in a month when the disease caused more than 300 deaths in London alone. Before his death he told his daughter, by now the Hon Mrs Jasper Ridley, of his earnest wish to be buried in Westminster Cathedral where he had worshiped regularly. This wish she conveyed not only to the Cathedral but also to the British Government.

The only people buried in the Cathedral at the time were the first two Archbishops of Westminster, Cardinals Wiseman and Manning. After the completion of the Cathedral in 1903, their remains had been transferred to the crypt in 1907 from an initial place of rest in Kensal Green Cemetery. Cardinal Bourne, the Fourth Archbishop of Westminster, had left for Rome in December 1916 and did not return until April 1917.

Communications between London and Rome had to pass through several war-torn countries. Letters could take a week to arrive and telegrams two days. Meanwhile in Russia the Imperial Family was in turmoil, and communications

The Hon Mrs Jasper Ridley, Count Benckendorff's only daughter, as a child.

subject to strike action. With these difficulties, together with the fact that the Count had died at 10pm on a Thursday, *The Times* reported on Monday 15 January that 'up to a late hour no reply has been received from Cardinal Bourne in Rome to the request that the body might be interred in the Cathedral'.

Solemn Requiem Mass

On Saturday, 13 January 1917, a private memorial service was held for members of the Count's family and staff at the Russian Embassy. On Sunday the body was brought to the Cathedral to lie overnight before the high altar under the Russian flag, prior to a Solemn Requiem Mass the following day. Count Benckendorff's Requiem Mass must have been one of the most unusual in the Cathedral. On a cold, gloomy winter's day, a Guard of Honour of Grenadiers, together with the band of the Irish Guards, was drawn up outside. Within the Cathedral the coffin lay before the sanctuary steps covered with a black pall and white cloth embroidered with the Imperial arms of Russia. On a cushion at the foot lay Count Benckendorff's medals and other decorations. On each side of the coffin stood three tall candles. A few paces from each, a British soldier leaned on his reversed rifle while an officer stood at the foot of the coffin.

Despite the problems of arranging the Requiem Mass at short notice during a weekend in wartime, members of both the British and Russian Royal Families attended or were represented. King George V was represented by the Duke of Connaught, Queen Alexandra by Earl Howe, the Tsar by his brother, the Grand Duke Michael. The Grand Duchess George of Russia was present and the Prince of Wales and five royal princesses sent representatives. Mrs Lloyd George (wife of the Prime Minister) was there and Cabinet members included Mr and Mrs Asquith, Mr Balfour, Mr Austen Chamberlain, Lord Robert Cecil, Lord Curzon, Lord Derby and Lord Milner.

Count Benckendorff drawn by John Singer Sargent in 1911.

Count Benckendorff gets his wish

A week later, on Monday 22 January 1917, Count Alexander Benckendorff's wish was granted. 'By special request of the Government and permission of His Eminence Cardinal Bourne' (to quote the *Westminster Cathedral Chronicle*), he was buried in St Peter's Crypt in Westminster Cathedral where he had been a constant worshiper during the last fourteen years of his life. At this simple service his wife, Countess Sophie, too distressed to attend earlier ceremonies, was the chief mourner, together with his only daughter who had played such a key role in bringing the Count to his last resting place. It was the Count's daughter who also commissioned Eric Gill (then working on the Cathedral Stations of the Cross) to produce the memorial slab which lies above the ambassador's tomb in the crypt. Made of dark green Cumberland slate, it was finally installed early in 1939. In Russian and Latin, the inscription reads: 'Count Alexander Philip Constantine Ludovic Benckendorff, Ambassador Extraordinary and Plenipotentiary for Russia to the Court of St James's. August 1 1849 - Jan 11 1917. Requiescat in Pace'.

Cardinal Bourne must have been under considerable government pressure to agree to the interment in Westminster Cathedral. Russia was a military ally and its seemingly imminent collapse would release many German divisions to fight Britain and France on the Western Front, for America did not enter the war against Germany until April 1917. It was a time to show solidarity with Russia, not for a snub, real or imagined. The Count's daughter knew what she was doing when she publicly declared her father's wish to the British Government. Soviet Russia has passed into history, as did the Russia of the Tsars, and an era of greater religious and political freedom has dawned in Eastern Europe. In 1991 the first post-Soviet Russian Ambassador since Count Benckendorff was appointed to the Court of St James's.

With many thanks to Mrs Humphrey Brooke, grand-daughter of Count Benckendorff, also to Count Constantine Benckendorff and Sir Adam Ridley, his great-grandsons, for their help with preparing this account.

Count Benckendorff's tomb in the Cathedral Crypt, inscribed by Eric Gill in both Cyrillic and Latin.

9. The Parish Priest of Westminster

John Southworth, known as the 'Parish Priest of Westminster', was hanged, drawn and quartered at Tyburn (near Marble Arch) on 28 June 1654. His only offence was to be a Catholic priest, which he freely admitted. His body now lies in St George's Chapel in Westminster Cathedral, close to where he lived and worked. But in between there lies a journey, shrouded in secrecy, which covered some 400 miles and took 276 years.

The Road to Martyrdom

John Southworth was born of a Catholic family in Lancashire in 1592 during the reign of Queen Elizabeth I, at a time when harsh penal laws were being enforced against Catholics. In July 1613, at the age of 21, he travelled to Douay English College (Collège des Grands Anglais) in the town of Douai, near Lille in northern France. There, under the assumed name of John Lee, he studied for the priesthood and was ordained a secular priest before being sent to England in 1619. After a short spell back at Douay College and then as chaplain to Benedictine nuns in Brussels from 1624-25, he returned to his home county of Lancashire. By this time King Charles I had ascended the throne and there was a more tolerant attitude to Catholics.

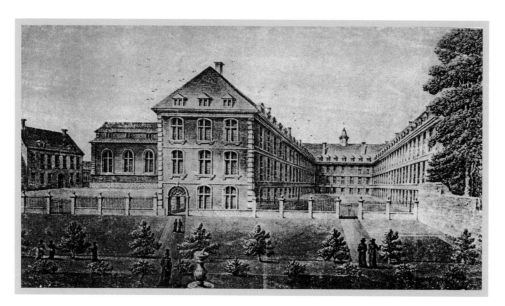

Douay College in the 18th century.

However, the penal laws remained in force and in 1626 (according to a subsequent warrant of 28 May 1630) John Southworth was arrested, tried for the priesthood (a treasonable offence) and condemned to death. He was reprieved, but not pardoned, and transferred from Lancaster Castle to the Clink prison in Southwark and then to the Gatehouse prison in Westminster where, though technically still a prisoner, he was allowed out on parole. For the rest of his life, when not confined in prison, he spent his time ministering to the spiritual and practical needs of the unhealthy and desperately poor Catholics in the parish of St Margaret's, Westminster, close to the site of the present Westminster Cathedral. His duties included administering the Sacraments, gathering and distributing alms, and visiting the sick and dying, particularly during the severe plague of 1636 when over 12,000 died in London.

But it was too good to last. The Civil War was followed by the flight of Queen Henrietta Maria, who had done much to help English Catholics, and the execution of her husband, King Charles I in 1649, accompanied by a more rigorous enforcement of the anti-Catholic penal laws by the Puritan government and parliament. John Southworth was arrested in his bed on the 19th June 1654, tried for the priesthood on the 24th, sentenced on the 26th and executed two days later. Lorenzo Paulucci, the Venetian Secretary to England, recorded that, after the rope had been put around Southworth's neck and the cart drawn away, 'in a fashion worse than barbarous, when he was only half-dead, the executioner cut out his heart and entrails and threw them into a fire kindled for

The site of the Tyburn executions, now near Marble Arch.

that purpose, the body being quartered, one for each of the quarters of the city'. But the Venetian's last supposition was to be proved wrong.

Someone with inside knowledge was Richard Symonds, a Royalist and antiquarian. He confided to his notebook that the Spanish Ambassador had bought the body from the executioner for 40 shillings. This would have been made easier by the fact that there were ten prisoners executed at Tyburn that day - including five coiners who suffered the same treatment for treason as John Southworth. A faded piece of paper identifying a relic relates what happened next. It refers to 'Mr James Clark, surgeon, who embalmed the body'. Both the Royal College of Physicians and Cambridge University record a James Clarke (or Clerke) who was awarded his medical doctorate in 1656-57.

The procession carrying the body of John Southworth to Westminster Cathedral. 1 May 1930.

Back to Douay

On 5 June 1655, George Leyburn, President of Douay English College, reported that Southworth's body had been sent there by two English Catholics of the highest rank. Leyburn had known Southworth well for many years in London. Bishop Richard Challoner later confirmed the arrival. Challoner was at Douay for 25 years from 1705. He was thus able to study the records and perhaps speak to those alive in 1655. He writes that 'Mr Southworth's body was sent over to the English College of Douay by one of the illustrious family of the Howards of Norfolk, and deposited in the church (the College chapel) near St Augustine's altar.'

Almost certainly it was Philip Howard, third son of the fifteenth Earl of Arundel and later Cardinal Protector of England, who organized the body's embalming and despatch to Douay. To the dismay of his family he had become a Dominican. A letter from him of 7 September 1654, and another of 1 October 1655, to the master-general of his order, stated that he had been called home to London on urgent business and had had no time to seek permission. His father was dead, his eldest brother Thomas (later fifth Duke of Norfolk) was mentally ill in Padua and Henry, the second son (later sixth Duke), was occupied with family affairs and possibly also abroad. Three of Philip's younger brothers had arrived to study at Douay in 1653 and in 1656 one of them, Francis, a youth of 17, fell seriously ill of a quartan ague and malignant fever and was given up for dead by his doctors, but made a miraculous recovery after prayers were offered to John Southworth and flowers and a pillow from the martyr's head brought to the youth to rest his own head on.

Such was the devotion of the townspeople of Douai at Southworth's shrine and the benefits reported to have been received that Leyburn was forced 'to mitigate the veneration and public concourse of people' - presumably by covering or otherwise removing the body from public view. In this he was obeying a decree of Pope Urban VIII on the veneration of martyrs. It was not until 1741 that relics of the Douay martyrs were allowed to be placed in altars and after this Southworth's body, in a leaden coffin, was placed under the altar table of St Augustine, about half-way down and probably on the left-hand side of the church. There it remained until 1793.

England and France went to war in January 1793. The National Guard arrived at the college, seals were set on objects and rooms and three guards (known to the students as 'the three spiders') were posted. Despite this, much valuable property was spirited away and buried by students while the relics, including the hair-shirt of St Thomas of Canterbury, the biretta of St Charles Borromeo and the body of John Southworth, were buried by the priests. It is fortunate that two records were left. Bishop Douglass wrote 'Mr Southworth's body in the Kilns exactly in the middle - six feet deep'. Father Thomas Stout, the Prefect General of the College, who seems to have been responsible for the relics, went one better and left a plan showing their position in the malt-kilns, (used for beer-making). Later that year, in August 1793, the English were expelled from the college and they returned to England two years later. The college buildings were employed as a French military hospital, then let to a cotton spinning company, and finally used as a military barracks (Caserne Durutte).

The portrait of John Southworth by John Trinick. February 1934.

A Remarkable Discovery

Not until 1863 was there a serious search for the buried objects. Some table silver was found near the refectory but nothing else. Sixty years later, in 1923, the town council of Douai decided to build a new road to the railway station, crossing the area where the old college had been. In 1926 the site was cleared, the road was then built and the surrounding land sold. In July 1927 workmen began to dig a cellar (the only one planned), for a shop at the corner of Rue Durutte and the new road (now Avenue Clèmenceau). On the 15th a pick struck a leaden coffin 5ft 8in long, moulded to the shape of a human body with the head towards the south-east. It was buried about 5ft down and a hole about 1½ inches across was in the centre. There was also a smaller hole at the head, caused by the pick. The authorities were notified, a priest (Fr Albert Purdie) summoned from England and the coffin, which was in two halves, the upper fitting tightly over the lower, was opened at the local morgue.

Inside lay the body of a man swathed in brown linen bandages. These had been treated with preservative and were very strong. Water penetrating through the larger hole (almost certainly caused by a metal probe used in the 1863 search) had badly damaged the chest and stomach but the head, which bore a slight moustache and beard, was well preserved and had been roughly severed from the trunk. The hands, ears and crown of the head were missing (presumably taken as relics). The brain and the internal organs had been removed and carefully replaced with preservative material. No expense had been spared in embalming the body in accordance with a method described in 1629. Subsequent X-ray results confirmed that the body had first been quartered and then meticulously sewn together.

The day after the discovery of the body a workman found a wooden box some 8 feet away. Inside were the remains of the relics of St Thomas Becket and St Charles Borromeo. Comparison of the position of this box and the coffin with Fr Stout's plan confirmed that the body was that of John Southworth. The complete absence of any identifying marks suggests that this simple leaden coffin may have been used to carry the body from England in 1655, when anonymity was essential. Tape binding the coffin, reported in 1786, indicates that it was normally kept closed but could be opened when necessary - as when Francis Howard was close to death.

The Return to Westminster

On 20 December 1927, accompanied by Fr Albert Purdie, John Southworth came back to England, his right forearm and left clavicle remaining as memorials at La Collégiale Saint-Pierre (Douai's largest church). From Dover the body travelled to St Edmund's College, Ware, the successor to Douay College in England. In April 1930 it returned to London, first to Tyburn Convent, and then, on 1 May, accompanied by a great procession led by Cardinal Francis Bourne, to the Chapel of St George and the English Martyrs in Westminster Cathedral. In December 1954 the body was clothed in vestments in the style of his time, a silver mask and hands added, and the martyred priest revealed to the public gaze.

Two portraits have been produced of John Southworth. The first was made by the artist John Trinick, who also designed the panel of Our Lady of Walsingham on the Cathedral pulpit. Trinick based his portrait, which appeared in the *Westminster Cathedral Chronicle* of February 1934, on a study of photographs made for Fr Purdie shortly after the body was discovered in 1927. Southworth's head was to some extent mutilated and damaged by earlier rough handling, but Fr Purdie was convinced that by studying the bone structure of the face and following certain well-defined characteristics which appeared in the photographs, John Trinick had recaptured the living look of the martyr. The second portrait was made by Alexander Siderov in the form of an icon. It is currently in the Exhibition of Treasures at Westminster Cathedral.

There in the Chapel of St George and the English Martyrs St John Southworth now lies, canonized a Saint on 25 October 1970, in death his face curiously unlined beneath the silver mask, despite his 35 years as a Catholic priest in a largely hostile land. Perhaps he even crossed this spot as he ministered to the poor and plague-stricken of Westminster, walking the green fields between the Bridewell prison, now the House of Fraser department store, and the 'Five Houses' or 'Seven Chimneys', an isolation hospital for plague victims beside the Thames, at a place not far from the present Vauxhall Bridge.

The shrine of St John Southworth in the Chapel of St George and the English Martyrs.

10. Our Lady of Westminster

There is one statue in Westminster Cathedral which is far older than any of the others. It is also probably the most venerated. It is the medieval statue known as Our Lady of Westminster.

The flat-backed figure is enshrined below Eric Gill's Thirteenth Station of the Cross - in which the body of Jesus is returned to his Mother's arms. The figure is of alabaster and shows Our Lady enthroned and crowned, with a broken sceptre in her left hand. Traces of paint indicate that Our Lady's crown, sceptre and mantle-fastening were gilded. Her garments were edged with gold with interior folds painted blue and red. Her dark brown throne stood amidst daisies in a dark green field.

15th century figure in Westminster Cathedral known as Our Lady of Westminster. 92cm high.

Alabaster Production

The Holy Child's position on the right and the corded mantle fastening are characteristic of English alabaster figures made between 1440 and 1525, but it is not yet possible to say with certainty where individual statues were made. Nottingham appears to have been the production and distribution centre for the alabaster industry from 1340 to 1550. With nearby quarries, particularly at Chellaston, fifteen miles to the south-west, supplying the raw material, large numbers of altarpiece panels, plaques and statues were carved and painted there. Contemporary records also indicate that alabaster was carved both locally at Chellaston and Burton-on-Trent, and further afield at Lincoln, Coventry, York and London

The Synod of Exeter in 1287 had directed that each parish church should have at least two images - one of its patron saint and the other of the Virgin Mary. By the time of the Reformation many of the ten thousand and more conventual and parish churches and chapels in England must have possessed at least one alabaster figure or panel. But the systematic destruction of religious images at the Reformation, particularly during the extreme Protestant government of Edward VI (1547-53), resulted in few surviving in this country. An Act of January 1550, for example, directed against so-called superstitious books and images, ordered that any person holding 'any images of stone, timber, alabaster or earth, graven, carved or painted', either taken from, or still standing in, any church or chapel, should deface and destroy such images by the end of June, on pain of a heavy fine or imprisonment for non-compliance.

Alabaster Exports

Fortunately English alabasters, which were usually relatively easy to produce and cheap to buy, were much in demand abroad, both before and during this period. This was particularly so in the Normandy and Bordeaux regions of France which had close links with England and where carved alabaster figures and panels, as well as uncarved alabaster blocks to be carved locally, could be readily traded for wine. Thus eight months after the passing of the 1550 Act, the English ambassador to France was reporting to the Privy Council the arrival of three or four ships from England laden with religious images which had been 'eagerly purchased' in Paris, Rouen and other places. Of the forty or more English alabaster statues of the Virgin and Child now identified, the majority either are, or were, in France.

15th century figure in the St Mungo Museum of Religious Life and Art, Glasgow, Scotland. 40cm high.

At least twelve of these figures, including Our Lady of Westminster, depict Our Lady seated with the Child on her right knee. Of these, five are now in France, three in England, two in Glasgow, one in Germany and one in Houston, Texas. Only one of these appears to have survived the Reformation in England. This was found buried behind the Church of All Saints at Broughton-in-Craven, North Yorkshire in 1863, but Our Lady's head and left arm are missing. The statue in the Cathedral, one in the British Museum and one in Glasgow all appear to have been purchased in France between 1954 and 1956. The figure now in the Museum of Fine Arts, Houston, was also purchased at this time by a French immigrant couple living in America.

Our Lady of Westminster, with a height of 92cm, is one of the largest of the twelve seated figures. The smallest (40cm) is in other respects very similar and can be seen in the St Mungo Museum of Religious Life and Art in Glasgow. The Cathedral figure also bears a close resemblance to that found buried in the churchyard at Broughton-in-Craven which, at 75cm, would be precisely the same height were the head still in place. It seems a real possibility that they were made in the same workshop - perhaps even by the same craftsman.

All Saints, Broughton-in-Craven

Before the Reformation, All Saints Church, Broughton-in-Craven, was dedicated first to St Oswald and then to St Oswald and Our Lady. Originally Norman, the nave was enlarged in the fifteenth century and a chantry chapel built in the north-east corner in 1442. Chantry chapels in nearby churches were dedicated to Our Lady and this would account for the change of name at Broughton. A Lady Chapel would have needed a statue.

15th century figure in All Saints Church, Broughton-in-Craven. 75cm high without head.

In 1863 two alabaster statues of the Virgin and Child were found buried in the ground at the rear of All Saints. One was of Our Lady seated and suckling the Christ Child (with head and left arm missing) on the left. The style shows that it was made in the fourteenth century. The second dates from the fifteenth century and is remarkably similar to that in Westminster Cathedral. The Broughton statues were presumably defaced and buried at the Reformation. Statues, which were usually heavy, were quite often buried near the church from which they came.

The fourteenth century figure would have been positioned in the nave or chancel. The roof of the chancel is also fourteenth century so the statue could have been acquired at the same time. It seems extremely probable that the fifteenth century statue was acquired for the new Lady Chapel, built in 1442, and positioned above the altar. Alabaster figures were carved both for a specific customer and in quantity from a standard pattern. In either case the Broughton figure would date from the early 1440s. The statue in Westminster Cathedral, while very similar, is a little more ornate. It seems safe to say that it was made about 1450, most probably in Nottingham, or nearby. This appears to be confirmed by another English alabaster discovered in France. Depicting the murder of St Thomas Becket in Canterbury Cathedral and believed to have been carved in the second half of the 15th century, it includes on the altar a statue of Our Lady apparently identical to that in Westminster Cathedral.

The Westminster Alabaster

The Westminster figure was first recorded in 1930 when it came up for sale in Paris. It reappeared in 1954 in an Exhibition of 'Chefs d'Oeuvre de la Curiosité du Monde' at the Louvre, on loan from the Paris art dealers Brimo de Laroussilhe who state that it was acquired from the Baron de Saint Leger Daguerre, living in Paris, but have no further information. The statue was then bought by an English ecclesiastical art dealer, S W Wolsey, in November 1954 and exhibited by him in June 1955 at the Antique Dealers Fair in London. He subsequently displayed it at his premises at 71 Buckingham Gate, now replaced by a modern office block.

Cardinal Griffin, sixth Archbishop of Westminster, wanted to have the statue for the Cathedral. But first to bid for it was the Dean of York Minster. An appeal by him for funds failed, however, despite a substantial donation by Sir William Milner. The Dean then suggested that Westminster Cathedral should have it. In October 1955 it was announced

15th century depiction of the murder of St Thomas Becket, in the Musée Departmental des Antiquités, Rouen, France.

that the sale had been completed. It was fitting that York Minster was represented by Milner at the Solemn Evening Mass on 8 December 1955, the Feast of the Immaculate Conception, with the Cathedral Choir welcoming the statue with the *Salve Regina*.

In 1971 a modern alabaster figure of the Virgin and Child, based on that in Westminster Cathedral, was installed in the north ambulatory of Westminster Abbey. It was carved by Sister Concordia Scott OSB at Minster Abbey. It commemorates a 'precious alabaster image of Our Lady', known as Our Lady of the Pew, given by the Countess of Pembroke to Westminster Abbey in about 1375 for a chantry chapel where prayers might be said for her husband and herself. The position of the plinth and the outlines of the statue, which can still be seen on the wall behind the modern alabaster, indicate that it was a tall, standing figure typical of those produced in the later 14th century. This medieval statue was said, like so many such figures, to have been destroyed at the Reformation.

So how and where did our medieval alabaster - Our Lady of Westminster - survive the Reformation? Most probably the figure was exported to France soon after it was made, destined for a French church, abbey, chapel or shrine. The similarity with the Broughton figure might suggest that it was first made for the home market and only later sent to France to escape destruction. But there is no other evidence for

15th century figure in Teurtheville-Hague Church, Lower Normandy, France. 86cm high.

this and several English alabaster figures in French churches are very similar - notably that dating from the second half of the fifteenth century in the church at Teurtheville-Hague in Lower Normandy. During the French Revolution, when many shrines were destroyed or vandalised, it probably came into private hands.

Speculation will continue about the history of this serene and touching sculpture. Yet what really matters is that, more than five hundred years after it was carved and coloured, a very rare and beautiful English pre-Reformation portrayal of the Virgin and Child has pride of place in Westminster Cathedral. *Salve Regina, Mater misericordiae; vita dulcedo et spes nostra, Salve.*

11. The Cathedral in Wartime

A story is related that a volunteer at the Cathedral Information Desk, asked by a group of visitors if the blackened walls of the Cathedral had resulted from a fire, described how a bombing raid during the Blitz had set the building ablaze from end to end. Only the efforts of valiant, bucket-carrying priests, nuns and choirboys, directed by Cardinal Hinsley himself, had managed to save the building. Sadly, nothing so spectacular really occurred.

1914-1918

In fact, since the Cathedral was structurally complete by 1903, it lived through two major wars. The first, that of 1914-18, initially had little effect on Cathedral life, though some of the chaplains donned uniform and went off to the Western Front, as did most of the men in the Choir, the rules of abstinence were suspended, and in 1916

Lighting a candle for peace.

the Catholic Women's League erected a hut on waste ground beside the Cathedral to provide meals (including a hot dinner for sixpence) and sleeping accommodation for servicemen using nearby Victoria Station. In the early stages of the war the bombing was only by German Zeppelin airships which became increasingly vulnerable to attack by aircraft, priests on the Clergy House roof watching two being shot down on 3 and 24 September 1916.

But as the war progressed its effects increased. In June 1917 the first names of fallen Catholic servicemen were inscribed in St George's Chapel and in the same year the Germans introduced the much more effective Gotha bomber to replace the Zeppelin. The *Westminster Cathedral Chronicle* described a raid in July by about 40 'Taube' aircraft in two groups, as witnessed from the Cathedral roof. However, the Etrich Taube was an unarmed reconnaissance aircraft used operationally only in 1914-15 and subsequently confined to training purposes, so the aircraft seen must have been some of the first Gotha G.IV bombers, which first appeared over London in May 1917.

By October 1917 the *Westminster Cathedral Chronicle* was reporting that 'air raids now seem to be the normal condition of things rather than disagreeable incidents'. The Cathedral crypt was opened as an air-raid shelter for parishioners, inspected and approved for 2,000 - a very large number even allowing for the space in the store-room under the Blessed Sacrament Chapel. During one raid the choirboys, finding the crypt full of those sheltering, played 'Buzz one' in the Song School, their only fear being that of being 'Buzzed-out'. The Choir School remained open throughout the war.

Fr J A Couglan and Fr M J Moriarty 'roof-spotting' at the top of the Cathedral Tower. 18 September 1940.

Each morning the boys went looking for shrapnel in the playground and during the day they used the practice trenches dug by the London Scottish Regiment in preparation for the Western Front to conduct their own particular and rather dangerous form of warfare.

1939-1945

Clearly the threat of air raids was much greater during 1939-45. The Choir School was evacuated in September 1939, initially to Horstead House, near Uckfield in Sussex, where the boys listened to a description of the Battle of the River Plate read by Fr Moore, their headmaster. In May 1940, with the imminent threat of invasion, the school was closed and did not reopen until January 1946. The boys left London with good reason. There was sustained German bombing for nine months from September 1940 to May 1941 with bombs falling all around the Cathedral - at the corner of Carlisle Place and King's Scholars Passage, scoring a direct hit on the Anglican Church of St Andrew in Ashley Place, near Morpeth Terrace, on the mansion flats of Carlisle Place and Ashley Gardens, and on Victoria Street and what is now Cardinal Place, but was then Watney's Brewery.

Fortunately air raid precautions had been introduced at the outset of war in September 1939. The Cathedral baldacchino, sanctuary, tribunes and organ gallery columns had been buttressed with scaffolding and sandbags while the shrine of St John Southworth in St George's Chapel was also heavily protected. The mosaic pavements in St Joseph's and St Paul's Chapels, which had only been laid in 1939-40, were covered with wooden planks, and Fenning & Co, which had been responsible for most of the recent marble and mosaic work in the Cathedral, promised to have a lorry and six men available at any time, day or night, to salvage marble and mosaics in case of war damage.

An air-raid post was set up in Archbishop's House and a system of 'roof-spotting' was adopted so that services could continue after the air-raid warning sirens had sounded. A squad of 20 wardens, recruited from the clergy and lay staff, manned observation posts on the Cathedral tower and roof and reported back any bombing threat to those organising the services in the Cathedral below. They also formed fire fighting parties, though initially equipped only with stirrup pumps and buckets. High Mass, and all Masses after sunset, were suspended, as were the rules of fasting and abstinence.

Arrangements were made for Cathedral clergy to support nearby parish priests at first-aid posts and casualty clearing stations in the event of heavy casualties, and the crypt once again became an air-raid shelter. The remains of a Westminster City Council notice informing those spending the night there that they were entitled to use council washing facilities for a penny (including soap and towel), rather than the usual three pence, can still be seen on a wall in the crypt store room, despite post-war efforts to remove it.

The gutted remains of St Andrew's Church, Ashley Place, after a direct hit in late 1940, showing the proximity of the bomb to the Cathedral.

The Cathedral in the Blitz

That was the situation in the Cathedral when the nightly blitz began in September 1940. In October, Clergy House was hit, but only by a slab of concrete sent flying by a bomb in Vincent Square. In December it was hit again, ironically by an unexploded anti-aircraft shell which did considerable damage to external brick and stonework before ending up in one of the priests' rooms. Bombs hit Blocks 10 and 11 of Ashley Gardens on 16 November 1940, and Block 4 in Ambrosden Avenue on 11 May 1941, scarring the woodwork of Archbishop's House and the Cathedral Hall, breaking many of the large leaded windows in the Cathedral sanctuary and nave, smashing in doors and covering the Cathedral with debris.

Remarkably, the bomb nearest the Cathedral, a delayed action variety which fell on the Choir School playground in October 1940 and exploded after two hours, left a crater 30 feet deep, 30 feet wide and 30 feet from the Choir School, but did no other damage, even to the windows. The blast was absorbed by the soft clay (the area was originally Bulinga Fen) on which the Cathedral is built, and went up vertically. Bricks and refuse from the Cathedral allotments were thrown into the crater and it was filled

The Cathedral's bomb-crater garden in the Choir School playground. June 1944.

with soil over a period of nine months. The chief sacristan, Mr Hayes, then created a highly ornamental and productive garden, providing 130 pounds of tomatoes annually together with cabbages, cucumbers, beetroot, onions, beans, parsley, lettuces, peas and mint to supplement the wartime diet, all surrounded by flower beds. Pictures of the Cathedral's bomb-crater garden appeared in the national press and in *The Sphere*, *The Tatler* and *The National Geographic Magazine of America* and it featured on both *Pathé News* and the 'Grow More Food' campaign on *Movietone News*.

Beside high explosives, the Germans also used incendiaries, but once again the Cathedral was largely unscathed. When John Bentley, the architect, was 14, his own parish church in Doncaster burned down. In building the Cathedral he used largely fire resistant materials such as brick, stone and concrete on which incendiaries burned harmlessly until extinguished. Nevertheless one burned a large hole in the wood block floor of Cathedral Hall, another went through the roof of the Choir School gymnasium and a third set fire to St Peter's Hall run by the Catholic Women's League as a servicemen's canteen on the site now occupied by St Paul's Bookshop. Another reason for the failure of the incendiaries was a 50,000 gallon static water tank and a motor trailer pump in the Choir School playground, which had been provided to protect the Cathedral and the immediate neighbourhood against fire.

> # Night in the Crypt
> ## AUGUST 1944
> ### A SOLILOQUY AFTER BYRON.
> I slept on marble, guarded from the skies,
> A Cardinal-Archbishop on each hand;
> I saw the scarlet tassels pendant-wise
> Which the broad brows of noble prelates
>   spanned:
> Wiseman and Manning, who the helm once
>   manned
> In England; and a living glory smiles
> Over the times when Second Springs were
>   planned,
> Which summered in these soaring marble piles,
> Intrepid in the Faith, a glory in these isles.

Written by Fr G Wheeler, one of those sheltering in St Peter's Crypt at a time when V-1 flying bombs were falling on London.

Getting Back to Normal

Neither the V-1 ('doodle-bug') flying bombs nor the V-2 rockets of 1944-45 caused much structural damage in the Victoria area, though on 25 June 1944 a V-1 fell on Hudson's Place beside Victoria Station, killing 14 and injuring 82. As the threat from air attack subsided, things started to return to normal and Midnight Mass was resumed at the Cathedral on Christmas Eve 1944, for the first time since the war started. All in all the Cathedral was extraordinarily fortunate to survive the 1939-45 War almost unscathed, despite being close to targets such as Victoria Station and many government buildings. A happy, if unintended, consequence occurred after the war. As early as 1918 the domes, which consist of two layers separated by three inches of airspace, had been leaking, resulting in the white stains to be seen from the nave. Nearby bomb blasts during the war forced the concrete stone slabs forming the outer shells of the domes apart, resulting in further leaks. In 1948-49, with the help of a grant from the War Damage Commission, the domes were clad with copper sheeting. Over the years this has turned green and is now a particularly attractive feature of the Cathedral. Every cloud has a silver (occasionally copper) lining.

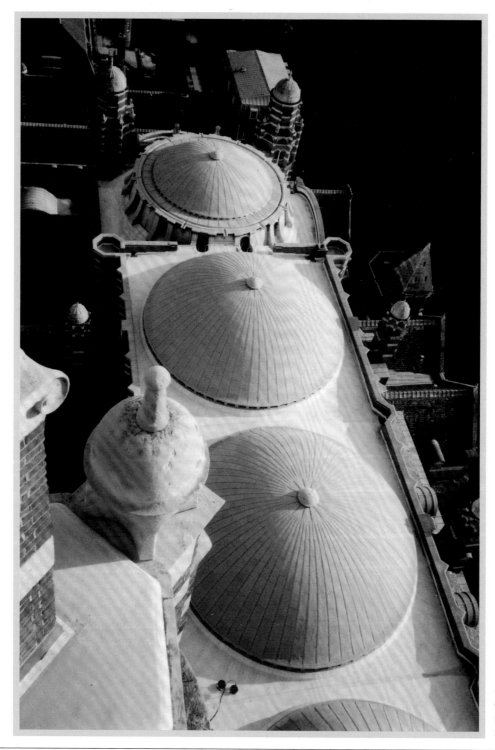

Looking down on the copper-clad domes from the top of the Cathedral tower.

Columns of Greek Cipollino and Italian breccia marble at the south transept.

1. A Tour of the Marbles

More than a hundred and twenty different varieties of marble and granite decorate Westminster Cathedral, almost certainly more than in any other building in England. Many of them were used in ancient Greece, Rome and Constantinople. They come from twenty-five countries on five continents.

On entering the Cathedral by the main entrance you are likely to be standing on light blue-grey Bardiglio Fiorito (floral blue) from the Carrara area of Tuscany in Italy. Immediately in front are two red columns, a reminder that the Cathedral is dedicated to the Most Precious Blood of Our Lord Jesus Christ. They are of Swedish Imperial Red granite*, with bases of dark grey Norwegian Larvikite showing iridescent flecks of silvery mica, and capitals of carved Carrara statuary marble. All the nave column capitals were meticulously designed by the architect, J F Bentley, in the Byzantine style and each one took two men three months to carve after it had been installed.

Looking down the nave the dark green columns on either side are Verde Antico marble from Greece. They come from a series of ancient quarries near Larissa in Thessaly which supplied the columns for Byzantine churches such as St John of Stoudios, Haghia Sophia (Santa Sophia) and Sts Sergius and Bacchus in Constantinople, now Istanbul. Between the columns are great brick-built piers. The smaller ones are clad with wavy green Greek Cipollino from the Island of Evia (Euboea), used extensively in ancient Rome. The larger ones are faced with Cork Red from near Midleton in County Cork in Ireland, and light green Campan Vert from the Campan Valley in the French Pyrenees.

Marbles from Ireland, Corsica, Greece, Italy, Portugal, South Africa, Chile and the USA decorate St Patrick's Chapel.

The archiepiscopal throne in the sanctuary consists of white Carrara marble inlaid with mosaic and marble from Greece, Italy, Yugoslavia (Croatia) and Egypt.

The Chapels of the South Aisle

Moving to the right down the south aisle we go past the Baptistry and come to the Chapel of St Gregory and St Augustine. Most of the marbles here are Italian - a lovely white marble panel from the Garfagnana district of Tuscany called Acquabianca (white water) on the floor above Cardinal Basil Hume's tomb. This is actually the third panel as the first broke when it was being delivered and the second broke when being cut to size. This one (the best) was inscribed by Ken Thompson of Ballycotton in Ireland and installed in 2000, the year after Cardinal Hume's death. More Italian marbles are nearby. Yellow and black Tuscan breccia from Stazzema clads the wall below the windows, with veined dark red Rosso Levanto from near Genoa for the bench below. The altar frontal is also from Italy, exceptionally beautiful slabs of Yellow Siena, but the great twin entrance columns are waxy Swiss Cipollino from the Canton Valais, while the altar table is Norwegian Pink from Fauske, with the rather attractive title of 'Midnight Sun' - you can see why.

On now down the south aisle to the Chapel of St Patrick where Irish marbles are much employed - wavy green Connemara from the Sky Road near Clifden for the altar frontal and floor, Cork Red for the little columns below the windows, the centre of the altar frontal and also much of the floor, and Kilkenny Black for the altar top. But marbles from many other countries also appear. On the floor below the altar is a design combining turquoise Amazon Green (Amazonite) from Colorado in America with dark blue Chilean Lapis Lazuli in a surround of green Verdite from Pemberton in the Transvaal of South Africa. Above the niches either side of the altar, French Red Languedoc encloses diamonds of red and grey Africano marble - certainly ancient since

A nave pier clad with light green Greek Cipollino, Cork Red, white Carrara, blue Azul Macaubas and dark green Verde Antico.

the old Roman quarry at Sigacik near Izmir in Turkey, had flooded, become a lake and remained undiscovered until 1966. It was called Africano by the Romans because of its colour, the colour of Africa, and in 74 BC it was one of the first coloured marbles which they imported.

Passing between more panels of yellow and black Siena breccia on the walls either side of the aisle, we come to St Andrew's Chapel with its 'pavement like the sea'. Besides being the patron saint of Scotland, St Andrew was a fisherman so the floor uses marble to remind us of this. The central floor panels represent a stormy ocean using great panels of swirling purple and white Fantastico Viola marble from Seravezza in Tuscany. The surrounding dark green wave is of Connemara and the light green and white marble, which is inlaid with twenty-nine sea creatures, is from the Iona marble quarry in Scotland. This closed at the outset of the 1914-18 War but the workings, marble blocks and abandoned machinery can still be seen there beside the sea. The altar in St Andrew's Chapel consists of three Scottish granites - the table of Alloa, the red pillars of Peterhead and the base of Aberdeen.

Opened-out Greek Cipollino panels in the south transept.

An English marble can be seen between St Andrew's and St Paul's Chapels. The skirting here is light grey Derbyshire Fossil limestone (rather demeaningly also used to build the M-1 Motorway), and contains a myriad of marine creatures such as crinoids which lived and died some 300 million years ago. The grey piscinas either side of the altar in St Paul's Chapel are from the same area - Wirksworth in Derbyshire, but they are made of Hopton Wood stone this time. However, the main marbles in this chapel are Turkish and Greek. Grey and white banded Proconnesian from the Turkish Island of Marmara lines the wall behind the altar, which is of translucent white Pentelic from Mount Pentelikon near Athens - used to build the Parthenon 2,500 years ago. Dusky grey Hymettian from Mount Hymettus, famous for its honey and also near Athens, lines the walls.

The floor of St Paul's Chapel provides another attraction. Designed by a writer on Italian art, Edward Hutton, it combines Greek Green Porphyry and Verde Antico with Egyptian Purple (Imperial) Porphyry and is modelled on the floor of the Palatine Chapel in Palermo, Sicily. In the twelfth century the Norman Kings of Sicily brought over Byzantine craftsmen to decorate their palaces and cathedrals with marble and mosaic. The Palatine Chapel in the Palace of the Normans is an outstanding example of their work. The Cathedral pulpit, which is near St Paul's Chapel, and the delightful floor panel (designed by Aelred Bartlett) below the statue of Our Lady of Westminster, are also in the Byzantine style.

From Our Lady to St Peter

Before the Lady Chapel stand two imposing columns of Red Languedoc marble from Caunes Minervois in southern France - so named because the people there once spoke Occitan (Langue d'Oc) - the tongue of the troubadours. The lower walls in the chapel display pink flushed yellow Giallo Antico from Kleber (Sidi Ben Yekba since independence from France in 1962) in Algeria and dark red Rosso Antico from the Mani in southern Greece. To the left of the chapel, in the Cathedral sanctuary, the side columns behind the wooden stalls are also French, Rouge Jaspé from near Toulon, alternating with Norwegian Pink. But the Carrara column capitals remain uncarved. The high altar, twelve tons of Cornish Penryn granite, stands beneath its great canopy, or baldacchino, of white statuary Carrara inlaid with coloured marbles, resting on eight columns of Yellow Verona. The archiepiscopal throne was made in Rome and modelled on that in the Basilica of St John Lateran there. It consists of marble from Italy, Greece, Yugoslavia (now Croatia) and Egypt. Looking back down the nave, our 1995 Centenary marbles can be seen fronting the piers high up at gallery level - dark red Rosso Laguna from Turkey** and light blue Azul Macaubas from Brazil.

Another Algerian marble from Kleber, the deeper pink, Rose de Numidie, lines the walls in the Blessed Sacrament Chapel, together with Yellow Siena. Further on, the Chapel of St Thomas of Canterbury, or Vaughan Chantry, encloses the effigy and tomb of the Cathedral's founder, Cardinal Herbert Vaughan, in carved white Pentelic, used

An English rose, made up of Rosso Antico, Lapis Lazuli, Yellow Siena, and Labradorite, in the centre of the floor of St George's Chapel.

by both Greeks and Romans in classical times. Two striking black-and-white columns, known as Grand Antique des Pyrénées or Bianco-e-Nero, stand outside the chapel. This French marble from the little village of Aubert in the French Pyrenees was also used in Roman and Byzantine buildings but the quarry is now abandoned and flooded. Next, to St Joseph's Chapel, where slabs of Greek Cipollino marble, cut from the same block, have been opened out or 'book-matched' against the north wall to create attractive patterns. The Cathedral is said to possess the best examples of opened-out marble in the country. In front of them below the windows is a central column of Tuscan Fior-di-Pesco, peach blossom marble, perhaps the most attractive in the whole Cathedral.

The next chapel is that of St George and the English Martyrs, so many of the marbles are the colour of blood - Greek Rosso Antico inlaid with mother-of-pearl roses on the wall above the altar, Rouge Sanguine from Kleber on the altar frontal, with dark red French Rouge Griotte (called 'Oeil de Perdrix' or partridge-eye because of its pearly white spots or eyes) on the floor, with a red English rose of Rosso Antico in the centre. The final chapel is that of the Holy Souls, with its themes of death and mourning. Here the colours are subdued - an entrance column of silver-grey Norwegian Larvikite below a mosaic of Adam, facing a column of veined cream Italian Pavonazzo below a mosaic of Christ - with floor and walls of grey Italian Bardiglio Fiorito and dark swirling green Verde di Mare (green of the sea) from Genoa. And so we come to the bronze statue of St Peter, the rock on which our Church is founded, and are back to where we started - which is always a good place to stop.

Red Grande Brèche de Kleber and Canadian Blue, inlaid with other marbles, make up the coat of arms of the donors on the floor of the Holy Souls Chapel.

Listed until recently as Norwegian, Norway's Geological Survey in Trondheim has confirmed that Norway is not a producer of red granite and has never produced granite of this type. It appears to be Swedish Imperial Red from Kalmar – see next Chapter.

**Not Italian as stated at the time of installation but Turkish from near Becin Kale. Turkish marble is often exported via Italy and described as Italian for commercial reasons.*

2. Identifying the Marbles

The first step for those researching the history and decoration of Westminster Cathedral is to read Winefride de l'Hôpital's book *Westminster Cathedral and its Architect*, published in 1919. This lists some fifty marbles which had been installed by that time - not far short of the number that her father (J F Bentley, the architect of the Cathedral) planned to use. It is clear from her book that she not only had access to her father's papers after his death in 1902, but was also provided with information by his successor as architect-in-charge, John Marshall, and by the Cathedral Clerk of Works (C H Mullis) and his assistant (Percy Lamb) together with representatives of the two marble merchants responsible for the early decoration (Henry Barnes of Farmer & Brindley and Joseph Whitehead of J Whitehead & Sons). As a result her identification of the marbles has been regarded as authoritative.

Two Italian marbles from the mountains of Lombardy, on display in the Natural History Museum, London.

Rosso Porfirico
Monte Verzegnes, Tolmezzo, Udine, Italy

Porfirico Bruno
Monte Verzegnes, Tolmezzo, Udine, Italy

Sources

The next person to study the Cathedral marbles was Francis Bartlett, Sub-Administrator at the Cathedral from 1954-64 and Administrator from 1967-77. In 1954-56 he produced a series of black-and-white photographs of the Cathedral annotated with the names of the main marbles and in 1989 he published two articles on the marbles in the newsletter of the Friends of Westminster Cathedral. But he freely admitted, as in a letter to the author of a book on Classical Marbles, Mary Winearls Porter, of 1965, that 'Nothing systematic has ever been done about the Cathedral marbles - when I was there I was always too busy to devote time to it.' Then there are the progress reports on decoration contained in the Cathedral periodicals - particularly the *Westminster Cathedral Record* (1896-1902) and the *Westminster Cathedral Chronicle* (1907-1967) which contain invaluable contemporary information. In the Cathedral archives there are the architectural plans and drawings of the building, sometimes annotated by Bentley and his successors with the names of marbles. And finally there are those who still remembered what happened - such as Aelred Bartlett (artist brother of Francis) who

Examples of English marble from Plymouth, Chudleigh and Totnes in Devonshire, in the gallery of the Oxford University Museum of Natural History.

went looking for suitable marbles for the Cathedral and then supervised the marble cladding of the nave, narthex and entrance porches from 1956-64. Shortly before his death in 2004, he recounted his memories to me deep into the night over Greek olives and Retzina.

After the Cathedral records the logical next step is to look at other written material on marbles, ideally that written while the Cathedral was being decorated. The main source here is John Watson's *British and Foreign Marbles and other Ornamental Stones* of 1916 as it refers on numerous occasions to the marbles in the Cathedral. Other useful books are those by Blagrove (1888), Renwick (1909), Davies (1939) and Grant (1955). The great advantage of Watson's book is that he describes the extensive collection of marble samples held in the Sedgwick Museum of Geology at Cambridge. Thus a colour photograph of an unidentified Cathedral marble can be compared both with Watson's description and with the sample at Cambridge. This was also done using some of the thousands of marble samples held by the Natural History Museum in London, at the Oxford University Museum of Natural History where columns of British and Irish marble are on display, and at Dublin's Trinity College Museum and the old Economic Geology Museum at 51 St Stephen's Green in Dublin where great panels of Irish marble line the foyer. There is also an extensive display of marbles at Bagnères-de-Bigorre in the French Pyrenees, and another at the Palazzo dei Conservatori in Rome.

Marble examples at the Sedgwick Museum of Geology, Cambridge.

Identification is much more reliable when columns or large slabs of marble are available for comparison rather than museum samples which are often only six inches square. Being naturally formed, no one piece of marble is completely identical to another. Examples may vary widely in colour and appearance and a single small sample can be misleading. This is another reason why the columns and slabs at Oxford and Dublin are so useful and the books by Watson and Renwick so valuable as these books also give examples of buildings using particular marbles for decoration - as they were intended. Many of these buildings have since gone - the marble-filled Holborn Restaurant in London, for example. But

The main quarry face for Rosso Antico marble - now a protected site - with a sheer drop below. Profitis Ilias, the Mani, Greece.

great slabs of Rouge Jaspé, Griotte de Sost and Vert des Alpes, together with columns of Campan Vert, can be studied in the foyer of the Hotel Russell in London's Russell Square; and many other marbles can be found in quantity in particular buildings - the National Gallery, the Victoria and Albert Museum, the Natural History Museum, the old booking hall at St Pancras Station, the Old Bailey, Drapers Hall, the Metropole Hotel (now government offices), the Norwich Union Headquarters in Norwich, Birmingham and Brompton Oratories, etc. - and so used for purposes of comparison. Another means of identification is to explore the quarries from which particular marbles may have come, gathering samples and taking photographs of quarry faces and marble blocks.

But often a definite match may be more complicated. To give just one example (and there are many more), the paired black and yellow columns in the apse alcoves above the choir in the Cathedral had never been identified. A visit to County Hall (the old Greater London Council (GLC) building by the Thames) revealed large columns and pilasters of an apparently identical marble in the deserted Council Chamber. These were on record there as Cipollino Dorato marble (also called Veine Dorée) from a little quarry near Valdieri in the province of Cuneo in Italy. In 1996 an Italian lady, Mrs Pia Bruno Allasio from the town of Moldovi nearby, had written to County Hall enclosing photographs of the columns leaving for England in 1925. The opportunity was taken to send photographs of the Cathedral columns to her and she referred these to Vanni Badino, Professor of Engineering at the Mining Department of the University of Turin, a specialist in this particular field. He confirmed that they were indeed Cipollino Dorato from Valdieri.

Involving the Experts

But written descriptions and photographs can only go so far in identifying marbles and once these are exhausted it is time to turn to marble merchants and other experts. Fortunately Gerald Culliford, Chairman of Gerald Culliford Ltd, and Ian Macdonald, Managing Director of McMarmilloyd Ltd, were willing to help. So was Monica Price, assistant curator at the Oxford University Museum of Natural History and author of the book *Decorative Stone: The Complete Sourcebook* which draws many of its examples and photographs from the Cathedral. It was with their help that the remaining Cathedral marbles and granites came to be identified.

A column of Cipollino Dorato from Valdieri in Italy, in an alcove overlooking the Cathedral Choir.

It was Monica Price, for example, who identified the sand-like disks which decorate the archiepiscopal throne as Breccia di Arbe from Arbe in what used to be Yugoslavia but is now Croatia, and it was Gerald Culliford and Ian Macdonald who finally resolved the problem of the eight beige and white columns below the windows in St Joseph's Chapel. These had been listed in the *Westminster Cathedral Chronicle* in 1933 as Hiberian Agate and, after installation in 1935, as Ibex Agate by the Cathedral architect-in-charge, Lawrence Shattock. But when Sub-Administrator of the Cathedral in 1954-56, Francis Bartlett had described them as Algerian Onyx. Fortunately the two marble merchants were able to identify the columns with certainty as Breccia Oniciata from the Nuvolento area of Lombardy in northern Italy.

Another problem with misidentification occurred with the twin red granite columns just inside the main entrance to the Cathedral, and the six red granite columns in St Peter's Crypt. In a supplement to *The Tablet* of 29 December 1900, Bentley had referred to the crypt columns as Norwegian red granite but had been less specific about the pair in the nave. However, in the first Cathedral guidebook, produced in 1902, they were described as 'red polished Norwegian granite', and Bentley's daughter and biographer, Winefride de l'Hôpital, described both those in the nave and those in the crypt as Norwegian red granite in her book of 1919. It was Gerald Culliford and Ian Macdonald who first challenged this, and photographs of the columns were sent to Norway's Geological Survey in Trondheim for identification. There Tom Heldal confirmed that Norway did not

One of eight columns of Breccia Oniciata from Lombardy, standing below the windows in St Joseph's Chapel.

produce red granite. The nave columns turned out to be Swedish Imperial Red from near Oskarshamn in Kalmar, a granite commonly employed in England in late Victorian times, while those in the crypt were of three types - Dark Shap from Cumbria, Carmen Red from near Kotka Koivuniene in Finland and, again, Swedish Imperial Red.

The Results of the Study

The process of identifying the Westminster Cathedral marbles lasted from 1995 until 2008 and resulted in the book *The Beauty of Stone: The Westminster Cathedral Marbles*. The study revealed that the Cathedral was decorated with 129 different varieties of marble and granite from twenty-five countries on five continents: Afghanistan, Algeria, Belgium, Brazil, Canada, Chile, Egypt, England, Finland, France, Greece, Ireland, Italy, Morocco, Norway, Portugal, Scotland, South Africa, Spain, Sweden, Switzerland, Tunisia, Turkey, USA and Yugoslavia (now Croatia). Just three of the total of 129 could not be positively identified - a black and grey breccia high on the west wall of the narthex (described by Aelred Bartlett as 'that awful Algerian conglomerate'), a dark green, cream and black vertical panel in the aisle outside St George's Chapel (probably an unusual form of Verde Antico) and a light grey marble on the floor below the altar of the Lady Chapel which Winefride de l'Hôpital listed simply as grey Greek marble.

3. The Lost Columns

When visitors enter the Cathedral an avenue of marble and granite columns stretches out before them - first two columns of red granite, then dark green marble, four on each side, then eight more columns in pairs as the nave crosses the transepts, and finally eight great yellow columns supporting the baldacchino over the high altar. One might assume that these columns were selected by the architect, approved by the Cardinal Archbishop, ordered, quarried, rough-hewn, transported, turned, ground, polished and installed as intended. But it didn't happen quite like that - not at all, in fact.

The eight dark green columns are Verde Antico marble from Thessaly in Greece. The same ancient marble appears throughout the Roman and Byzantine worlds, particularly in Rome, Venice, and Istanbul (Constantinople) in Turkey. After lying disused for well over a thousand years the quarries were reopened to provide the columns for the Cathedral. The first five marble blocks had been rough-hewn and transported the seven miles to the railhead at Larissa, when Turkey occupied Thessaly in April 1897 and held it until June 1898, preventing shipment for over a year. Thus it was that the Verde Antico columns, on which Cardinal Vaughan had set his heart, were not finally cut, polished and installed until late in 1899.

Trouble in the Transepts

But meantime worse had occurred. When one first looks at the eight paired columns where the nave crosses the transepts all seems well. But then one notices that on the left a column of wavy, light green Greek Cipollino has been paired first with a column of cream and purple Italian breccia (broken pieces of stone which have coagulated and solidified) and then with one of Verde Antico - not the lovely dark green Verde Antico of the nave columns but a duller, less attractive variety, possibly from a different quarry. Meanwhile on the right a column of the same Verde Antico stands beside one of Italian breccia while a little further on a column of breccia is paired with one of Cipollino. It all looks a bit cobbled together. Can this be the work of John Francis Bentley, the Cathedral architect, a man renowned for his scrupulous attention to detail?

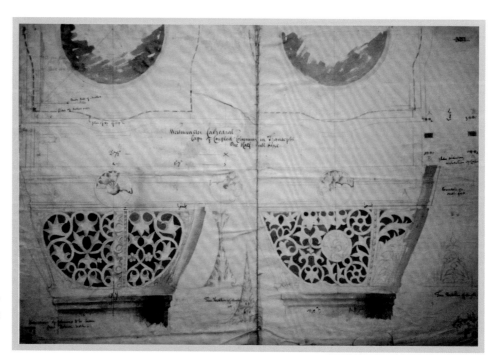

Bentley's design for the Greek Cipollino transept column capitals (F-65).

Well yes it was, but things had happened outside his control. Originally Bentley had wanted the transept columns to show the red and orange of Numidian marble – presumably the Marmor Numidicum, or Giallo Antico, marble of the Romans and Byzantines, which he described in the *Westminster Cathedral Chronicle* of February 1899, but clearly he was unable to obtain columns of this rare marble in the time available. So he turned to the other varieties of marble columns which were available at his marble merchants – Farmer & Brindley. But then, to his dismay, at Farmer & Brindley's marble yards at 63 Westminster Bridge Road across the Thames, three columns for the Cathedral, two of them of Greek Cipollino and one of Italian breccia, cracked while they were being

Columns of Verde Antico and Greek Cipollino marble in the north transept of the Cathedral.

worked on in 1899. To have ordered, quarried, transported, cut and polished similar replacement columns from the same quarries would have taken months. After waiting over a year for his Verde Antico nave columns Cardinal Vaughan was in no mood for further long delays. The columns were part of the structure and were needed at once to carry the galleries across the transepts. Besides, if Cipollino and Italian breccia were prone to crack could replacements of the same marble be relied upon?

What was available, however, were blocks of Verde Antico, released in 1898 from the log-jam caused by Turkish occupation. By 1894 William Brindley of Farmer & Brindley had discovered no less than ten ancient quarries for this marble and in 1896 he had set up the Verde Antico Marble Company to supply it. Verde Antico was the main marble used in Byzantine churches such as Haghia Sophia (Santa Sophia) in Constantinople. It was particularly liked by the Cardinal and had proved its durability and load-bearing strength over many centuries. It was most unlikely to crack as the other marbles had.

Three of the eight paired transept columns are now of Greek Cipollino and three of Italian breccia. The remaining two are of Verde Antico. A drawing (F-65) by Bentley to show the design of the transept column capitals (of which there are four types), shades all four columns a light Cipollino-like green. This suggests that four transept columns were intended to be of Cipollino and therefore, logically, the remaining four of breccia. It thus confirms that two of the columns which broke were intended for the transepts. So where would they have gone? I believe the present pattern tells us. All three Cipollino columns are on the inner (nave) side, blending in with the Cipollino-clad piers, while all three Italian breccia columns are on the outer (transept) side, reflecting the more varied marbles of the transept walls. This, I believe, was the planned pattern throughout.

Back to Bentley

But what of the other Greek Cipollino column which cracked and was discarded? There is only one obvious position for it - the aisle leading to the Blessed Sacrament Chapel, a position now occupied by a rather unattractive column of the same dull Verde Antico as in the transepts. A Cipollino column here would blend in perfectly with the surrounding Cipollino wall cladding. Indeed there is no other obvious position for it, for Bentley's columns are almost always paired - either side by side or (in the case of chapel entrance columns) across the nave - Languedoc with Languedoc, Swiss Cipollino with Swiss Cipollino, Greek with Greek. An exception is the Holy Souls Chapel where the sombre, silver-grey Larvikite entrance column is a fitting prelude for the silver mosaic and grey marble of the interior.

The Verde Antico column in the approach to the Blessed Sacrament Chapel was also 'lost' for a time - though it subsequently made a comeback. To facilitate processions moving down the aisle, in 1949 the Cathedral authorities had it removed and replaced by a marble-clad horizontal steel girder completely out of keeping with the Byzantine style of the building. The wall on either side shows where the girder was installed. The view of the *Westminster Cathedral Chronicle* in May 1949 that this 'will be welcomed by all' was very far from the case. In 1953 the Cathedral Art Advisory Committee, which had lapsed with the War, was reinstituted and the column, which fortunately was still in Fennings' builders yard at Hammersmith, was restored. It was said that it had been carefully chosen by Bentley. Well ... up to a point.

Finally to the eight columns of yellow Verona marble for the baldacchino. Cardinal Vaughan had a contact, Marius Cantini, who owned onyx quarries near Constantine in Algeria and had supplied Marseilles Cathedral. The Cardinal decided he wanted Algerian onyx columns for the baldacchino. In vain was he told that onyx was unsuitable for a heavy load-bearing role and that columns greater than five and a half feet had

Algerian Onyx columns intended for Westminster Cathedral's baldacchino, now in Birmingham Oratory.

The marble-clad horizontal steel girder installed in the approach to the Blessed Sacrament Chapel in 1949.

never been produced; he was adamant. At length, in 1902, soon after Bentley's death, the eight onyx columns arrived. Three were already broken and another badly cracked. Two of the others now support the pediment over Our Lady's altar in Birmingham Oratory. The yellow Verona columns originally planned by Bentley were ordered and arrived without mishap in 1905. His baldacchino, on which he had spent so much effort and which he had described as 'the best thing about the Cathedral' was unveiled on Christmas Eve 1906.

Some one hundred and fifty years ago, John Ruskin, an influential critic of art and architecture (and later of social conditions), compared the columns of a marble-encrusted building to its jewels. There are a hundred and thirty-four marble and granite columns in Westminster Cathedral, all of them monoliths, all of them solid, ranging in length from three to fifteen feet. They are its jewels.

4. A Pavement like the Sea

In the summer of 1901 Cardinal Herbert Vaughan was a disappointed man. The thirteenth centenary of St Augustine's landing in England from Rome in 597 had come and gone. So had the Golden Jubilee of the Restoration of the Catholic Hierarchy, on 29 September 1900 - a date provisionally fixed for the Cathedral's consecration and opening. Yet the building was unfinished. Writing in a supplement to *The Tablet* of 7 June 1902, the Cardinal explained that a further £16,000 was still required for work to be completed and to pay off liabilities. Under Canon Law a church must be free of debt before consecration can take place.

The Cathedral nave nearing completion in 1902, showing some of the visitors whose sixpences paid for the wood-block flooring.

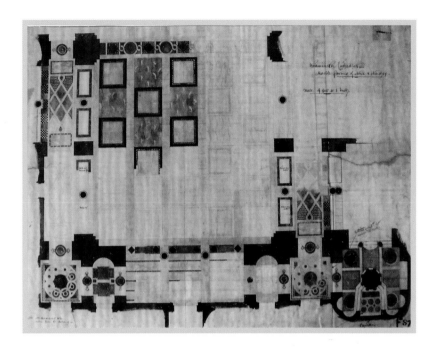

Bentley's design for the marble paving of the nave and narthex.

Meanwhile the Cathedral architect, J F Bentley, was working impossible hours. Since starting on the Cathedral in 1895 he had suffered two paralytic strokes - the first in November 1898 and a more serious one in the summer of 1900 which had affected his speech and memory. He had experienced considerable disappointment when the Cardinal had overruled him - ordering what Bentley regarded as an inappropriate altar of unadorned Cornish granite, Algerian onyx columns (subsequently rejected) for the baldacchino, and an unsuitable pulpit and archiepiscopal throne made in Rome. Knowing that time was running out for him, Bentley rapidly laid down a scheme for the marble revetment of the nave, sanctuary and side chapels. But his main concern was the floor. As early as February 1899 he wrote in the *Westminster Cathedral Record* that, 'the question of the floor of the Cathedral has not yet been decided, but we cannot suppose that any consideration for cold toes will secure for wood-blocks a preference over the legitimate marble'.

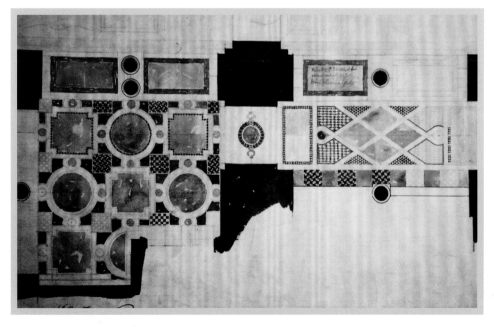

Bentley's design for the marble paving of the aisles and transepts.

After his European tour in 1894-95, Bentley had planned to study Byzantine architecture in Constantinople (Istanbul), particularly the church of Haghia Sophia (Santa Sophia). However, a serious epidemic of cholera there prevented this, and his knowledge of this sixth century church was drawn from a detailed study compiled by W R Lethaby and Harold Swainson and published in 1894. It seems probable that Bentley was also influenced by Lethaby's book of 1891 entitled *Architecture, Mysticism and Myth,* with its descriptions of the history and symbolism of features such as the labyrinth, pavements like the sea and ceilings like the sky, in ancient architecture. It seems very likely that Lethaby's book was the inspiration behind Bentley's determination to have a 'pavement like the sea' at Westminster Cathedral.

Bentley's Design

Bentley's plan for the nave floor consisted of wave-like Cipollino marble inset with many types of fish 'typifying all the varieties promised to St Peter's net' – an allusion to the Church as a ship carrying the faithful over the troubled sea of life. His designs show the floor divided into 10ft x 9ft sections, each containing five waved bands with inlaid fish. Alternate compartments of light grey marble framed by small black and white squares are interspersed at regular intervals by pink or blue tesserae set in a ground of golden yellow, all enclosed within a 9in dark marble border. Each 10ft panel is divided from its neighbour by a 2ft 9in strip of light marble running the length of each bay. Between bays in the breadth of the piers are 4ft circles of rose-red marble, alternating with lozenges of green enclosed in tesserae-filled squares of equal diameter.

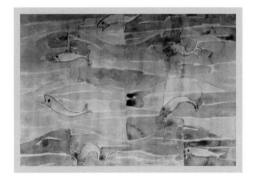

One of the panels in Bentley's design, showing the inlaid fish.

'What a grand floor!' wrote Cardinal Vaughan to Bentley when the design finally reached him in October 1901. The following December Bentley was able to write to a friend and fellow architect, Charles Hadfield, that 'the Cardinal, I am glad to say, has given in to the marble pavement'. But Vaughan was having the design costed. The estimate was £1 per square foot or £15,000 for the whole area. This would have doubled the sum outstanding on the Cathedral and postponed consecration indefinitely and Vaughan cancelled the scheme. Writing in June 1902, after the architect's death in March, he described attendance at a service on such a floor as 'synonymous with cold, rheumatism, influenza and every other bodily ailment', likely to result in beads of water forming on the floor and the unpleasant noise of chairs scraping on marble. But it is clear that the overriding factor was, as ever, economic.

Some concession was made in 1903 in the shape of marble paving, to Bentley's designs, in the narthex and between the piers and columns, at a cost of just over £1,000, but the nave was fitted out with wood-block flooring by the Acme Paving and Flooring Company (1904) Ltd ('Immovable Acme'). The cost of all the wood-block flooring in the Cathedral was met by the visitors who, at the instigation of the first Administrator, Mgr Patrick Fenton, each paid sixpence to view the work taking place in the building from 1900 to 1902. They were admitted through a turnstile by the 'Green Man', Sergeant Crooke the doorkeeper, who wore a green uniform. In this way £3,109 was raised, clear of expenses, which was more than enough to pay for the flooring.

The Surrey House Marble

Now the scene switches to Norwich, to the boardroom of the Norwich Union Life Insurance Society in December 1901. George J Skipper, architect for Surrey House, the company's new head offices, announces to the directors that a large consignment of very fine marble ordered for Westminster Cathedral has unexpectedly become available. A strike in the Italian quarries has resulted in it arriving too late to be used there. Skipper had inspected the marble and provided samples. The interior of Surrey House could be fitted out with it at the bargain price of no more than £8,139. The board approved. The marble was bought, decoration proceeded and Surrey House was completed and occupied in 1904. It is now a showcase of polished marble - and what marble! Column after column - six in the vestibule, forty more in the 60ft x 60ft Marble Hall - more main columns than in the whole of the Cathedral but in a fraction of the space. Slab after slab on the walls and galleries, many of them 2in thick; the columns in light green Greek Cipollino, very strikingly patterned, together with dark green Verde Antico, Rosso Antico, and lighter red Skyros on the 30ft-high walls. Also on the walls, staircases and floor are Italian varieties - pink and white alabaster, violet breccias, grey Bardiglio, veined Pavonazzo and Piastraccia, and white statuary from Carrara. Particularly attractive are the eight little pillars of rare Yellow Siena which support the air fountain in the centre of the hall.

Many of the marbles which suddenly came onto the market at the end of 1901 are the same as those needed by Bentley for his sea. The huge amount of wavy green Cipollino, smaller quantities of Verde Antico, Rosso Antico, Skyros, Bardiglio, Pavonazzo, Piastraccia and white Carrara (but not the alabaster which is too soft for paving) would have served him very well. The explanation of a delayed marble shipment in 1901 is at least possible. As described in the previous chapter, Cardinal Vaughan's impatience appears to have resulted in inferior marble columns being installed in the Cathedral transepts. The firm responsible, Farmer & Brindley of Westminster Bridge Road, was the one supplying Surrey House with marble and, in addition to Bentley's 'pavement like the sea', they also lost out on other marble work in the Cathedral at this time. Contracts for the decoration of the sanctuary arcades and tribunes, the Holy Souls Chapel and the Chapel of St Gregory and St Augustine, were all awarded to J Whitehead & Sons of Kennington Oval - a major competitor.

Almost all we have of Bentley's design – the marble paving outside the Gift Shop in the narthex.

Farmer & Brindley also lost a major contract elsewhere in London. Work on Edward Mountford's new Old Bailey courthouse started in 1902 and was finished in 1907. Inside, the two great halls and connecting stairway are lined with marble, including a large number of Verde Antico and Cipollino columns similar in size and appearance to those now at Surrey House. Farmer & Brindley were the leading marble merchants in London and may well have assumed that the Old Bailey contract would be theirs, ordering the stock which would be needed including column blocks. Instead the contract went to a newcomer on the scene, the recently formed firm of Arthur Lee of Hayes, Middlesex.

Conclusion

We will probably never be sure how and why the Surrey House marble suddenly became available in 1901. As a pamphlet on Skipper's firm of architects put it in 1980, 'The reasons have never been adequately elucidated' - perhaps in order to avoid embarrassment for Bentley's family or Westminster Cathedral. The firm of Farmer & Brindley carried out much of the early marble work, including the 1903 paving, in the Cathedral. Clearly they had excess stock, perhaps resulting in cash-flow and storage problems. They could have imported the marble on Bentley's instructions or simply anticipated that contracts for the Cathedral pavement, sanctuary arcades, tribunes and chapels would be theirs. It seems quite possible that Bentley, knowing that the sands were running out for him and being determined to supervise as much of the work as he could, ordered the marble for his 'pavement like the sea' before it was formally and finally approved by the Cardinal. The cancellation of the project clearly came as a bitter blow.

In a letter to Lady Herbert of Lea, just after Bentley's death in March 1902, Cardinal Vaughan wrote that he expected 'financial trouble in consequence of his (Bentley's) latterly unbusiness (sic) ways. His nerves were shattered and his memory almost as affected as his speech'. As he later wrote in Bentley's obituary in *The Tablet* on 7 June, 'Mr Bentley was a poet ... he cared little for economy'. So what would his 'pavement like the sea' have looked like? Bentley's three drawings of the paving of the nave, narthex, aisles and transepts (F-52, F-86 and F-87) and the marble paving which we see today in the narthex, together with Robert Weir Schultz's stormy marble sea inlaid with twenty-nine fish and other marine creatures in St Andrew's Chapel, give us some idea of what might have been. For the rest we can only imagine.

The Marble Hall at Surrey House, Norwich.

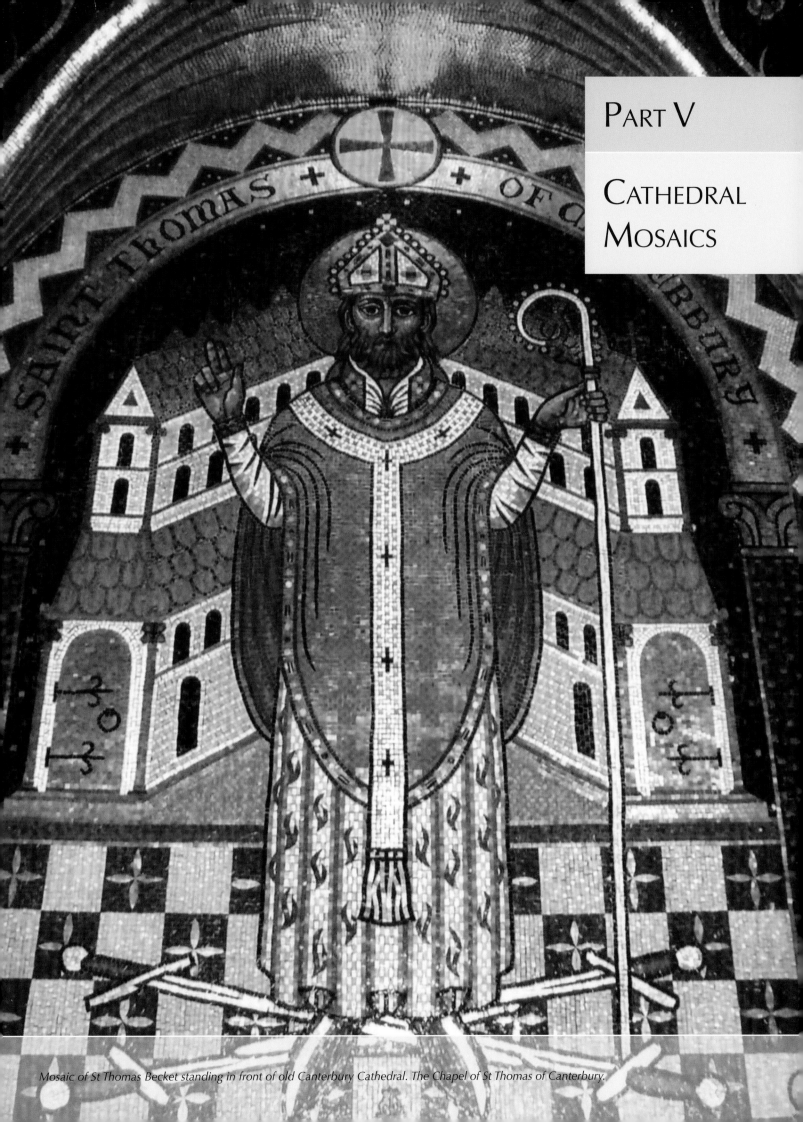

PART V

CATHEDRAL
MOSAICS

Mosaic of St Thomas Becket standing in front of old Canterbury Cathedral. The Chapel of St Thomas of Canterbury.

1. Mosaics and Methods

Westminster Cathedral was built from 1895 to 1903 in the style of an early Byzantine basilica - constructed and faced with brick and decorated internally with marble and mosaics. The marblework is now effectively complete but only a small part of the Cathedral has yet received its mosaics - nine of the twelve chapels, the great sanctuary arch and the smaller arch in the crypt, one of the confessional recesses and a few smaller recesses and panels elsewhere. Yet already some fourteen million pieces of mosaic have been laid. To complete the decoration in the manner originally intended would require perhaps seventy-five million.

Fourth Century Roman wine-making mosaics on the vault of the Church of Santa Costanza, Rome.

History of Mosaics

Mosaic consists of small pieces of marble, stone, terracotta or glass known as tesserae (or smalti in the case of opaque Venetian glass), which are applied (fixed) to a prepared surface. When the practice first began is unclear but by the third millennium before Christ coloured terracotta cones were being pressed into damp mud to decorate buildings in Mesopotamia (modern-day Iraq) and by the start of the fourth century BC coloured pebbles were being used by the Greeks to produce regular patterns and representations of human figures and animals on floors. The Romans also used mosaic extensively on floors and in the first century BC they began decorating the walls of their natural or artificial rustic grottoes, often containing a water feature such as a spring or fountain, with marble chips, sea-shells and eventually stone and glass tesserae.

In the first century AD the Roman use of decorative coloured glass on walls increased though it is only in a few places such as Pompeii and Herculaneum, engulfed in cinders, ash and mud by the eruption of Vesuvius in 79 AD, that these early wall mosaics have been preserved. For when a building collapses the walls fall in, protecting any floor mosaics but shattering those on walls and vaults. It was the mosaicists of Christian Constantinople (previously Byzantium, now Istanbul) and its empire who mastered the technique of decorating walls and vaults with glittering gold, silver and coloured glass tesserae during the eleven hundred years (330-1453) of Byzantine rule. The early figure

Sixth Century Byzantine apse mosaic in the Church of San Vitale, Ravenna.

mosaics of Constantinople itself were largely destroyed in the period of iconoclasm (726-843), and most of those subsequently restored were plastered over or defaced after the city's capture by the Ottoman Turks in 1453, handfuls of tesserae being given to visitors to Justinian's great sixth century church of Haghia Sophia (Ayasofia or Santa Sophia) as late as 1840. But early Byzantine mosaics still exist in places such as Ravenna in Italy, Porec in Croatia, and Thessaloniki (Salonica) in Greece, while outstanding examples of later Byzantine mosaics can be found in Istanbul, in Palermo, Monreale and Cefalu in Sicily, in Venice and in Greece. It is these Byzantine mosaics that Westminster Cathedral mosaic designers have usually turned to for inspiration and which they have often attempted to emulate.

Tenth Century Byzantine tympanum mosaic in the Church of Haghia Sophia (Santa Sofia), Istanbul.

Cathedral Mosaics

The opaque glass tesserae used in the Cathedral average one square centimetre in size and are half a centimetre thick. Thus they are about the same size as those used by Byzantine mosaicists in the church of Haghia Sophia (now a museum) in Istanbul, and later in St Mark's Basilica in Venice. They come mainly from Venice and the island of Murano nearby. Some have gold, silver or platinum leaf fused onto clear or greenish glass with another thin sheet of glass (cartellina) on top to protect the metal from the atmosphere. Normally 500-700 tesserae are used to the square foot, depending on their size and proximity, so the blue sanctuary arch mosaic in the Cathedral consists of about a million and the Lady Chapel has about three million. The first Cathedral mosaics were laid in the Chapel of the Holy Souls in June 1902 using the direct method. In this, full-size coloured drawings (cartoons) of the designs are outlined, pricked or traced onto the working surface. The tesserae are then inserted directly into the fixing medium of adhesive cement, using the cartoon as a guide to their positioning and colour.

The Cathedral architect, John Francis Bentley, was not concerned whether the fixing medium was water or oil-based (which allows more time for adjustment before setting), providing it was durable and the tesserae were worked in situ on the walls. In fact oil based mastic was used for all the early Cathedral mosaics. The potential advantages of the more traditional, direct method are precision, the glittering effect of gold and silver tesserae inserted individually and thus at different angles to the light (demonstrated spectacularly in the vault of St Andrew's Chapel), and the difficulty of judging the effectiveness of a mosaic in terms of colour and proportion when it is produced under

Twelfth Century Sicilian-Byzantine mosaic in the apse of Monreale Cathedral, Sicily.

a bright light (and possibly upside down) in the studio, rather than in its final position high on a wall or vault and dimly lit from below. In the Cathedral the direct method was used for the Holy Souls Chapel, St Andrew's Chapel, the Lady Chapel, the Sacred Heart Shrine, the sanctuary arch, the main arch in St Peter's Crypt, the inner crypt panel of St Edmund blessing London, the south transept confessional recess, the panel of St Joan of Arc in the north transept and the RAMC (Royal Army Medical Corps) memorial in St George's Chapel.

The direct method was the one normally used in antiquity though prefabrication did sometimes occur when working on very detailed panels (emblemata) for insertion in a larger mosaic. One way of doing this is to assemble the tesserae face upwards in a temporary bed of damp sand etc, paste them with water-soluble gum and cover them with gauze or similar material. Attached to this by the gum the mosaic is lifted from its temporary bed and secured in its final position. The gauze or other material is then soaked and removed. This method is used with the direct method at the Mosaics School in Ravenna to copy ancient mosaics. Another method is to cement the tesserae, again face upwards, onto a permanent backing of thin reinforced concrete slabs, board or mesh. This is then transferred from the studio and secured in its final position with screws or adhesive cement. Both board and fibre-glass mesh are used at the Friuli Mosaics School at Spilimbergo. Concrete slabs are used for mosaics intended for outside.

Thirteenth Century Venetian-Byzantine apse mosaic in the Basilica of Torcello, Venice.

The indirect or reverse method, disliked by Bentley, is to assemble the tesserae face downwards onto gummed, full-size reverse cartoons. The tesserae attached to the cartoons (often cut into numbered segments) are then pressed into the permanent fixing medium on the wall or vault, the cartoons subsequently being soaked and removed to reveal the mosaic (now face up), below. The mosaic is then usually grouted to produce a level surface. In the Cathedral this method was employed for all the mosaics not listed in the previous paragraph except for the panel of St Patrick in the south aisle which was produced by Trevor Caley on board in the studio, and that of St David, also in the south aisle, which was produced by Tessa Hunkin on nylon mesh in the studio before being transferred to its final position in 2010.

2. The First Mosaics

When the Cathedral architect, John Francis Bentley, died on 2 March 1902, he left no finished mosaics in the Cathedral and very little in the way of mosaic drawings and designs. It was thus left to future architects, designers and donors supervised, from 1936, by the Cathedral Art Committee, to decide on the mosaics. Between 1902 and 2010 twenty different designers and at least sixty mosaicists have worked on the Cathedral mosaics, and the work continues today.

Initial Ideas

Bentley's architectural drawings of the west and north elevations, drawn up in 1895-96, include small pencil sketches by him of mosaics above both the main and north-west entrances. In the *Westminster Cathedral Record* of February 1899 he provided a written outline for the decoration of the Lady Chapel 'by an artist' and in the same magazine in May of that year an anonymous illustrated scheme for one of the chapels of the north aisle. But the only one of these schemes to be adopted was that above the main entrance which was reworked first by John Marshall and then by Robert Anning Bell and installed in 1915-16.

Cardinal Vaughan, the Cathedral's founder, had also been considering the question of the mosaics, and between 1899 and 1901 a total of twelve prominent Catholics, half of them clerics and half laymen, had been asked to provide written suggestions for a scheme for the nave. Vaughan had expressed the view that the nave should tell the history of the Catholic Church in England, while the Lady Chapel and St Peter's Crypt should illustrate the devotion of the English people to Our Lady and St Peter respectively. Most of the responses (the most comprehensive of which was from Revd Herbert Lucas SJ, published in *The Tablet* of 28 December 1901), consisted of lists of scenes and saints illustrating the story of Christianity in England from the martyrdom of St Alban in about 304 AD or the arrival of St Augustine in 597, down to the return of the Catholic Hierarchy in 1850 or the building of Westminster Cathedral. But Bentley's death in March 1902, followed by that of the Cardinal in June 1903, put an end to this initiative.

The Chapel of the Holy Souls

Meanwhile Bentley had concluded that it would be best to start work first on the mosaics in the side chapels. His ideas can best be seen in the Chapel of the Holy Souls for which, together with the artist William Christian Symons, he helped to design the mosaics. Symons was an old friend and fellow convert, and in 1899 Bentley had asked the Cardinal that he should decorate one of the chapels, with John Sargent (who turned it down) and Bentley himself each doing another. Correspondence in 1900 on the themes for the mosaics of the Holy Souls reveals that Symons suggested the Three Youths in the Burning Fiery Furnace for the west wall - symbolic of redemption, but it was Bentley who suggested the Purgatory scene above the altar with the archangel Raphael

*Adam and the serpent.
The Chapel of the Holy Souls.*

(believed by him to be the angel of death) leading the souls in, and the archangel Michael welcoming them out and up to Paradise. Symons also suggested portraying Adam and Eve on the south and north walls, though Eve was rejected in favour of Christ for the north wall (I Corinthians: 15). Bentley's 1899 scheme for a north aisle chapel stated that 'the vault forming the ceiling will be covered with silver mosaic, glazed with golden green and enriched with wreaths of green and gold'. The sketch accompanying this showed a bishop (apparently St Patrick) above the altar and a monk surrounded by snakes above that. So it looks as if the silver vault with its green wreaths was Bentley's idea and unrelated to the subsequent dedication of this chapel to the Holy Souls.

Even though he died before mosaic installation began, Bentley's influence in the Holy Souls is very evident. He wanted a 'severe and very Greek' character and supervised the sketches and subsequent full-size cartoons in Symons' riverside studio on Grosvenor Road in Pimlico. To install the mosaics they chose George Bridge and his 26 young lady mosaicists who had a studio at 139 Oxford Street to which Bentley was a frequent visitor. Initially it was intended to prepare much of the mosaic face downwards on canvas in the studio (the indirect method). But this was not a success and was soon abandoned. Instead the direct method was adopted in which the irregularly shaped glass tesserae were inserted directly and individually into the oil-based, salmon-tinted mastic. Instead of the usual Byzantine background of gold or dark blue, here silver-coloured tesserae were used to suit the sombre colour scheme, with wide gaps between them to tone down the effect. A report in *The Universe* of 25 April 1903 described how Bridge's girls were given circular coloured slabs of mosaic material which they chipped into pieces and inserted into the mastic using as a guide the coloured cartoon pasted up in sections beside them.

Blessed (now Saint) Joan of Arc. The north transept.

Installation of the Holy Souls mosaics took eighteen months, from June 1902 to November 1903. The *opus sectile* panels for the altarpiece and above the niches either side of the altar, were made by George Farmiloe & Sons of St John Street, West Smithfield. They were painted by Symons in 1903 and installed in 1904. *Opus sectile* was used here because, except when very small tesserae are used - as in late Byzantine micromosaics of icons and in the mosaic copies of Renaissance paintings in St Peter's, Rome - mosaic is less effective to the eye at close range. But with a wife and nine children to support, Symons wanted the work to continue. Advised in a letter of April 1903 from George Bridge, who also wanted more work, that a rival, the Venice and Murano Glass Company, had bid to execute the tympanum mosaic above the main entrance to the Cathedral, Symons submitted his own design for this to the Cardinal in May. But Vaughan died in June. So, urged on by Revd Herbert Lucas - one of those who had drawn up a scheme for the nave mosaics and who wanted Symons' support for its implementation - Symons approached Vaughan's successor, Francis Bourne, seeking an interview to discuss his own mosaic designs for both the entrance and the Blessed Sacrament Chapel.

*The Holy Face.
The Shrine of the
Sacred Heart and
St Michael.*

But the only commissions Symons received from Bourne were to design a mosaic panel of St Edmund blessing London in the inner crypt, another of St Joan of Arc in the north transept and the Holy Face (Vernicle) in the Shrine of the Sacred Heart and St Michael, all executed in 1910-12 by George Bridge and his young ladies using the direct method. When the Joan of Arc mosaic was first revealed in 1910 Bridge was accused of not following Symons' cartoon and was forced to alter it. Symons' design for the Holy Face was a death mask, disliked by the donor (Mrs Evelyn Murray), but he refused to change it. He died in 1911. Five years later, in 1916, all the mosaics in the Sacred Heart Shrine, installed by George Bridge and his girls in 1911-12 but which by 1913 had become loose enough to fall out, were replaced by James Powell & Sons of Whitefriars using the direct method at a cost of £780. The simple and attractive floral pattern for the vault mosaics was designed by John Marshall, Bentley's successor as architect-in-charge of the Cathedral, the new Holy Face being based on one in St Mary's, Cadogan Terrace, Chelsea, of which there is now no trace.

The Chapel of St Gregory and St Augustine

The decoration in the Chapel of St Gregory and St Augustine was installed at the same time and by the same group of mosaicists as that in the Holy Souls Chapel across the nave. But despite this it is in complete contrast - the result of having a very different donor, designer, producer and method of installation. Lord Brampton, the donor, was a distinguished advocate and judge and a friend of Cardinal Manning, the second Archbishop of Westminster. He joined the Catholic Church in 1898 and paid £8,500 (£400,000 today) for the decoration of St Gregory and St Augustine's Chapel, which was intended to be both a thanksgiving offering and a chantry chapel for his wife and himself. The theme is the conversion of England from Rome, with the saints who brought this about portrayed in *opus sectile* above the altar, and those who subsequently kept the faith alive in this country shown in mosaics on the side walls and vault.

The east wall mosaics. The Chapel of St Gregory and St Augustine.

The story starts with the panel on the right of the entrance. Here is St Gregory the Great, then a Benedictine monk in about the year 587, with three English children in the Roman slave market and remarking "Not Angles but Angels if Christian". It was said that it was then that he conceived the idea of the evangelisation of England. Next Pope Gregory, as he had become, is shown above the altar with the dove of divine inspiration, together with another Benedictine in black, St Augustine, carrying the picture of Christ which he and his companions brought to England in 597. On either side are Saints Paulinus (Bishop of York), Justus (Bishop of Rochester), Mellitus (Bishop of London) and Laurence (successor to St Augustine as Archbishop of Canterbury). Both Mellitus and Justus also subsequently held this position.

The upper mosaics above the altar show an enthroned Pope Gregory sending St Augustine and his companions off on their journey to England, while above that they are seen meeting Ethelbert, King of Kent, and Bertha, his Christian wife, after their arrival. Opposite, above the entrance to the Baptistry, are St Augustine and St John the Baptist with the four Rivers of Paradise (Euphrates, Gehon, Phison and Tigris), emphasising the link between baptism and conversion. The other saints portrayed in mosaic are (facing the entrance) Wilfred, Bishop of York, and Benedict Biscop, founder of Benedictine monasteries at Wearmouth and Jarrow, who together consolidated the link with Rome at the Synod of Whitby in 664. On the right is Cuthbert the 'Apostle to the Lowlands' and later Bishop of Lindisfarne, who attracted many Northerners to Christianity. He is shown carrying the head of St Oswald, Christian King of Northumbria, killed by the pagan king Penda of Mercia in 642, after which his head was placed in St Cuthbert's coffin on Lindisfarne. St Oswald himself appears opposite above the entrance and beside him are St Bede, a Benedictine monk and the 'Father of English history' and St Edmund, Christian King of East Anglia, slain by Danish archers in 870.

Opus Sectile and the Italian Method

The donor of the chapel, Lord Brampton, selected Clayton & Bell of 311 Regent Street, renowned for their ecclesiastical stained glass, to design the decoration. It was decided to use *opus sectile* for the panels above the altar showing St Gregory, St Augustine, his companions and successors, and these were made by James Powell & Sons (Whitefriars Glass), of 26 Tudor Street, Whitefriars. *Opus sectile* was originally a term for flat pieces of naturally coloured stone, larger than tesserae, (i.e. more than 5cm across), which

'Not Angles but Angels'. Opus sectile panel in the Chapel of St Gregory and St Augustine.

were cut to shape to form geometrical patterns and pictures on Greek and Roman pavements from the second century BC. In the Cathedral, examples laid in 1903 can be found on the floor outside both the Baptistry and the Gift Shop. But in the 1860s Powells had started grinding up waste glass and baking it, to produce panels of opaque material with an eggshell finish which were then cut into suitable shapes, painted with ceramic paint, fused in the kiln to bond the paint to the panel and assembled to form pictures and patterns. These manufactured tiles were also named *opus sectile*. Those above the altar were made by Powells in 1901 and designed and painted by Clayton & Bell. The panels either side of the entrance are later: 'The Just Judge' - Clayton & Bell's memorial to Lord Brampton, who died in 1907, and 'Not Angles but Angels' - given by the Choir School in 1912 from the proceeds of a nativity play.

John Richard Clayton, who had co-founded Clayton & Bell in 1865, believed that any attempt to revive the dead in art was a profound mistake and he ignored the wishes of the Cathedral architect, J F Bentley, that the Byzantine style should be adopted. Instead his designs were similar to those he produced for Victorian Gothic churches. Clayton & Bell's standard procedure with mosaic commissions was to produce full-size, coloured cartoons in reverse which were then passed to Salviati & Co (Compagnia Venezia-Murano, or Venice and Murano Glass and Mosaic Company). They in turn employed a technique practised in Venice from the mid-19th century, and hence popularly known as the 'modern Italian method', and attached standard sized, glass smalti of matching colour, face downwards onto the cartoons before returning them in sections to Clayton & Bell in England. George Bridge later confirmed that J R Clayton wished the mosaics in the Chapel of St Gregory and St Augustine to be made using this method, which Bridge personally disliked and believed 'rendered the work flat and lifeless'. Nevertheless from December 1902 to May 1904 his young mosaicists, already working in the Holy Souls Chapel, hammered each section into place with mallets and flat pieces of boxwood, before soaking and removing the drawings to reveal the mosaics, now face up.

Comparing the Chapels

In the Holy Souls Chapel opposite, Bentley and Symons were clearly given a pretty free hand in the designs by the donors, Mr & Mrs Walmesley, who are portrayed in the lower corners of the altarpiece, though the result is more Victorian (verging on the Art Nouveau in the case of the mosaic of Adam) than the Byzantine which Bentley sought. After an unsuccessful attempt at prefabrication in the studio, installation of the mosaics was by the traditional, direct method and the tesserae were inserted individually into oil-based mastic on the chapel walls and vault. George Bridge had installed the mosaics for the façade of the Horniman Museum in 1900-01, using tessarae he had largely made himself. However it is unlikely that he made tesserae for the Holy Souls Chapel, on some of which the protective glass layer (cartellina) had flaked off by 1918, since these were described as Italian. Among those working on the Holy Souls mosaics was twenty-two year old Gertrude Martin, later to become a well known mosaicist in her own right, while working on the figure of St Oswald in the Chapel of St Gregory and St Augustine was seventeen year old Ethel Linfield, a student at the Slade School of Art. So the more experienced of Bridge's girls may well have been given the more demanding direct method work in the Holy Souls.

The Chapel of St Gregory and St Augustine is in complete contrast to that of the Holy Souls. Lord Brampton knew exactly what he wanted and chose Clayton & Bell to carry it out. J R Clayton disregarded Bentley's instructions to avoid anything Gothic and used the style he normally used. James Powell & Sons had perfected the modern technique of *opus sectile* and were expert at it. The Venice and Murano Glass and Mosaic Company was equally accomplished at producing mosaics and Antonio Salviati claimed to have invented

'The Just Judge'. Opus sectile panel in the Chapel of St Gregory and St Augustine.

the 'modern Italian method' in which they were prepared face downwards on paper in reverse - the method employed here. Bentley much preferred the direct method but approved of *opus sectile* and, before his premature death, intended to use it for the Cathedral Stations of the Cross. In the event the Holy Souls Chapel mosaics are sombre, funereal, late Victorian pictorial on a background of silver. Those of the Chapel of St Gregory and St Augustine are glowing, vibrant, late Victorian Gothic on gold. Both are impressive in their own way, but they have little in common.

3. The Arts And Crafts Men

The decoration of the Cathedral in the period 1912-16 was largely the work of members of the Arts and Crafts Movement, notably Robert Anning Bell and Robert Weir Schultz. Eric Gill was also associated with the movement, though he had distanced himself by the time he produced the Stations of the Cross in 1914-18. The work of these men is among the best in the Cathedral.

Robert Anning Bell

The Arts and Crafts Movement, originating in mid-nineteenth century Britain with the ideas of John Ruskin, William Morris and others, believed that industrialisation and mechanisation dehumanised those involved and debased craftsmanship. The movement advocated social reform, individualism and creativity in art and design and a return to traditional materials and working methods. The Art Workers Guild, founded in

Robert Anning Bell.

1884, provided a forum for architects, designers and craftsmen who supported these ideals. One of these, who subsequently became Master of the Guild in 1921, was Robert Anning Bell RA. Experienced in art, sculpture and architecture and a designer of stained glass, mosaics, fabrics and wallpaper, in 1900-01 he produced a 32ft by 10ft mosaic for the façade of the Horniman Museum at Forest Hill in London. Also in 1901 he presented a paper entitled *Notes on the Practice of Pictorial Mosaic* to the Royal Institute of British Architects in which he explained the practicalities of mosaic designing and making

and praised the virtues of the direct method 'as I cannot think that a good result can possibly be obtained by other methods'. He was Professor of Decorative Art at Glasgow School of Art when John Marshall, then architect-in-charge at Westminster Cathedral and a fellow Nonconformist, approached him.

In 1899 two designs, one by the Cathedral architect, J F Bentley, had been produced for the mosaics of the Lady Chapel but at that time the chapel was intended to occupy the position now occupied by the Blessed Sacrament Chapel and neither design was adopted. In 1908 the walls of the Lady Chapel were clad with marble, and by 1910 Cardinal Bourne had decided on the Virgin and Child as an *opus sectile* altarpiece and W C Symons had produced a sketch of a seated figure. But instead Marshall turned to Anning Bell who in 1912 produced a mosaic design portraying Our Lady standing and holding the Holy Child, which Marshall believed 'would make the best bit of mosaic in the Cathedral'. The cost was £120 (about £6,000 today). For the four niches set into the chapel walls Anning Bell designed mosaic portrayals of Isaiah, Jeremiah, Ezechiel and Daniel, all Old Testament prophets who had foreseen the Incarnation. The predominantly blue mosaics were installed in 1912-13, under the supervision of Anning Bell and Marshall. The traditional, direct method was employed by the mosaicist, Gertrude Martin, who had worked for George Bridge on the mosaics of the Holy Souls Chapel ten years earlier but had received her first commission as an independent master mosaicist in 1911. She returned to the Cathedral in 1921 to execute Anning Bell's designs for the mosaics in the twin alcoves in the apse above the choir. These were finished the following year, again using the direct method.

Robert Anning Bell's mosaics in the Lady Chapel were generally praised but Cardinal Bourne himself was disappointed. Anning Bell and Gertrude Martin were among eight artists to produce designs for the Cathedral Stations of the Cross in 1913, but the commission went to Eric Gill who was determined to secure it and produced by far the lowest estimate. Nor did Anning Bell secure approval for his 1913 design for the Lady Chapel apse. But Bourne did agree that he should design the 24ft wide tympanum mosaic over the main entrance of the Cathedral. Bentley had provided a small sketch in pencil for this in 1895-96 and Symons, Frank Brangwyn and Professor Seitz had produced subsequent designs. But Marshall preferred Bentley's original, showing Christ enthroned and displaying his wounds, thus reminding us of the dedication of the Cathedral to the Most Precious Blood. On either side of Christ are the principal saints to which the Cathedral is dedicated - on the left St Peter with the keys of the Kingdom of Heaven, together with Our Lady, and on the right St Joseph carrying the lily of purity. Next to him is St Edward the Confessor with royal crown and sceptre, to whom the Cathedral tower is dedicated.

Robert Anning Bell's altarpiece in the Lady Chapel.

Marshall worked up Bentley's pencilled sketch in colour and the result appeared in the *Westminster Cathedral Chronicle* in March 1907. Christ is now shown fully clothed in red and white with hanging drapery behind the throne, Our Lady in blue and white, St Joseph in dull red, St Peter in russet and brown, and St Edward in purple, white and green. Both St Peter and St Edward are shown kneeling (a consequence of the reduced headroom at either side of the arch). Marshall's design was in turn very largely followed by Robert Anning Bell in his own sketch of 1913, but the open book held by Christ showing the words (in Latin) 'I am the gate, if anyone enters by Me he shall be saved' (John 10:9) is a new theme, and the mosaic is considerably simpler and more austere, with more subdued colours. It is clear that Anning Bell devoted considerable thought to the mosaic, rejecting gold as liable to frost damage, and bright colours as too great a contrast with the drab brick and stone background, darkened by smog, coal fires and smoke from trains at nearby Victoria Station. The mosaic, grouted up to a level surface to ensure durability, was installed in 1915-16 by James Powell & Sons of Whitefriars, who also replaced the mosaics in the Sacred Heart Shrine at this time.

The main entrance tympanum, designed by Robert Anning Bell.

Robert Weir Schultz

Meanwhile other members of the Arts and Crafts Movement were at work in St Andrew's Chapel. Robert Weir Schultz (R W S Weir after the outbreak of the 1914-18 War) was an architect and a pioneer in Byzantine studies. His chief client was the Fourth Marquess of Bute, whose father, the Third Marquess, had also employed him and had earlier assisted him (together with Sidney Barnsley) to undertake the overseas study of Byzantine architecture. On his return Schultz wrote *Byzantine Architecture in Greece* together with Barnsley, in 1897 he produced a two part article entitled *Byzantine Art* for *The Architectural Review* and in 1901 (again with Barnsley) *The Monastery of St Luke of Stiris in Phocis*. The Fourth Marquess, a prominent Catholic, had agreed to pay for the decoration of St Andrew's Chapel providing that Schultz designed and supervised this. His mosaic designs portray St Andrew himself, the cross of his martyrdom and cities connected with him - a fisherman born in Bethsaida, Bishop of Constantinople, finally crucified in Patras in Greece. Then the journey of his relics after being taken by the Crusaders from Constantinople in 1204 - to Milan, Amalfi and St Andrews in Scotland. Schultz's choice of marbles was criticised in *The Observer* as 'positively freezing in its colourless coldness' but the mosaics were generally praised, notably in *Country Life*. They cost £3,617 (about £150,000 today).

The designs for the east and west walls of St Andrew's Chapel as drawn by Robert Weir Schultz.

Besides Schultz himself, other Arts and Crafts colleagues who worked on the chapel were: George Jack (the full-size mosaic cartoons), Thomas Stirling Lee (crucifix and low relief wall carving), Ernest Gimson (brown ebony stalls inlaid with ivory) and Sidney Barnsley (matching kneelers made nearly ten years later in 1923-24). The marble 'pavement like the sea' refers to St Andrew's occupation. It was made by Messrs Farmer & Brindley and is inlaid with 29 fish and other marine creatures. This form of decoration, which Schultz had employed in 1893 for the floor of a chapel at St John's Lodge, Regent's Park, for the Third Marquess of Bute, was commonly used for Roman mosaic floors and also appears in Byzantine and early Italian churches. Like the Regents Park chapel, the floor of St Andrew's Chapel was probably inspired by the 1891 book *Architecture, Mysticism and Myth* written by W R Lethaby, whom Schultz acknowledged as his mentor.

The mosaic of the west wall of St Andrew's Chapel as executed.

Schultz's designs were approved by Cardinal Bourne in 1910 and the mosaics installed in 1914-15 by six mosaicists (one a Venetian) who had previously been working for Sir Ernest Debenham on mosaics for his department stores and private house at 8 Addison Road, Holland Park. Before that two of them had worked on Sir William Richmond's mosaics for St Paul's Cathedral. Directing the mosaics team in St Andrew's Chapel was Gaetano Meo, who had been Sir William Richmond's assistant at St Paul's and had also then worked for Debenham. They employed gold, red, blue and black slabs of mosaic material supplied by James Powell & Sons, and the tesserae were cut and inserted by the traditional, direct method into cement of the same composition as used at St Paul's Cathedral. The mosaics of St Andrew's Chapel include trees, shrubs, flowers, sheep and deer* reminiscent of the apse in Ravenna's Sant' Apollinare in Classe, and are outstanding examples of quality and craftsmanship, particularly the shimmering fish-scales (or 'golden clouds screening Paradise from earthly view') on the vault, and the arch soffits where 33 different birds perch amidst the foliage.

---

* A plover and a rabbit in the extreme corners of the west wall mosaic were removed in 1916, possibly because they were thought to be distracting from the main composition.

4. A Dream and a Petition

By the end of the 1914-18 War four of the Cathedral chapels had been decorated with marble and mosaic - The Holy Souls, St Gregory and St Augustine's, St Andrew's, and the Shrine of the Sacred Heart. In addition the main entrance tympanum, the Lady Chapel altarpiece and a few panels elsewhere had also been completed. Seven different artists, including J F Bentley, the Cathedral architect, had been responsible for a wide variety of mosaic designs but, with the possible exception of St Andrew's Chapel, Cardinal Francis Bourne was satisfied with none of them.

A Dream of Monreale

In November 1905, two years after his installation as fourth Archbishop of Westminster, Francis Bourne was in Rome and from there travelled to Sicily specifically to see the twelfth century Byzantine mosaics in Palermo's Capella Palatina and in the great

Gilbert Pownall and his wife.

Cathedral of Monreale nearby. There at last Bourne found what he wanted, telling the Pope on his return of his intention to reproduce the mosaics he had seen there in Westminster Cathedral. Writing later in the *Westminster Cathedral Chronicle* of January 1934, Bourne admitted that he had found the whole question of the mosaics most perplexing. After W C Symons' death in 1911 he had been persuaded by John Marshall, then Cathedral architect-in-charge, to commission Robert Anning Bell to design mosaics for the altarpiece and four wall niches in the Lady Chapel (executed in 1912-13) and then the main entrance tympanum (1915-16). But Bourne regarded the altarpiece as a disappointment and the tympanum as 'the greatest disappointment which I have received in connection with the work of the Cathedral'. By now he had convinced himself that no non-Catholic artist could be trusted with work of this type.

To commemorate his twenty years as Archbishop of Westminster, Cardinal Bourne had his portrait painted in 1923. The artist was Gilbert Pownall, a Catholic who had exhibited regularly at the Royal Academy from 1908. Bourne believed that at last he had found the right man to design the Cathedral mosaics. As Pownall had little or no experience in this medium, Bourne arranged for him to go with Marshall to Ravenna, Rome, Venice and, of course, Palermo and Monreale, to study the masterpieces in mosaic there as Bourne himself had done. During 1926 Pownall set about planning the Cathedral decoration, obtaining a sketch of the main apse and details of Bentley's 1899 plan for the Lady Chapel mosaics from Archbishop's House. By the spring of 1927 Pownall had produced a model showing his own designs for the Lady Chapel mosaics which, according to the *Westminster Cathedral Chronicle*, received much well-deserved praise.

In January 1928 Cardinal Bourne announced that he was considering setting up a workshop and school of mosaics since, 'in all probability the mosaic decoration of the Cathedral will occupy a century or more, and when the work is finished it will, as is the case in Venice, constantly call for renewal and repair, so that mosaic workers will be a necessary part of the establishment of the Cathedral for all time'. In 1930 the workshop was established on the third floor of the Cathedral tower with Basil Carey-Elwes and Thomas Josey, both of whom had worked on the mosaics of St Andrew's Chapel fifteen years before, as the first mosaicists, and boys from Canon Craven's Crusade of Rescue (subsequently renamed the Catholic Children's Society) as apprentices.

The Mosaics Installed

Bourne asked the mosaicists to work first on the mosaics above one of the confessionals in the south transept near the Lady Chapel, and then on the Lady Chapel itself. Pownall's first designs, showing the penitent St Peter and St Mary Magdalen, were executed in 1930, using the direct method. A start was then made on the Lady Chapel, supervised by Pownall and Lawrence Shattock, the new Cathedral architect-in-charge. By now the team of mosaicists had grown, to three with the arrival in 1930 of Carlo de Spirt (previously apprenticed to Zanelli), and then to five with the arrival of Filippo Mariutto and Gian-Battista Maddalena in 1931. Both were originally from Udine near Venice but they had been working for the German mosaics firm Diespeker on the decoration of Selfridges.

Gilbert Pownall's mosaics in the Lady Chapel. Installed 1930-35.

The Lady Chapel mosaics took the first three mosaicists five years, being completed in June 1935. The apse shows Christ as the Tree of Life with Our Lady as Patroness of London beside the Tower of London, and St Peter as Patron of Westminster beside Westminster Cathedral, together with the Archangels Gabriel and Michael and other saints. On the west wall opposite is Our Lady's Coronation as Queen of Heaven. Around the walls of the chapel is a garland of flowers held by angels and representing a great rosary culminating in Christ above the altar. In amongst the garland and Tree of Life are over a hundred animals, insects, fish and birds. Below are scenes such as the declaration of the Immaculate Conception and the appearance of Our Lady to Bernadette at Lourdes. The lower frieze consists of a series of scenes from Our Lady's life, starting with her parents (Anne and Joachim) with King David, and finishing with St Luke writing his gospel.

The Flight into Egypt scene in the Lady Chapel.

While the work was going on in the Lady Chapel, Mariutto and Maddalena were working on the blue sanctuary arch mosaic of Christ in Glory surrounded by the four Evangelists (Matthew, Mark, Luke and John), with the twelve Apostles on either side and a blue background consisting of perhaps a thousand little faces - the host of heaven. After eighteen months work this had been finished and late in 1933 the two Italians started on the mosaic in St Peter's Crypt with its scenes of St Peter enthroned, attempting to walk on the water and being presented by Christ with the keys of the Kingdom of Heaven. This was completed by the autumn of 1934 and the pair then turned their attention to the apse mosaic above the Cathedral choir. In July a three foot wide, coloured cardboard model of Pownall's design for the apse had been placed in the Cathedral crypt with a request for comments, one of which, from sixteen-year-old Aelred Bartlett, resulted in Cardinal Bourne telling Aelred's father that he needed his bottom smacked! The centre of the design consisted of a circle of angels while an outer ring was made up of the apostles. In rectangular panels below were biblical scenes including the Sacrifice of Isaac, The Presentation in the Temple, The Agony in the Garden, the Crucifixion (centre), the Scourging at the Pillar, the Crowning with Thorns, Cain and Abel, Moses in the Bulrushes, the Burning Bush, Pharaoh in the Red Sea, the Tables of the Law and Moses drawing water from the Rock.

Gilbert Pownall's 1931 design for the Cathedral sanctuary arch mosaic.

Edward Hutton and the Petition

Initial reactions to Pownall's mosaics were generally favourable, the design for the confessional alcove being viewed by *The Times* of 22 September only as a little too pictorial. Similarly the mosaic in St Peter's Crypt was, and is, generally considered to be Pownall's best. But before this was completed, storm clouds were gathering with the unveiling in February 1932 of the Lady Chapel apse mosaic which was described in *The Catholic Times* as 'sprawling meanly and anaemically over the vault'. Then at the end

Edward Hutton, aged 92, in 1967.

of 1933 the great blue Cathedral sanctuary arch mosaic was unveiled. On 7 December *The Daily Telegraph* published a letter from Edward Hutton, introducing him as a critic of Italian and Byzantine art. Hutton described the Lady Chapel apse mosaics as 'meaningless, weak and incoherent', the small Flight into Egypt scene in the chapel frieze as 'so puerile and unmasterly that it might decorate a commercial Christmas card' and the mosaics of the freshly unveiled blue sanctuary arch as displaying empty puerility, weakness and clumsiness in drawing, and ugliness and crudeness in colour 'seeming to involve the whole great church in little less than ruin'.

However, it was not Hutton's letter that caused the furore, it was Cardinal Bourne's furious response to it in the *Westminster Cathedral Chronicle* of January 1934, in which Pownall was defended and Hutton's credentials as an art critic challenged. The confrontation attracted headlines in the national press and Hutton had achieved the publicity he sought, writing again to *The Daily Telegraph* in January to point out that Our Lady in the Lady Chapel had been inaccurately portrayed as patron saint of London, thus depriving St Paul of that title. He followed this up in August 1934, attacking Pownall's coloured cardboard model showing his designs for the Cathedral apse as 'very feeble, ugly and confused in design, without dignity or beauty', consisting of subjects having little connection with one another and little relevance to any central or main subject, and with an amazing circle of winged creatures 'easily mistaken for a beauty chorus because of their bare legs'. This time Cardinal Bourne refused to respond. Preparations for the apse mosaics went ahead, the scaffolding being erected by the end of 1934. Bourne died shortly afterwards, in January 1935.

But Hutton was not to be put off. His private papers, given to the British Institute of Florence after his death in 1969, reveal that as early as January 1933 *The Burlington Magazine* had suggested to him that he draw up a protest petition to be signed by influential people in the world of art. They also show that the publicity he had attracted in 1933-34 had resulted in wide support, including that from two chaplains at the Cathedral, though one was mainly concerned about the discomfort of the Canons' stalls. Hutton therefore formed a committee of five and prepared a petition to the newly appointed Archbishop of Westminster, Arthur Hinsley, to be signed by leaders of the world of art and architecture, urging him to stop the work on the mosaics and form a committee to advise him. A preliminary letter, which Hinsley ignored, was followed in August 1935 by the petition signed by the Presidents of the Royal Academy and the Royal Institute of British Architects, the Directors of the National Gallery, Tate Gallery, Victoria and Albert Museum and many more, including Eric Gill. This time Hinsley responded.

Archbishop Hinsley Gives In

Hutton's papers include both a formal, noncommittal response from Archbishop Hinsley and also a conciliatory hand-written letter from him of 4 September 1935, agreeing strongly that a committee of experts should be set up to carry out the ideas of J F Bentley, the Cathedral architect. Hinsley also asked Hutton to convey to those signing the petition his heartfelt thanks for enabling 'me to take up a firm decision in this very important question. There can be no doubt that the Cathedral cannot be allowed to be the happy hunting ground of amateurs'. Hinsley followed this up with a meeting with Hutton and another member of his committee on 23 September at which Hutton repeated his demands. It is clear from Hinsley's notes and letters that he had decided by now that only money specifically so dedicated should be used for the decoration of the Cathedral and that other available income should go to Catholic schools. But to be so frank with Hutton about the situation was a tactical error which was to have repercussions.

At the end of October 1935 Hinsley received another letter from Hutton, again calling for the mosaic work to be stopped and a committee of experts set up, 'the names for which were submitted to your Grace at your request'. Hutton warned that 'the pressure for public expression in this matter is so strong and widespread that unauthorised publication in some form or other might appear at any time'. On 30 November, in the mistaken belief that the contract between the Cathedral and Pownall was merely verbal and from year to year, Hinsley suspended work on the apse mosaics, to the dismay of Pownall who claimed he had a contract for another three years. Shortly before 10pm on 2 December Hinsley's secretary telephoned Hutton with the news. Hutton records in his notes that, as suspected, he immediately passed on the news to the press revealing details not only of the petition and those who had signed it but also of Hinsley's appreciative response to it. Next day it was all over the newspapers.

A fortnight later a statement was issued that the petition had been published without Archbishop Hinsley's knowledge or consent. But at the same time it was reported that Pownall's designs and the Cathedral school of mosaics had been abandoned. Hutton remained in contact with Hinsley and met with the Cathedral solicitors regarding the terms of the contract which Pownall was now able to produce. After initially being sent just £100 in compensation, he secured £2,000 in July 1936 after taking steps to sue for breach of contract, a charge which Hinsley was in no position to challenge in open court. It was also Hutton who provided Hinsley with the names of three Catholic laymen for the new Art Advisory Committee. They were Henry Harris (a trustee of the National Gallery), Frederick Griggs RA, FSA (an etcher, illustrator and architect), and Professor Ernest Tristram FSA (a leading authority on medieval wall-painting). The names were accepted and the appointments made in October. Hutton had not nominated himself but was nevertheless put out at not being invited. He finally became a member in 1938. Meanwhile Pownall's apse mosaic, by then still only about 25 per cent complete, was taken down and only the inability of the new advisory committee to agree on a new design, followed by the 1939-45 War, saved the sanctuary arch.

So how much of Cardinal Bourne's dream of bringing Palermo and Monreale to Westminster was achieved? The main theme of the Lady Chapel - the Tree of Life and the vine - are clearly taken from the twelfth century apse of San Clemente in Rome and many of the animals, including the unusual fish-like creatures at the termination of tendrils, are virtually identical. The mandorla of Christ on a rainbow in the Lady Chapel apse may well have been inspired by the Ascension dome in St Mark's Basilica in Venice, while the blue entrance arch of the chapel may derive from the 'Mausoleum of Galla Placidia' in Ravenna. Other features - Gabriel and Michael, the Coronation of Our Lady, and the Virgin Martyrs (Cecilia, Catherine, etc) appear in Bentley's scheme of 1899. We know from Cardinal Bourne that the Cathedral sanctuary arch mosaic of Christ enthroned among evangelists and apostles was inspired by the late fourth (or early fifth) century apse of Santa Pudenziana in Rome - Bourne's titular church, though the treatment is vastly different. It must be admitted that only certain features of the engagingly simple yet effective arch mosaic in St Peter's Crypt, and perhaps the confessional alcove, have any real affinity with the mosaics of Palermo and Monreale. But then dreams often are impossible.

Gilbert Pownall's model for the Cathedral apse mosaic.

With many thanks to Jane Buxton, Gilbert Pownall's daughter, and Alyson Price at the British Institute in Florence, for giving access to the notes and papers of Gilbert Pownall and Edward Hutton respectively.

5. Russian and Roman

The Art Advisory Committee established by Cardinal Arthur Hinsley in 1936 lapsed during the 1939-45 War and was not re-established until 1953. Meanwhile two mosaic panels had been installed - the first of Ste Thérèse of Lisieux in the south transept in 1950, which was replaced by a bronze of the saint in 1958, and the second a war memorial to the officers and men of the Royal Army Medical Corps (RAMC), installed in St George's Chapel in 1952.

The period between the re-establishment of the Cathedral Art Advisory Committee by Cardinal Bernard Griffin (Hinsley's successor) in December 1953 and the conclusion of the Second Vatican Council in 1965 witnessed a series of major decorative projects. The nave, narthex and porches were all clad with marble from 1956-64, the medieval alabaster statue of Our Lady arrived in 1955 and the Lady Chapel floor was laid the following year, a gilt bronze figure of St Patrick was installed in his chapel in 1961 and the Blessed Sacrament Chapel and St Paul's Chapel were decorated with mosaics between 1960 and 1965.

Cardinal Griffin's new advisory committee consisted of Professor Thomas Bodkin (an Irish authority on the Fine Arts), Professor Goodhart-Rendel (a past President of RIBA), Sir John Rothenstein (Director of the Tate Gallery) and Arthur Pollen (a sculptor). They were joined in 1955 by Sir Albert Richardson (an architect) and Sir John Betjeman. Many of their proceedings and recommendations were concluded amicably - the restoration of the Verde Antico column in the north transept in 1954, the installation of the medieval alabaster of Our Lady in 1955 and the replacement of the mosaic of Ste Thérèse of Lisieux by Manzu's bronze of the saint in 1958. Others, particularly the marble cladding of the nave, were only arrived at after considerable discussion and argument.

Boris Anrep and the Blessed Sacrament Chapel

The man chosen by the advisory committee to design the Blessed Sacrament Chapel mosaics was Boris Anrep, a larger-than-life artist and mosaicist associated with the Bloomsbury Group. A Russian by birth, in 1914 Anrep was responsible for the unfinished mosaic of angels and a book near Cardinal Manning's tomb on the vault of the inner crypt. This work was interrupted by the First World War and the design was lost when Anrep returned to Russia to lead his troop of Cossacks in the Imperial Russian Guard -

Boris Anrep (on right) with Justin Vulliamy, his assistant.

in the process retrieving religious icons most of which are now in the Hermitage Museum in St Petersburg. In 1917 he returned to England and in 1924 he produced the Cathedral mosaic of St Oliver Plunkett outside St Patrick's Chapel, using the indirect method but adjusting the tesserae in situ. In 1937 he produced mosaic designs for this chapel but at £10,400 his estimate for the finished mosaics was regarded as too high. In 1954 Sir John Rothenstein proposed to the new advisory committee that Anrep be asked to design a replacement for the blue sanctuary arch mosaic designed by Gilbert Pownall. Anrep produced a coloured model showing the Last Supper and provided an estimate of £26,000, more than twice the £10,000 anticipated. This, coupled with concern at how the public, and potential donors, would react to the destruction of the existing mosaic, which had been cleaned in 1952, resulted in Cardinal Griffin abandoning the plan to replace it. Rothenstein then proposed that Anrep should design the mosaics for the Blessed Sacrament Chapel.

A peacock (symbol of immortality). The approach to the Blessed Sacrament Chapel.

Both Anrep's inner crypt mosaic and that of St Oliver Plunkett have every sign of being produced in situ by the direct method. Despite this, Anrep's technical assistant, Justin Vulliamy, tells us that Anrep always used the indirect (transfer) method, preparing the mosaics in reverse in the studio. This is confirmed in a letter from Anrep to Mgr Gordon Wheeler, the Cathedral Administrator, of 14 February 1955, in which he justifies the use of this method for the sanctuary arch. Anrep writes: 'Yet various means can be employed to enrich the surface texture of the mosaic while using the transfer method, e.g. angular concave and convex tesserae, uneven rendering of the wall surface. Such devices can be used in the preparatory as well as the fixing stages in order to avoid flatness … In view of the above considerations it is my humble opinion that my usual methods, supplemented with in situ work, will give an adequate result … The discovery of Portland cement has confirmed the advantage of the transfer method over the in situ medium which, in present circumstances, has become extremely onerous … For an example of a mosaic made by the transfer method, albeit on a minor scale, might I draw the attention of the committee to my panel of Blessed Oliver Plunkett in Westminster Cathedral'.

The advisory committee were convinced, and were 'deeply impressed' when, in 1956, Anrep produced a model of his designs for the Blessed Sacrament Chapel with three main themes, illustrated by scenes from the Old Testament in the nave and from the New Testament in the apse. The first theme is Sacrifice - on the left Abel offering up a lamb, then Abraham about to kill Isaac, then Malachi, last of the prophets, and finally Samuel, last of the judges, with an abandoned sacrificial knife. On the right Noah with his three sons, Shem, Ham and Japheth, about to sacrifice after the flood. Interwoven with this theme is that of the Eucharist, with the Hospitality of Abraham and Sarah to the three angels (on the tympanum facing the altar), the Gathering of Manna, Abraham and Melchisadech (crowned) and an angel persuading Elijah to eat. This theme continues

The sacrifice of Noah. The Blessed Sacrament Chapel.

with ears of wheat at the springing of the tympanum arch and grape vines in the window arches. Then into the apse with the Wedding Feast at Cana and the Feeding of the Five Thousand. Also in the apse are shown the Resurrection and the Liberation of Captured Souls. The third theme is the Trinity - Abraham's guests again, the three youths in the Burning Fiery Furnace, and the Trinity itself high in the apse with Christ between the Hand of God and the Dove representing the Holy Spirit. The twelve doves on the sanctuary arch signify the apostles. Finally, in the centre, a triumphant, jewelled cross is set over the globe of the universe and the Church, embedded in a rock from which the Rivers of Paradise flow.

Anrep chose a traditional, early Christian, style and a pale pink background to give a sense of light and space and to blend in with the colour of the marbles - mainly panels of Yellow Siena and Rose de Numidie. Together with his assistants, Justin Vulliamy and Leonide Inglesis, and using the indirect (reverse or transfer) method, Anrep then produced full-size coloured cartoons and working drawings in his Paris studio and sent these to Venice. There Antonio Orsoni attached smalti from Angelo Orsoni's glass factory to the working drawings using the cartoons as a guide, and the results were crated and sent to London. The mosaics were then revised and adjusted by Anrep and Vulliamy to bring them into their final shape.

Installation started in November 1960 with Peter Indri doing the fixing and Anrep himself, wreathed in smoke from his habitual Gauloises, making constant adjustments on a huge work table 'as big as a dance floor' partitioned off in the north transept of the Cathedral. Twenty-two year-old Lucio Orsoni, from the Orsoni family firm in Venice, came over to assist them. The niche mosaics of a peacock (signifying immortality), and a phoenix (resurrection) were the last to be completed and were paid for by the Guild of the Blessed Sacrament at a cost of £450 each. Installation was completed in December 1961 with the final adjustments being made early in 1962. Anrep wanted to continue at his own expense - perhaps because Malachi and Samuel, though in the correct chronological order in his original scheme of May 1955, have been transposed in the finished mosaic. But the Cathedral authorities insisted that the chapel be reopened. The total cost of the mosaics came to about £45,000.

Aelred Bartlett and the Roman Style

While Boris Anrep and his technical and artistic assistant, Justin Vulliamy, were working on the mosaics for the Blessed Sacrament Chapel from 1955-62 and St Paul's Chapel from 1961-65, another artist and mosaicist, Aelred Bartlett, was supervising the decoration of the Cathedral nave. In the process he designed and produced a number of small mosaics and put forward his own mosaic designs for St Paul's Chapel, to the annoyance of some members of the Cathedral Art Advisory Committee who resented his influence.

St Nicholas.
The north aisle of
the Cathedral.

Aelred Bartlett came from a family closely associated with the Cathedral. His elder brother, Francis, was Sub-Administrator in 1956 when Cardinal Griffin decided that work should resume on the decoration of the nave, using the designs of the Cathedral architect, J F Bentley, and Aelred was called in to supervise the project. As the marble decoration proceeded down the nave, Aelred began to design mosaics to accompany it. By early 1960 the work had passed the pulpit and Aelred designed a mosaic floor panel, combining purple and green porphyry in the Roman and Byzantine style, to lie below the English medieval alabaster statue known as 'Our Lady of Westminster' and emphasise its importance as a shrine. At about the same time he also produced the vine and star mosaics which decorate the transept arch soffits - 'just practising' as he disarmingly put it. His final work, and that of which he was the most proud, was the niche mosaic of St Nicholas at the end of the north aisle. Produced at home in 1960 using the indirect method and installed by himself and his assistant (Ron) in March 1961, this is a memorial to Dame Vera Laughton Matthews, head of the WRNS during the 1939-45 War, so it includes a small wren. In making it, Aelred employed his children to cut up the mosaic material into pieces of the appropriate size. The mosaic is in the early Roman style and is influenced by the examples of fifth century mosaics to be found in the Basilica of Santa Maria Maggiore in Rome.

Justin Vulliamy and St Paul's Chapel

But Aelred's style was not universally appreciated. Some members of the Cathedral Art Advisory Committee resented the influence of the Bartlett brothers and their determination to adhere to Bentley's designs. One member, Arthur Pollen, initially doubted Aelred's competence in architectural matters, particularly regarding his

*St Christopher.
The north aisle of
the Cathedral.*

scheme for the gallery balustrade. Another, Sir John Rothenstein (who Aelred later described as 'a pain in the neck'), threatened to resign over his mosaic of St Nicholas, even after it was pointed out to him that Aelred had been chosen by the donor. So when Aelred put forward designs for the mosaics of St Paul's Chapel in late 1960 the committee turned them down. Instead, Rothenstein suggested that Boris Anrep be asked to produce a scheme, which was accepted by the committee in 1961. But then Anrep, now almost 80, asked that his assistant for thirty years, Justin Vulliamy, should take on the commission while he himself would advise and assist him. Meanwhile Vulliamy, perhaps to demonstrate his competence, was producing the niche mosaics of Saints Christopher, Anne and Joachim in the Cathedral aisles.

Naturally enough Aelred Bartlett took great umbrage. He believed he had been promised St Paul's Chapel and had produced his carefully worked-out designs for it mindful of the need for economy and intending to use the stocks of glass smalti held in store in the Cathedral. Even his arch critic, Sir John Rothenstein, had praised his design for the barrel vaulting, though he had reservations concerning the designs for the end walls. Aelred's assessment of Vulliamy's ability was dismissive, describing his mosaic of St Christopher (with some justification) as 'looking as if both Christ and St Christopher were wearing bathing costumes'. Nevertheless Vulliamy undertook the commission for St Paul's, designing and producing the mosaics from 1962-64 with Anrep detailing the principal figures. They worked in Paris (where Anrep had his studio), and Venice (where the firm of Angelo Orsoni made the glass smalti) using the indirect method. The finished mosaics were then returned to England for final adjustment followed by installation by Peter Indri in 1964. St Paul's Chapel reopened in January 1965.

Vulliamy described the mosaics of St Paul's Chapel in an article in the *Westminster Cathedral Chronicle* of February 1965. Above the altar the domed surface of the apse shows a grey-blue sky sprinkled with stars - such 'ceilings like the sky' feature in early Byzantine buildings such as the fifth century 'Mausoleum of Galla Placidia' in Ravenna. In the tympanum above the arch is the inscription *Dominus Legem Dat* (the Lord gives the law) with the four Gospels and above that Christ is shown carrying the scroll of the law, between St Peter and St Paul. On either side are pavilions and through vaulted openings may be seen four streams of living water, flowing in a rocky landscape. On the opposite wall is shown the conversion of St Paul on the road from Jerusalem to

Damascus (Acts 9). Paul kneels, temporarily blinded, with the light of heaven shining about him as he is told by the Lord to arise and go to Damascus. Below is a Latin inscription meaning 'Stand up and go into the city and there you will be told what you must do'. A sword lies beside him showing both that he travelled armed and that this was to be the instrument of his martyrdom.

Facing the entrance, Paul is shown shipwrecked off Malta (Melita). The ship has run aground, traditionally at a place called St Paul's Bay, and the saint has been cast into the sea (Acts 27). Above the entrance runs an inscription meaning 'Out of the strong came forth sweetness' with six bees and a lion. This is the riddle of Samson and refers to bees producing honey in the carcass of a lion (Judges 14). It refers to Paul, originally called Saul and a persecutor of Christ's followers, being converted and becoming a Christian apostle himself. The basket refers to his night-time escape down the walls of Damascus in a basket (Acts 9). Above the inscription are three churches against a wide expanse of sky, referring to the tradition that when Paul's head was severed by a sword outside the walls of Rome in about 64AD, it bounced three times. Where it touched the ground there appeared fountains over which churches were subsequently built. The spot is still known as Trefontane (Three Fountains). Covering the vault, or ceiling, over almost all the chapel, and billowing upwards to the sky, is shown an iridescent pink, blue and gold tent. It refers to St Paul's trade as a tent-maker (Acts 18) and is embroidered with a Star of David motif and central Christogram (the Greek Chi-Rho). This can be viewed as the initial of St Paul and is shown between the palm leaves of martyrdom. The mosaics were the last to be installed in the Cathedral for many years.

The conversion of St Paul.
The west wall of St Paul's Chapel.

6. Recent Mosaics

After all the activity of the early 1960s, when both the Blessed Sacrament Chapel and St Paul's Chapel, together with four nearby wall niches in the north and south aisles, were all decorated with mosaics, and the Cathedral nave, narthex and entrance porches were clad with marble, there was a prolonged lull in the Cathedral decoration which really only came to an end as the millennium itself drew to a close.

The Great Pause

The Second Vatican Council had been held from 1962-65 and underlying themes were simplicity, Christian unity and world poverty. At the same time, Cardinal John Carmel Heenan had succeeded Cardinal Godfrey as eighth Archbishop of Westminster in 1963, and although he allowed the work then underway in the Cathedral to continue, he believed that there things should end. In the words of his new Cathedral Administrator (Mgr George Tomlinson) in 1964, 'It is time to turn our minds to the plight of men and women in undeveloped countries .... One way of decorating the Cathedral would be a wholehearted participation on the part of those who worship in it in the Freedom from Hunger Campaign'.

St Patrick.
St Patrick's Chapel.

Thus it was that no new mosaics went up until 1982 when one was installed to commemorate the celebration of the first Papal Mass in the Cathedral by His Holiness Pope John Paul II on 28 May that year, at the beginning of his six day pastoral visit to England, Scotland and Wales. The mosaic, consisting of superimposed lettering of varying sizes, designed by Nicolete Gray, was installed in the arch over the now disused north-west entrance from Ambrosden Avenue (which gives onto the Cathedral Gift Shop). In 1895 John Bentley, the Cathedral architect, had produced a pencilled sketch for a mosaic here, showing Our Lady and the Christ Child seated with a saint on each side. This sketch was now ignored in favour of the mosaic inscription *Porta Sis Ostium Pacificum Per Eum Qui Se Ostium Appellavit Jesum Christum* (May this door be the gate of peace through him who called himself the gate, Jesus Christ). Besides the Cathedral north-west entrance, Nicolete Gray also designed the memorial of the Pope's 1982 visit for the floor in front of the main sanctuary, and designed and carved the inscription on Cardinal Heenan's tomb which dates from 1976 and lies below the Twelfth Station of the Cross.

Nicolete Gray's mosaic for the north-west entrance of the Cathedral was made by the mosaicist Trevor Caley and installed by Art Pavements and Decorations Ltd in 1982. Fifteen years later, in 1997, Caley was commissioned to design a panel at the entrance to St Patrick's Chapel in the Cathedral. He initially envisaged an interpretation of the seventh century tall stone Celtic cross at Carndonagh in Donegal known as 'St Patrick's Cross'. This was based on the assumption that the chapel vault might eventually be decorated by a mosaic representation of the four Evangelists to be found in the Book of Kells and other Celtic manuscripts. But in 1998 this idea for the panel was changed to a representation of St Patrick shown holding a shamrock and crozier with writhing snakes intertwining into a Celtic pattern adorning his vestment. In deliberate contrast to Arthur Pollen's austere, gilt bronze of St Patrick above the altar, installed in 1961, Caley has aimed for a more human interpretation. The face of the saint derives from early Byzantine mosaics, which Caley believed provided an appropriate balance between stylisation and natural likeness. Using a combination of unglazed, non-reflective ceramic material and glittering glass smalti from Cathedral stocks, Caley produced the mosaic on board in the studio and installed it himself in March 1999.

A New Millennium

The following year, the first of the new millennium, the Cathedral Art and Architecture Committee asked the designer Christopher Hobbs to produce a full-scale cartoon of St Alban for a mosaic panel in the aisle near St George's Chapel, and this was then approved by the Historic Churches Committee. St Alban was a young Romano-British martyr and Hobbs's portrayal is in the early Byzantine style, though the face is inspired by Late Antique Egyptian Faiyum (Al Fayoum) mummy portraits of St Alban's time. The red line around his neck signifies decapitation. The symbol at the top left of the mosaic refers to the donor's family. The mosaic was assembled in the studio by Tessa Hunkin of Mosaic Workshop of London and installed by her and Walter Bernadin by June 2001 when it was unveiled.

St Alban.
The north aisle.

Ceramic tile adhesive with an additive to improve cohesion was used and the gold smalti of the halo were worked in situ to produce a glittering effect.

The next mosaics were those of St Joseph's Chapel, a major undertaking costing some £300,000. As early as 1999 the Cathedral Administrator (Mgr George Stack) had suggested a Holy Family scene and one of St Joseph the Worker, the carpenter. After his success with St Alban, Christopher Hobbs was chosen as the designer. In 2001 he produced his proposals for a scene of the Holy Family in the apse, of which he also made a scale model. Because of the curve of the apse he proposed that the direct method be used. But he subsequently accepted the reverse method for all but the gold background which was to be laid in situ at different angles so that it would glitter in the light. In 2002 the mosaicists, Mosaic Workshop again, started work in the studio, initially on the arch mosaic with its stylised dove representing the Holy Spirit - two versions of which made it look very sinister indeed! Then work commenced on the Holy Family mosaic, which is clearly influenced by the Byzantine and was first traced on the apse wall using a slide projector.

The Holy Family.
The apse of
St Joseph's Chapel.

By April 2003 St Joseph's apse mosaics had been completed and installed, reaction being one of 'delight and appreciation'. There was then a pause while attention shifted to the Chapel of St Thomas of Canterbury, for the Friends of the Cathedral had undertaken to raise the £200,000 needed for the mosaics in this chapel and were getting impatient at the lack of progress. St Thomas's Chapel was also the chantry of Cardinal Vaughan, founder of the Cathedral, and his body was to be reinterred there. Ever since his death in June 1903 Vaughan, at his own request, had lain at Mill Hill Missionary College which he had also founded, his Cathedral chantry containing only his effigy and empty tomb. So St Joseph's Chapel had to wait until late in 2004 for work to start on the repeated wattle, or basket-weave, pattern for its vault. This consisted of

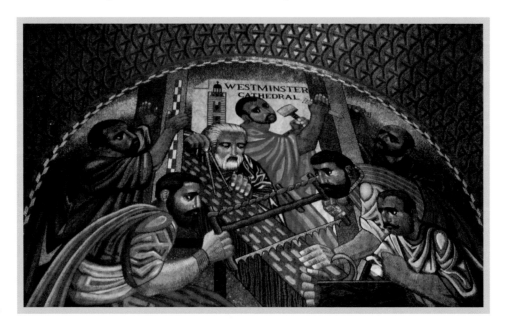

Workmen building
the Cathedral.
The west wall of
St Joseph's Chapel.

just over a thousand small, identical, interlocking sections and much of the work was done by the mosaicists at home. By October 2005, after three months back-breaking installation work by Walter Bernadin and his assistant, the vault mosaic was up and the west wall mosaic of workmen building the Cathedral had been assembled and lay on the studio floor in sections. During 2006 it was installed in the Cathedral, ready for the chapel decoration as a whole to be unveiled on 30 September of that year.

St Anthony of Padua preaching to the fishes. The narthex.

And so to the chapel which had caused the delay. In March 2002 Christopher Hobbs had produced designs for the east wall showing St Thomas Becket standing before the old Canterbury Cathedral, and of his martyrdom at the hands of Henry II's knights for the wall opposite. Because the chapel was closed off from the rest of the Cathedral, Hobbs took the opportunity of moving the style of the mosaics away from the Byzantine and towards the Romanesque of St Thomas's time. Hence the Norman arches with their zigzag decoration, the lovely roundel of the saint at sea (based on a thirteenth century original) on the vault and the crossed staffs and scallop shell, symbol of a pilgrim, on the north wall. Hobbs also wanted the richness of the decoration, which included glass jewels and mother-of-pearl, to suggest St Thomas's reliquary in Canterbury Cathedral. Work by Mosaic Workshop started in the studio in mid-2003. By February of the following year the scene of St Thomas before his cathedral was up, to be followed by the vault, the north wall and finally the splendidly atmospheric portrayal of the martyrdom, completed by Christmas 2004. In March 2005 Cardinal Vaughan's body returned from Mill Hill to his chantry in the Cathedral which he had founded. The Vaughan Chantry was formally reopened and blessed on 29 April 2005.

Subsequent mosaics have been on a smaller scale. The Bartlett family spent several years fundraising for memorials to Francis and Anthony Bartlett who played key roles in the history of the Cathedral. Mosaics of St Francis of Assisi and St Anthony of Padua, designed by Leonard McComb RA and executed by Mosaic Workshop, were installed by Walter Bernadin and Tessa Hunkin facing the side entrances either side of the main doors in October 2008 and March 2010 respectively. The features of the two saints are modelled on those of two of McComb's students at the Royal Academy Schools. St Francis is shown surrounded by birds and St Anthony by fish to which, according to the fourteenth century book *The little Flowers (Fioretti) of St Francis*, the two saints preached. McComb found some of the fish for his mosaic of St Anthony in Billingsgate Market. One of the fish carries a ring - a reference to St Anthony finding things that are lost. In September 2008, a mosaic panel of Cardinal John Henry Newman (now Blessed) was installed. It was designed by Tom Phillips RA who, in 2003, also designed two inlaid marble panels commemorating the first London performance (in 1903) of Edward Elgar's *The Dream of Gerontius*, based on a poem by Cardinal Newman. These panels are either side of the Holy Souls Chapel and the mosaic of Cardinal Newman is on the aisle wall nearby. The panels were made by Taylor Pearce of London and the mosaic by Mosaic Workshop.

St David of Wales

The most recent mosaic to be installed (as of June 2012) is that of St David, patron saint of Wales, which was installed in the south aisle of the Cathedral in September 2010 and blessed by His Holiness Pope Benedict XVI after celebrating Mass in the Cathedral on the 18th of that month. The mosaic was designed by Ivor Davies, himself a Welshman

*St David of Wales.
The south aisle.*

from Penarth, after considerable research into the life and miracles of St David. The saint is portrayed standing on the Hill of Brevi (Llandewi Brefi in Cardiganshire), with the dove of the Holy Spirit on his shoulder, in reference to the 'Miracle of Brevi' in which a hill rose miraculously below him so that he could be seen, while he became endowed by the Holy Spirit with eloquence to address a synod of bishops. Also featuring in the mosaic are Saint David's Cathedral in Pembrokeshire, the ship in which he travelled to Rome, and a leek - symbol of Wales. The mosaic itself consists of tesserae and larger pieces of glass assembled on nylon mesh by Tessa Hunkin before being installed in the Cathedral by her and Walter Bernadin. Finally, mosaic designs by Tom Phillips for St George's Chapel have also been approved and preparation is currently underway. They celebrate the Forty Martyrs of England and Wales represented as tongues of flame on the vault, with the three empty crosses of Golgotha reworked as Tyburn gallows on the west wall. A fundraising campaign to raise the £500,000 needed has been undertaken by the Friends of the Cathedral.

PART VI

MAKERS
OF THE
CATHEDRAL

Westminster Cathedral in 1903

1. John Francis Bentley

John Bentley, as the architect of Westminster Cathedral was christened, was born in Doncaster on 30 January 1839, the son of Charles Bentley, a wine-merchant. One of his most memorable experiences as a boy was when the local Anglican parish church, dedicated to St George, burned down in 1853. He made two cardboard models of it from memory, complete in every detail, and sold the first for five guineas. A regular haunt was the workshops of carvers and joiners in Doncaster, and when work started on rebuilding the parish church in 1853, in the Decorated Gothic style to a design by Sir George Gilbert Scott, he assisted the clerk of works.

John Francis Bentley aged 60.

Bentley left school at sixteen and at first wanted to be a painter, but he was indentured to the London building firm of Winslow & Holland by his authoritarian father. However, Richard Holland realised that Bentley's skill as a draughtsman qualified him for the profession of an architect. In 1857 he moved to the office of Henry Clutton, a well-known architect who, as described in an earlier chapter, produced a series of designs for a Gothic-style Westminster Cathedral for Cardinal Manning ten years later. It was at Clutton's that Bentley learned to design in the French Gothic and Italian Lombardesque styles and from where he exhibited at the Royal Academy in 1861 a coloured 'Study for a Chancel', glowing with marble and painted decoration. It was also there that he first encountered Catholicism, while supervising the enlargement of the Jesuit church at Farm Street and the building of the church of St Francis of Assisi, Pottery Lane in Notting Hill.

Going It Alone

In 1860 Bentley finished his five-year pupilage at Clutton's and although only twenty-one he was offered a partnership. But he was determined to strike out on his own and in 1862 he took chambers at 14 Southampton Street in the Strand. In between his first, rare, early commissions he studied at the Architectural Museum and developed lifelong friendships with architects, artists and craftsmen such as Charles Hadfield, Thomas Willson, William Christian Symons and Thomas (T C) Lewis. Many of them were Catholics for by this time Bentley was becoming increasingly drawn to Catholicism, and on 16 April 1862 he was baptised a Catholic by Cardinal Wiseman. He was the first person to be baptised in the baptistry which he himself had designed in 1861 for the church of St Francis of Assisi, Pottery Lane, taking the baptismal name of Francis. He also designed the font, and added a polished oak cover for it in 1865, in thanksgiving for his baptism and reception into the Catholic Church.

Bentley's admission into the Church, and his friendship with the Oblates of St Charles Borromeo (founded by Cardinal Manning in 1857), was followed by commissions to design church furniture and decorative features in several Catholic churches. Between 1861 and 1865 he was given a series of commissions by the parish priest at St Francis, Pottery Lane, designing a curved Lady Chapel, porch, presbytery and school in the thirteenth century French Gothic style which he had used for the baptistry, together with altars and other church furniture and decoration. For St Mary's Church, Chelsea, he designed an alabaster altar, together with a pulpit in the Romanesque-style. On 6 October 1874 Bentley was married in the church of St Peter and St Edward, Palace Street. In 1863 and 1867 he had provided two altars (one of them the high altar) for this church, situated a stone's throw from the site of the future Westminster Cathedral.

Bentley's Churches

In 1875 Bentley returned to St Mary's, Chelsea, to rebuild the church in the Early English Gothic style and this, his first church, was completed in 1879 and contains the altar and pulpit he had designed in 1864. Hs next church was Our Lady of the Holy Souls, Kensal New Town, which he built for the Oblates of St Charles Borromeo in 1881. Once again the style was Early English Gothic but, unlike St Mary's, Chelsea, which was faced with white stock bricks, the church of Our Lady of the Holy Souls was built of red brick dressed with Bath stone. Bentley played no part in the internal decoration which was undertaken by the rector. Similarly Bentley's third church, that of Corpus Christi, Brixton Hill, was never completed because of a lack

The pulpit in St Mary's Church, Chelsea.

of funds. His plan, which the parish priest described as 'simply magnificent', was for a nave of five bays with north and south aisles, a chancel with ambulatory, two transepts with an organ loft, two sacristies, three side chapels, a presbytery and a tower. The present church, which is in the Early Decorated Gothic style and was opened in 1887, consists only of a chancel, transepts, two eastern chapels, a sacristy and an organ loft.

The Fourteenth Station of the Cross. Designed by Bentley for the Sacred Heart Church, Wimbledon in 1900. Painted by Innes Fripp on canvas in 1900-1903.

After Westminster Cathedral, Bentley's finest church is that of the Holy Rood, Watford. The founder, Stephen Taprell Holland, was a wealthy member of the building firm for which Bentley had worked as a youth and was wholly in sympathy with his ideas. Described as a 'summary of Bentley's knowledge and resources', the church was designed in the Late Perpendicular Gothic style for a congregation of 450-500. The sanctuary, nave, transepts and south aisle were structurally complete and opened for worship in 1890, the foundations of the baptistry and tower were laid by Cardinal Vaughan in 1894 and the church was completed and consecrated in 1900. The materials used are flint facings and Bath stone, with red tiles for the roofing. Some internal features are echoed in Westminster Cathedral - the arcades running across the transept openings, the dominance of the painted rood, the pierced bronze lighting pendants. But the timber roof, the gilded and painted wood and plaster, the stained glass and carved stone tracery of Holy Rood, are, of course, entirely different.

The only other church built by Bentley is the simple and attractive Anglican village church of St Luke's, Chiddingstone Causeway, in Kent, built in the local style of the early

The Church of the Holy Rood, Watford.

The interior of the Church of the Holy Rood, Watford.

sixteenth century and opened in 1898 for a congregation of 180-200. The materials are Bath stone ashlar with red tiles for the roofing. The interior is plastered, with wood block flooring and encaustic tiles patterned with leopards' heads putting out their tongues, 'because you are Protestants' remarked Bentley humorously to the founder. Bentley also designed a Late Decorated Gothic cathedral for Richmond, Virginia, in 1883, and another for Brooklyn, New York, in 1898-99, but neither came to fruition. By now he had a large family and was living next to Clapham Common and working at 13 John Street in the Adelphi, off the Strand. He had been appointed by Cardinal Vaughan to be the architect of Westminster Cathedral in July 1894 and, as recounted in earlier chapters, he had spent the winter months from November to March of 1894-95 studying Romanesque and Byzantine architecture in Italy

The Cathedral Architect

By the spring of 1895 Cardinal Vaughan had decided on the early Christian Byzantine style for his new cathedral, in preference to the Gothic style preferred by Bentley, and that of an Italian basilica which he himself had favoured. As Bentley later admitted, 'Personally I should have preferred a Gothic church; yet, on consideration, I am inclined to think that the Cardinal was right'. Vaughan's attitude was that, 'Having laid down certain conditions as to size, space, chapels and style, I left the rest to him. He offered me the choice between a vaulted roof and one of saucer-shaped domes; I chose the latter. He wished to build two campaniles; I said one was enough for me. For the rest he had a free hand'. Of course it was not quite as simple as that. Vaughan disliked the arcades and galleries crossing the transepts which Bentley insisted upon, and he wanted 'something warmer' instead of the greenish tinted Venetian roundels for the window glass. He gave in to Bentley over these but ordered a pulpit and archiepiscopal throne from Rome without consulting him, and overruled both his design for the altar and, to Bentley's dismay, his 'pavement like the sea' for the nave.

The last years of Bentley's life were devoted to the building of Westminster Cathedral which *The Pall Mall Magazine* described in October 1902 as 'the greatest material expression of religious faith given to England by devout Catholics since the Reformation'. In the words of a cabby to a Cathedral visitor, 'The architec's inside. E's 'ere day and night'. Never of robust health, Bentley suffered a first slight paralytic stroke in November 1898, and a second in June 1900 which also affected his speech.

He was constantly needed at the Cathedral to oversee construction and decoration and was being pressed by Cardinal Vaughan for progress reports and estimates of cost. He was also worried about his family. It was not the workload but 'worry that kills me' he is reported to have said. Nomination for the Royal Gold Medal of the Royal Institute of British Architects provided a temporary glow of achievement, but he was never to receive the medal. He suffered a third paralytic stroke while visiting friends on 1 March 1902 and died the following morning. In Cardinal Vaughan's words, 'He put the whole of his life and soul into the Cathedral and it killed him'.

On 5 March 1902 Vaughan preached Bentley's funeral oration at the church of St Mary's, Clapham, which Bentley had attended for the last twenty-eight years of his life and for which he had built an ornate side chapel dedicated to Our Lady of Perpetual Succour. In the Cardinal's words, 'Bentley was a poet; he saw and felt the beauty, the fancy, the harmony of his artistic creations. He had no love of money, he cared little for economy; he had an immense love of art, a passion for truth and sincerity in his work. He was not ambitious to get on; he was not self-assertive, but he coveted to do well. He went in search of no work, but waited for work to come in search of him. He was the best of architects for a cathedral, or for any work that was to excel in artistic beauty. He was no mere copyist and no slave to tradition. Whatever he produced was stamped with his own individuality; it was alive and original; and he had a genius for taking infinite pains with detail'. John Francis Bentley is buried in the churchyard at St Mary Magdalene's Church, Mortlake, with his wife and three of his eleven children, two of whom died in infancy.

Westminster Cathedral in 1903.

2. William Brindley

As described in previous chapters, Westminster Cathedral is not a conventional late-Victorian building but is modelled on a Byzantine basilica - built of brick with the interior decorated with marble and mosaics. The Cathedral authorities were unusually fortunate in having, just across the river, a marble merchant not only well-versed in Byzantine architecture but who knew where Byzantine materials could be obtained. His name was William Brindley.

William Brindley in 1890.

William Brindley was born in Derbyshire in 1832 and educated locally. As a boy he developed a talent for sketching, designing and carving and, appropriately enough in a county renowned for its building stone, when he left school he became a stone carver. By the 1850s he was working for William Farmer, another stone carver from Derbyshire nine years his senior, on the decoration of churches and other buildings and in 1868 the two formed a partnership at 67 (later 63) Westminster Bridge Road in London. By this time they had become established as architectural sculptors in stone and wood and were the preferred choice of well-known architects such as George Gilbert Scott and Alfred Waterhouse. Scott chose Brindley for the capitals and other decorative stone carving on the Albert Memorial in Hyde Park and described him in 1873 as 'The best carver I have met with and the one who best understands my needs'. Brindley was also successfully employed by Scott on the decoration of Preston Town Hall, Wellington College Chapel in Shropshire, and the magnificent capitals at Kelham Hall in Nottinghamshire, all of which were described by Scott in his memoirs as 'examples of carving of a high order'.

The Albert Memorial - decorative stone-carving by William Brindley.

Brindley Goes Exploring

George Gilbert Scott died in 1878 and William Farmer died the following year, leaving Brindley in sole charge of the firm. By this time the marble decoration of prestige buildings such as the Albert Chapel at Windsor, the Royal Mausoleum at Frogmore and the Opéra Garnier in Paris had convinced Brindley that coloured marble was becoming increasingly fashionable. So he embarked on a mission to seek out the old Roman quarries in Europe, Africa and Asia. As he put it twenty years later, 'As my delight is in old quarry hunting and as I knew the very high price fragments dug up in Rome fetched, I determined to try to find the lost quarries, and see if they were worked out or not'. After previously listing themselves in the Trades Directories simply as sculptors, in 1881 the Farmer & Brindley firm began to advertise as marble merchants.

Animals modelled by Farmer & Brindley decorate the Natural History Museum in London.

In preparing for his mission of rediscovery, Brindley studied all the contemporary accounts he could find of the use of marble in antiquity, such as Strabo's *Geography*, Pliny the Elder's *Natural History* and Paul the Silentiary's description of the Byzantine Church of Santa Sophia (Haghia Sophia) in Constantinople. Then, during the 1880s and early 1890s, he travelled widely through Greece, Turkey and North Africa, discovering the ancient workings of Cipollino marble on the Greek Island of Evia, Porta Santa on Chios, Verde Antico near Larissa on the central Greek mainland and Imperial Porphyry at Gebel Dokhan in the Egyptian Eastern Desert, which he travelled through with his wife, nineteen Bedouin and fifteen camels and where he recorded that his goatskin of drinking water 'tasted like hot, rancid bacon broth'. Whenever possible his discoveries were followed by the negotiation of a concession to reopen the quarries and extract any workable marble. He also purchased examples of ancient marble which he discovered during his travels and presented a number of papers to the Royal Institute of British Architects, accompanied by articles in trade journals such as *The Builder* and *The Building News*. As a result of his research Brindley was elected a Fellow of the Geological Society in 1888.

The mountains of Gebel Dokhan in the Egyptian Eastern Desert – location of the Imperial Porphyry quarries.

Meanwhile demand for decorative coloured marble was increasing as Brindley had foreseen. There was a building boom in England and marble was in growing demand. A major customer was John Francis Bentley, the architect of Westminster Cathedral, who required twenty-nine structural columns for the nave, aisles and transepts and large amounts of marble cladding for the chapels. In 1899 Brindley invited visitors from the Cathedral to his works to watch the 13ft main nave columns being turned on lathes with steel blades, ground with sand and polished with oxide of tin before being installed in the Cathedral. The white Carrara capital for the top of each column, however, was only roughly shaped at the works and received its detailed carving after installation, two of Brindley's stonemasons taking an average of three months to carve each one.

Bentley died in March 1902 and Cardinal Vaughan, the Cathedral's founder, died in June 1903 but work on the Cathedral continued. The Cardinal had set his heart on eight 15ft onyx columns to support the baldacchino (canopy) over the high altar. Both Bentley and Brindley had advised against onyx and, sure enough, when the columns arrived from Algeria four were already broken. So Brindley replaced them with Bentley's choice of eight columns of yellow Verona marble. The baldacchino, which Bentley had described as 'the best thing about the Cathedral', was installed by Farmer & Brindley from 1905 and unveiled on Christmas Eve 1906. Then followed the marble decoration of the Blessed Sacrament Chapel (completed 1907), Lady Chapel (1908), Sacred Heart Shrine and Vaughan Chantry (1910), Baptistry floor (1912), St Andrew's Chapel (1915) and St Paul's Chapel (1917).

The Verde Antico marble quarries near Larissa in central Greece - located by William Brindley in 1888-89.

Brindley in Retirement

Farmer & Brindley became a private limited joint stock company in 1905 when Brindley sold the firm for £50,000 (though retaining a majority shareholding) and transferred control to his nephew, Ernest Brindley, and his son-in-law, Henry Barnes. Now aged 74, Brindley moved down to his house, 'Eastercourt', in St John's Road, Boscombe, near Bournemouth in Hampshire. He presented a major paper on the use of marble in architecture to the Royal Institute of British Architects in 1907 and continued to travel to distant countries such as Canada, the United States (twice) and Japan (three times).

He corresponded with academics and architects, allowing them to consult his extensive architectural library and collection of photographs, and he arranged for, and often led, groups such as the Architectural Association and the Geologists' Association on tours of the Farmer & Brindley premises. These included its marble museum containing an extensive collection of ancient and modern granites, porphyries and 'lumps of marble that you wanted to eat' according to Edward Burne-Jones after a visit in 1891. Brindley died in 1919 at the age of eighty-seven leaving an estate valued at £60,000.

From 1908-23 Farmer & Brindley advertised as 'Largest establishment and with greatest variety and stock of choice coloured marble and rare stones in the Kingdom' but the 1914-18 War disrupted markets and Brindley's death seemed to take the heart out of the firm. London's County Hall and Glasgow's City Council Chambers provided work until 1928 but the demand for wood, stone and marble decoration never picked up to pre-war levels. In Westminster Cathedral the apse wall (1921), the organ screen (1924) and the south transept (1926) were clad with marble, while work on St Patrick's Chapel, using some of Brindley's last remaining stock, which he had collected during his travels, took place intermittently from 1923-29. But standards were starting to slip. There was an accident at the works in 1924, and in 1929 the carved marble screen at the entrance to St Patrick's Chapel was rejected and had to be recarved. The same year, the year of the 'Great Crash', Farmer & Brindley went out of business. On its site at 63 Westminster Bridge Road an unimposing block of flats now stands.

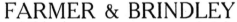

FARMER & BRINDLEY
Ltd.

MODELLERS, SCULPTORS, CARVERS & ART WORKERS IN MARBLE, STONE, WOOD, ETC.

The largest Assortment of Marble in the world on view.

The greater part of the Marble Work in the Cathedral (including the Baldacchino) has been executed by this firm.

STUDIO, WORKS, ETC.:

63 Westminster Bridge Road,
LONDON.

A Farmer & Brindley advertisement of 1913.

3. Sir Richard Runciman Terry

No history of Westminster Cathedral would be complete without an account of the contribution of Sir Richard Terry to its choir and its music. His rediscovery and revival of forgotten Tudor church music gained him a doctorate in 1911 and a knighthood in 1922, but of equal importance is the influence he exerted through a quarter of a century as Director of Music and Choirmaster at Westminster Cathedral.

Richard Terry (in boater) with the choir of Westminster Cathedral in its heyday in 1913.

Learning the Ropes

Richard Runciman Terry was born in 1865 at Ellington in Northumberland, not far from the North Sea. His mother's family were seafarers and he grew up with a love for the sea, its sailors and their music. At the age of eleven he started playing the organ in church. After school he went up to Oxford and then to King's College, Cambridge on an organ scholarship. There he became music critic to *The Cambridge Review* and both the Professor of Music, Charles Villiers Stanford, and Dr A H Mann, who was also at King's and taught him the techniques of choral singing and the training of boys' voices, took a lasting interest in him. By this time Terry was becoming increasingly drawn to unaccompanied choral singing which was to lead him to sixteenth century English polyphony.

In 1890 Terry left Cambridge and became organist and choirmaster first at Elstow School near Bedford and then at St John's Cathedral in Antigua. He loved the West Indies and while there he met an Irish Catholic priest, a meeting which resulted in him converting to Catholicism in 1896 after his return to England. As a consequence, he was appointed Music Master at Downside School by Prior Hugh Edmund Ford of the Benedictine Monastery there. It was Prior Ford, later first Abbot of Downside, who, in Terry's words, 'realised that the church music of Tye, Tallis, Byrd and their contemporaries was fit for better things than the occasional performance as concert items. He realised that it was as true an adjunct to public worship today as it was in the sixteenth century'.

Richard Terry robed as a Doctor of Music in 1919.

Sir Richard Terry being congratulated by the Cathedral choir on his knighthood in 1922.

Ford gave Terry a virtual free hand with the Downside music which was generally recognised as having become moribund, and Terry remembered his five years there as the happiest he ever spent. He started gradually, holding popular concerts and encouraging interest in folk songs, sea shanties and music for the theatre, accompanied by a ruthless purge of the existing choir. Meanwhile curiosity about English Tudor music had led him to spend almost all his holidays in the British Museum, discovering and scoring the work of composers forgotten since the Reformation, gradually inserting their music into the repertory of his new choir. It was at Downside, under Abbot Ford and Richard Terry, that the revival of Tudor church music really got underway, and that the first recorded performances were held of Byrd's Masses for five and three voices, Taverner's *Western Wynde* Mass, the *Gradualia* and *Cantiones Sacrae* of Byrd and Philips, motets by Tye, Shepherd etc.

From Downside to Westminster

On 25 November 1899 Terry took the Downside choir to sing at the opening of the new Benedictine church at Ealing. They sang Byrd's *Mass for Five Voices*, three motets by Palestrina, Philips's *Hodie Sanctus Spiritus* and an *Adoremus* by Allegri. The celebrant and preacher was Cardinal Herbert Vaughan, a member of an old English recusant family, devoted to the principles and practices of the pre-Reformation Catholic Church. His reaction on hearing the Downside choir was 'This is the music I want for my Cathedral'. By now Downside's music was exclusively polyphonic. It included many new pieces provided by Terry, such as Tallis's *Lamentations*. Already it was attracting considerable attention in music circles, as was its choirmaster, Terry, who had started to write a series of strongly polemical articles about sixteenth century music, dispelling popular myths and widely-held illusions, a practice which he continued all his life.

Cardinal Vaughan had initially wanted to appoint Sir Charles Santley as Director of Music at Westminster Cathedral but when this proved impossible he selected Terry, who moved into Archbishop's House in 1901 to plan the music and form the choir. In October eleven boys were selected as the nucleus of the Cathedral Choir School and by June 1902, when regular services started in the Cathedral Hall, the choir had swelled to twenty-five trebles and fifteen men, as well as the clergy. During his first five years Terry not only had to train voices but to teach his choir in a totally unfamiliar idiom and to initiate them in the singing of plainsong in which his own ideas were only half-formed. But at all times he had the complete support of Cardinal Vaughan until the latter's death in June 1903, which came as a severe blow to Terry both personally and professionally.

Sir Richard Terry rehearsing with the Cathedral choir in 1922.

Music at Westminster

Away from the choir Terry's research continued unremittingly. He was preoccupied with plainsong, which was new to him, and finally created from the Solesmes system his own interpretation based on the fundamental rules of the restored chant. Meanwhile his choir had to perform hundreds of Masses and motets annually, largely from the works of Palestrina and the sixteenth century school of Italian polyphony, together with those of the Spaniard, Vittoria, and the Flemish composer, di Lasso. To this Terry added examples of English Tudor music which his own researches had brought to light. He believed it was important to hear the unknown Byrd beside the acknowledged Palestrina, the unknown Taverner and Tallis beside the recognised Vittoria and di Lasso. During his first ten years at Westminster his work with the choir, together with his research, occupied all his time. But the results were becoming increasingly well-known. In Christmas week of 1906 *The Daily Telegraph* called his choir 'one of the most beautiful choirs in Europe' and the following year both *The Daily Telegraph* and *The Times* began regular reviews of the Westminster Cathedral music.

Terry's admiration for Palestrina, whom he regarded as the greatest of all Italian composers, was based not just on his music, but on his 'rightness' as a composer of liturgical music. As Terry put it 'the reason why he remains - as truly today as in the sixteenth century - the ideal composer for the Roman Rite is that he was steeped in the spirit of the liturgy'. A similar message was contained in Pope Pius X's 1903 encyclical on the improvement of church music entitled *Motu Proprio*, made more explicit in his *Regolamento* addressed to his Vicar-General in Rome. In these the Pope condemned the, then popular but non-liturgical, Viennese type of Mass of Haydn, Mozart and others, and praised the sixteenth-century composers of polyphony, especially Palestrina, 'for the music is merely a part of the liturgy and its humble handmaid'.

At the International Music Congress of 1911, a special session was held at Westminster Cathedral to hear early English music sung by the choir. In the same year Terry received the *honoris causa* degree of Doctor of Music at Durham University. The years leading up to the 1914-18 War saw a great increase in the performance of unpublished Tudor music at the Cathedral, particularly during Holy Week, with a series of Masses and motets unheard since the Reformation. Terry's choir reached its peak in 1914, but the war resulted in only one of his permanent men-singers (too old to be called up) remaining by 1918, and the alto parts were performed by the boys. By this time Terry was preoccupied with reviving the work of John Taverner, who lived during the reign of Henry VIII and whom Terry regarded as the greatest discovery in English music. His *Western Wynde* Mass was first performed at the Cathedral in 1913. In 1917 five of his Masses were heard; Holy Week 1921 was declared a Taverner Festival, and all eight of his Masses had been performed many times by March 1924 when Terry resigned.

Sir Richard Terry with Dr Ralph Vaughan Williams and the Cathedral choir after the first performance of the Vaughan Williams Mass in G minor in 1923.

After Westminster

In 1922 Terry was knighted for his research in early English music manuscripts, but Holy Week 1923 was his last as Director of Music and Choirmaster at Westminster Cathedral. During the week the Byrd *Mass for Five Voices* which had brought him from Downside to Westminster was sung, as was the *Mass in G minor* by Ralph Vaughan Williams in its first performance. When he left the Cathedral it was after a prolonged period of tension. With Cardinal Bourne he never developed the similarity of views on church music and the easy working relationship which he had with 'the great founder of the Cathedral, my ever revered master, Herbert Cardinal Vaughan', as he put it in an article in *The Morning Post* of 9 April 1924. He had seen the permanent men-singers of his choir cut from fifteen in Vaughan's time to four (plus one part-timer) in Bourne's and he clearly resented it.

Terry's refusal to brook interference with the choir, coupled with prolonged absences from the Cathedral engaged in other activities, meant that colleagues did not always find him easy to work with. Cardinal Bourne also clearly found him difficult to control, writing in 1911 of 'criticisms which reach me from every side' and urging him to observe the choir rules. Yet Terry's achievements in discovering and reviving English Tudor music are unequalled. As Choirmaster at Westminster he was a hard taskmaster, not above using his baton to rap the head of an offender, but the boys whom he taught clearly had a profound respect and often a genuine affection for him. After leaving the Cathedral he spent his time travelling, writing, broadcasting, lecturing, examining, adjudicating at music festivals and conducting community choirs. He published books of Tudor motets, hymns, carols, sea shanties and nursery rhymes. He clearly enjoyed himself. He died on Easter Sunday of 1938.

4. John Arthur Marshall

While the name of John Francis Bentley is almost synonymous with that of Westminster Cathedral, the name of John Arthur Marshall is known only to a few. In fact Bentley only worked on the building from 1895 until his death in 1902. As his chief assistant for almost twenty-five years, Marshall worked closely with him during these years and was subsequently responsible, over the next twenty-five years, for bringing to fruition many of Bentley's plans which the architect had left unexecuted, plus many of his own. It is Marshall whom we must thank for much that we see in the Cathedral today. He died on New Year's Day of 1927.

In 1868 Bentley moved to larger premises at 13 John Street in the Adelphi (off the Strand) and it was there that Marshall, then aged twenty-five, joined him in 1878. In the paper which he read to the Architectural Association in 1907, Marshall recounted how he was not expected to design, but to exercise care and judgement and take an interest in the work. 'The annual holiday was a reprehensible undertaking rather than a recognised institution. Smoking, whistling and gossiping were strictly prohibited and to take off one's coat for greater freedom or coolness was pre-eminently disrespectful, not to say vulgar'. Nevertheless Marshall admitted that whenever a suitable opportunity occurred 'conventionality was cast aside for uncontrollable bursts of boyhood', resulting in 1879 in a note from Bentley calling for less noise. It appeared that Mr G, in an office downstairs, had complained.

Marshall Takes Charge

Marshall remained Bentley's chief assistant until the latter died on 2 March 1902. His last service to Bentley was to design his tombstone, and he succeeded him as architect in charge of the Cathedral, which was by then structurally almost complete. But Bentley had left no provision for the firm which he had founded and it was Marshall who took on that responsibility. Quietly and conscientiously he set about ensuring its continuation, initially as J F Bentley & Son, then (from 1906) as John F Bentley & Son and (from 1909) as John F Bentley, Son & Marshall. The firm remained at 13 John Street and Marshall worked in partnership with Bentley's widow, Margaret, and his second son, Osmund. But in 1912 the partnership broke up, and from 1913 until his death fourteen years later, Marshall worked from his home at 5 Church Lane, Edgware.

Marshall's design for the mosaic of the main entrance tympanum.

THE TYMPANUM.

The success of the Cathedral results in no small part from the fact that Marshall knew what Bentley intended and remained absolutely faithful to his vision. Thus the baldacchino, which was unveiled on Christmas Eve 1906, and which Bentley had described as the 'best thing about the Cathedral', is exactly according to Bentley's drawings, although the blue and gold patterned mosaic lining, which blends in perfectly, is of Marshall's design and the whole structure is slightly smaller than originally intended. Then the lighting, for which Bentley had left no plans, combines the style of Byzantine oil lamps with Bentley's designs for lighting elsewhere. The little pendants in the Chapel of the Holy Souls and that of St Gregory and St Augustine, for example, are remarkably similar to those in Bentley's neo-Gothic Church of the Holy Rood, Watford, and the main chandeliers in the nave and sanctuary, installed in 1909, resemble descriptions of those in the great Byzantine church of Haghia Sophia (Santa Sophia) in Constantinople.

The Blessed Sacrament Chapel. Metalwork designed by Marshall.

Bentley had left drawings for the marblework in the Blessed Sacrament Chapel. But it was Marshall who designed the carved wooden canopy above the altar, the silver gilt tabernacle and all the other metalwork, including the pendant lights and the extensive bronze gilt screens around the chapel, completed in 1914. The seven great bronze gilt candlesticks and crucifix behind the high altar in the Cathedral sanctuary, first used at the Mass of Consecration in 1910, must also have been designed by Marshall - he would never have entrusted such an important task to anyone else. Other metalwork designed by him can be seen in the twelve lovely bronze consecration sconces, each one in the shape of an arm bearing a candle, put up on 1 July each year in the nave aisles and transepts to commemorate the dedication of the Cathedral. They remind one of Jean Cocteau's film *La Belle et la Bête* in which arms bearing candles also project from the wall of the enchanted castle. But there the arms *move* to provide illumination as the visitor passes by. Marshall's versatility was also demonstrated in his plan for a pulpit. Realising that the original marble pulpit was both unsuitable and increasingly insecure, his 'temporary' wooden pulpit, erected in 1914 in the position occupied by the present one, was used for twenty years. Other examples of Marshall's work are the painted decoration of the Cathedral Hall - now restored to his original design - and his work on Clergy House and the Choir School.

Both in the Shrine of the Sacred Heart and nearby in the Vaughan Chantry (the Chapel of St Thomas of Canterbury), all the work, including the simple but effective red, green and gold mosaics in the barrel-roofed shrine, and Cardinal Vaughan's effigy and sarcophagus carved in white Pentelic marble for the chantry, are also to Marshall's designs. Similarly, although Bentley had prepared preliminary, partly coloured, designs for the marblework in St Paul's and St Joseph's Chapels, the detailed work fell to Marshall. During the 1914-18 War traditional Greek and Turkish marbles - Verde Antico, grey Hymettian, white Pentelic and streaked Proconnesian from the Island of Marmara - went up in St Paul's Chapel, the work in St Joseph's Chapel (the apse) being carried out in 1914, though Marshall's design for a baldacchino over the altar has never been executed.

Working With Others

Another reason for remembering Marshall is for his choice of artists - the Nonconformist Robert Anning Bell RA, who designed both the lovely blue altarpiece in the Lady Chapel (1912) and the great tympanum mosaic over the main entrance doors (1916), for which Marshall had also produced a design in 1907. And Eric Gill, the controversial

sculptor, who carved the Stations of the Cross from 1914-18. In both cases Marshall, a Nonconformist himself, faced opposition from Cardinal Bourne who distrusted non-Catholics and was disappointed with both the blue altarpiece and the tympanum mosaic, describing the latter as 'the greatest disappointment which I have received in connection with the work of the Cathedral'. As to the Stations, Gill, a Catholic convert from 1913, writes in his autobiography that Marshall told him that he only got the job because he was cheap and Cardinal Bourne was threatening to give it to the first Catholic he met in the street.

In the mid-1920s Bourne conceived the idea of forming a permanent school of mosaic workers to decorate the Cathedral and maintain existing mosaics. He had been impressed by the work of the artist, Gilbert Pownall,

One of the twelve large consecration sconces designed by Marshall.

who had painted his portrait in 1923, and arranged for him, together with Marshall as Cathedral architect, to study the mosaics and methods of Venice, Ravenna, Rome and Sicily with a view to the design and production of mosaics for the Cathedral. Pownall clearly enjoyed the trip but it is less certain that Marshall did. He was by then over seventy and not accustomed to overseas travelling. He may also have been feeling unwell from the cancer and heart failure which killed him a year or so later. In February 1926 Lawrence Shattock (his eventual successor) was appointed to assist him.

The Final Years

Marshall's later work for the Cathedral included the design of St Patrick's Chapel (1919), the marblework of the apse (1922), the great marble organ screen above the narthex at the other end of the Cathedral (1924), the Lady Chapel aisle and transept and the

gates and grille of the Baptistry (all 1926). One of his last projects was designing the two bronze gilt angels, each bearing a trumpet, for the organ screen. They were installed on 23 December 1926. A little over a week later, on 1 January 1927, Marshall was dead. He was seventy-three and had been complaining of a persistent cough since October. Although he had completed other projects which Bentley had left unfinished - marble and mosaic work in the Church of Our Lady of the Assumption, Warwick Street, additional accommodation for St Thomas's Seminary, and a wooden altar for St John's Anglican Church (both in Hammersmith) - the last thirty years of his life had centred on Westminster Cathedral.

A bronze gilt angel decorating the organ screen. One of Marshall's last projects.

A quiet and self-effacing man, Marshall was known to few outside his own family circle and immediate friends and colleagues. He was content to give all the credit for the Cathedral to Bentley and walk in his shadow. His intimate knowledge of Bentley's ideas, the structural problems presented by the building and how these were solved, are shown in a paper read by him to the Architectural Association in January 1907. The proposal of thanks to him afterwards described the paper as 'one of the most remarkable they had ever had on what must be considered to be one of the most remarkable buildings of modern times'. Unfailingly courteous, he consistently refused to respond to often ill-conceived, and sometimes deliberately offensive, criticism of the Cathedral and its decoration. He has no memorial there, but just as Bentley's memorial is the Cathedral itself, so Marshall's consists of much of the decoration, including two bronze angels bearing trumpets.

The triptych of St Paul in St Paul's Chapel. Designed by Marshall.

5. The Bartletts

A mosaic near the Cathedral entrance, installed in October 2008, portrays St Francis of Assisi. Another mosaic, installed nearby in March 2010, shows St Anthony of Padua. They commemorate the lives of Francis and Anthony Bartlett and were donated by members and friends of the Bartlett family, a family intimately bound up with the life of the Cathedral since its opening more than a hundred years ago. It has provided an Administrator, two ceremonial swordbearers to six Cardinal Archbishops, and an artist whose work on the marble and mosaics of the Cathedral can be seen all around us.

Joseph Henry (Harry) Bartlett was born the son of a Bristol vintner (purveyors of Bartlett's whiskey) and converted to the Catholic faith at the age of seventeen. He moved down to London as the representative of John Hardman, Church Furnishers, and started the Art and Book Company at 22 Paternoster Row. From 1902 until 1971 his company occupied premises at 28 Ashley Place, then opposite the main entrance of Westminster Cathedral which itself opened in 1903. On one occasion he ejected Eric Gill from the shop for showing salacious sketches. Harry gradually formed a close friendship with the newly appointed Cardinal Archbishop, Francis Bourne, and became his *Gentiluomo*, or ceremonial swordbearer. Marriage to Eleanor Mackie, from a longstanding Catholic family who lived next door to Birmingham Oratory, was followed by the birth of twelve children.

The Bartlett family with Harry Bartlett at the top right and his wife seated in front of him.

Francis Bartlett, the ninth child of the marriage, was born in 1912 in Kensington, and named Francis after his godfather, the Cardinal. Educated by the Jesuits at Wimbledon, at first he wanted to be a Dominican but was dissuaded by Cardinal Bourne who sent him off first to Allen Hall, then based at Ware, and then to St Sulpice in Paris. He was ordained priest by Bourne's successor, Cardinal Hinsley, in 1935 and appointed curate at the Church of St Anthony of Padua, Edgware. At the end of the War, which he spent as a curate at Kenton and found galling 'with five brothers in uniform and me on a bicycle in the suburbs', he returned to the Cathedral as a Chaplain in 1944 and then as Sub-Administrator from 1954-64. It was then that he persuaded the Cathedral authorities to recommence the decoration of the

Cathedral. Then, after a short break as parish priest at Our Lady of the Assumption, Warwick Street, he was appointed Cathedral Administrator from 1967-77, doing his best to protect the Cathedral Treasures from Cardinal Heenan who wanted to sell them to raise money for the Third World. Francis Bartlett died on 12 February 1992.

An advertisement of 1910 for the Art and Book Company at 28 Ashley Place.

Anthony Bartlett, Francis's younger brother, was born in 1913 on the Feast of St Anthony of Padua and worked at the Art and Book Company in Ashley Place, taking over on the death of his father in 1936. He also took on his father's role as *Gentiluomo* and served five Cardinals in this capacity until the death of Cardinal Hume in 1999 – the last to do so for the Second Vatican Council had decided to end the tradition of *Gentiluomo*. As Anthony put it 'I am a sort of Dodo, I am officially extinct'. After returning from the War, which he spent driving a fire engine during the Blitz and then shooting at V-1 flying bombs on the South Coast, Anthony continued as manager of the Art and Book Company. But in 1971-75 the area in front of the Cathedral was redeveloped, producing the Piazza and the view we have today from Victoria Street. The old Ashley Place buildings disappeared and the Art and Book Shop moved to new premises at 28 Buckingham Palace Road.

Anthony, who retired at the age of eighty and died on 25 October 2000, will probably be remembered best for his tireless work for the elderly, the unemployed and the homeless with the Society of St Vincent de Paul, the Passage Day Centre and Providence Row night shelter – work for which he received the OBE in 1991. He was also a Eucharistic Minister, Reader and Server at Mass. Working with his elder brother, Francis, he installed in the Cathedral both the medieval alabaster statue of Our Lady of Westminster and the 17th century wooden figure of St Anthony, hewn from a tree trunk. In the aftermath of Vatican II and the changes this instituted, sometimes together with his younger brother Aelred, and sometimes with the artist Douglas Purnell, he undertook the re-ordering and redecoration of sanctuaries in Catholic churches such as Our Lady of Victories in Kensington, St James in Spanish Place, the Holy Redeemer in Chelsea and Our Lady of the Assumption in Warwick Street, together with chapels at Heythrop and Mayfield Colleges.

*Aelred and
Anthony Bartlett at
Victoria Station
in 1937.*

Aelred, the youngest of the three brothers, was born in 1918 and grew up, like them, in the shadow of the Cathedral. He went to Ampleforth and then trained as an artist at the Slade but World War II interrupted his studies and he was sent off to be an anti-aircraft gunner in the Orkneys, and then to Africa, Austria and to Italy as an interrogator in the Intelligence Corps. Fortunately he was based in Italy at L'Aquila in the Abruzzi and its many imposing Romanesque and Renaissance churches and palaces increased his interest in church architecture and decoration. On his return to England he obtained his Slade diploma and then worked as a restorer of paintings, as a church decorator and as a designer of theatrical sets. In early 1956, on the advice of the Cathedral Art Advisory Committee, Cardinal Griffin decided that work should resume on the decoration of the Cathedral nave and Aelred was brought in. Both he and Francis, the Sub-Administrator, were determined that the work should be in accordance with the original designs of the architect, J F Bentley, despite opposition from some members of the Committee and the architect in charge of the Cathedral whose favourite colour, according to Aelred, was beige.

So it was that Aelred travelled to Italy, Greece, Turkey and Ireland to find the marbles and mosaics of which Bentley would have approved. Together with Cecil Whitehead of the marble merchants John Whitehead & Sons, Aelred visited Cipollino marble quarries on the Greek Island of Evia and insisted on the opening of a new quarry face to produce the wavy, light green marble which clads the Cathedral nave piers today. It was Aelred who contacted the Geological Survey of Ireland through the Irish Embassy, and arranged for the reopening of the abandoned Cork Red marble quarry at Baneshane, previously used by

*Francis Bartlett as
Sub-Administrator
of Westminster
Cathedral in 1960.*

the Cathedral before the 1914-18 War. This mottled red marble is now combined with Cipollino throughout the nave. Finally it was Aelred who supervised the nave, narthex and porch decoration and the marble floor in the Lady Chapel from 1956-64.

Other examples of Aelred's work in the Cathedral consist of the vine and star mosaics in the soffits of the transept arches, the Byzantine-style inlaid marble panel set into the floor below Our Lady of Westminster, and the Roman-style mosaic depiction of St Nicholas in the niche at the end of the north aisle - complete with a wren for it commemorates the wartime head of the WRNS. He also prepared mosaic designs for the decoration of St Paul's Chapel but, to his intense annoyance and frustration, and at the insistence of Boris Anrep who had just finished the mosaic decoration of the Blessed Sacrament Chapel, it was Anrep's assistant, Justin Vulliamy, who received the commission. Aelred's reaction was to lock himself in the Cathedral and engage in other work. He then returned to Greece where he built his own house and on one occasion, after a good lunch, fell out of a tree onto the village orchestra below. Aelred's last work for the Cathedral was to select marble panels for the front of the nave piers at gallery level. He chose deep red Rosso Laguna from Turkey and pale blue Azul Macaubas from Brazil and the panels went up in time for the 1995 Centenary.

Anthony Bartlett as Gentiluomo to Cardinal Hume in 1995.

Working sometimes together and sometimes alone, the three Bartlett brothers gave much to the Cathedral, spiritually, practically and artistically. At the centre was Francis, to whom both Anthony and Aelred were very close. Francis combined a great love for humanity, the Catholic Faith and the Mass with a full appreciation for what life in London had to offer - opera, theatre, art galleries, good food and wine. He loved telling stories, not always strictly truthful. As his brother Aelred said of him, 'If Francis did not know something he simply made it up', and many of the Cathedral legends originated with him. He was an accomplished photographer and enjoyed travelling, particularly in Greece, Turkey and Italy. As for Anthony, his life was one of service, of helping people he saw as less fortunate than himself. In the words of Aelred Bartlett, who died on Good Friday 2004 and is much missed, 'Francis combined a deep faith with a love of the world and its people, Anthony was a saint, and I am just an artist'.

Aelred Bartlett in 1995

A winged ox, traditional symbol of St Luke. The sanctuary arch tympanum mosaic.

1. Thomas More's Monkey

In the summer of 1938 Eric Gill, the sculptor who had carved the Cathedral Stations of the Cross in 1914-18, was approached by Cardinal Arthur Hinsley's Art Advisory Committee and commissioned to carve a stone altarpiece (reredos) for the Chapel of St George and the English Martyrs. It was to be a memorial to Mrs John Boland who founded the Catholic Truth Society (CTS) Box-Tenders Association and who died in 1937. Gill spent three days in October 1938 designing the altarpiece and produced his revised drawings in July 1939. Two of England's most famous martyrs, Sir Thomas More who had been Henry VIII's Chancellor, and John Fisher who was Bishop of Rochester and a Cardinal, were to be portrayed either side of the crucified Christ. The two men had been executed at Tower Hill in June and July 1535 for refusing to accept the Act of Supremacy of 1534 under which Henry VIII was declared 'the only supreme head on earth of the Church in England' (thus depriving the Papacy of its authority). Thomas More and John Fisher were canonised as martyr-saints in 1935.

Eric Gill, self-portrait. 1927

In July 1940, while the altarpiece was being carved, Gill provided a description for the *Westminster Cathedral Chronicle*. He wrote: 'As this is the chapel of the English Martyrs, it seemed appropriate that the altar panel should have a crucifix, and figures of St John Fisher and St Thomas More, and it seemed appropriate to portray Our Lord reigning from the Cross as Priest and King. The Cross is held up by two angels and has moulded finials; this is to show that it is a symbolic cross and not a picture of the Crucifixion. St John Fisher is clothed in the chasuble and wears a mitre and holds a crosier. St Thomas More is clothed in his long coat, and his favourite monkey is crouching at his feet with hands uplifted. St Thomas had a little zoo of his own at his house in Chelsea and among the inhabitants was a little monkey of whom (sic) he was very fond. The sculptor has introduced the little animal as indicating by its very incongruity the deeply human character of the saint - so completely unlike the conventional stained glass window figure. Moreover the animal does by its caricature of humanity remind us of our own lowly state.'

Cardinal Griffin Objects

Gill started to carve the altarpiece from Hopton Wood stone on 29 September 1939 and continued throughout 1940, assisted by Laurie Cribb. He worked on it until 29 October by which time all the essentials, including the monkey, had been carved. But he was feeling increasingly unwell. He died in hospital during an air-raid on 17 November 1940 after an operation for cancer. The work was finished by his assistant, Laurie Cribb, but remained in Gill's studio at High Wycombe until November 1946 when it was installed in the Cathedral by the firm of Fenning & Co of Hammersmith. It was when it was revealed to the public that the controversy started, for the monkey had been removed. Although Cardinal Hinsley and his Art Committee had authorised and approved the altarpiece in 1938-39, the committee had lapsed with the War and Hinsley had been succeeded by Cardinal Bernard Griffin in 1943. Soon after it arrived Griffin was given a private viewing. He saw the monkey, didn't like it and peremptorily ordered Fenning & Co to remove it.

Then the storm broke. During February and March of 1947 *The Catholic Herald* was deluged with letters on the subject, some of them unpublishable. They revealed that no-one had been consulted before the Cardinal's decision - neither Mary Gill (Eric's widow and executor) nor Lawrence Shattock (the Cathedral architect-in-charge who was on holiday at the time), nor even Laurie Cribb, who was still carving the altarpiece when part of it inexplicably disappeared, overnight so to speak. As Mary Gill wrote to Lawrence Shattock from Gill's studio at High Wycombe on 22 November 1946, 'The feeling here about the matter is very acute'. She subsequently pointed out that the altarpiece had not been fully paid for (£400 had been paid of the £500 total) and that she would not have parted with it if she had known of its fate.

Among the first to write to *The Catholic Herald* was Denis Tegetmeier, Gill's son-in-law. He stressed that Gill intended to give the monkey a special symbolic significance. It was an integral part of his conception, not a mere accessory to the saint. David Jones, a close friend and discerning critic of Gill's work, wrote that when the design was executed, the monkey turned out to be one of the more lively parts of the whole work. He explained that Gill 'seemed to be thinking of the ape-ishness in man and, further and more important still, of the whole animal creation, suppliant at the Tree'. Graham Greene, the author, described the removal of the monkey as 'the latest example of clerical ignorance and lack of taste'. Robert Speaight, later Gill's biographer, pointed out that 'if there was no place for the ape at Westminster, perhaps Liverpool, Prinknash or Campion Hall would have been more hospitable'.

Two letters supported the Cardinal's action. One suggested that a monkey never fails to raise a smile and was therefore inappropriate in a Crucifixion scene. The other was from Fr Arthur Rivers, writing from Westminster Cathedral. He believed that Gill's intention was indeed to portray the 'apeishness of man', for the monkey, 'whilst it possessed the limbs of its kind, had no tail, and its head and torso were those of a boy. It was also to be noted that its arms were raised - apparently in prayer - towards the Figure on the

Thomas More and his family. Copied from Hans Holbein's portrait of c.1527 and showing the monkey at bottom right.

Cross'. He added that the adornment of a church had to be in accordance with the laws of sacred art and with accepted Christian tradition. The monkey would 'have achieved little more than a series of distractions, revolutionary and evolutionary'.

The Administrator of the Cathedral, Canon Martin Howlett, was 84 at the time and the Sub-Administrator, Canon Charles Brown, was 79 and had been described as 'ancient' in *The Catholic Times* in 1943. The priest actually running things in the Cathedral was the relatively junior Fr Arthur Rivers who had worked as an architect and then as a banker before becoming a priest. Ordained in 1939 and Prefect of the Sacristy at

The Gill altarpiece as designed. 29 July 1939.

the time he wrote the letter in 1947, the following year Cardinal Griffin made him an honorary Canon at the early age of 37 and appointed him Financial Secretary for the Diocese, (resulting in him being known to the Bartlett children as 'Mr Moneybags'). There seems little doubt that the views in his letter were those of the Cardinal.

Eric Gill's Intentions

So what were Eric Gill's intentions in including the monkey? Clearly the first was to show St Thomas More as a human being. Included in More's household at Chelsea were the monkey, two dogs, rabbits, a fox, a ferret, a weasel and an exotic collection of songbirds in an aviary. In the family portrait which More commissioned from Holbein in 1527, the monkey and a dog are included. More detested blood sports and liked animals. It was just such human characteristics which appealed to Gill. Indeed his own extended family has been compared with that of More. He was fully conversant with More's masterpiece of humanist philosophy *Utopia*, and prepared the lettering for two editions, including proposals for More's *Utopian* alphabet. Gill was not the man to portray a plaster saint.

Eric Gill working on the altarpiece. June 1940.

Secondly, Gill was also reminding us of our own lowliness. Both he and More were essentially humble men. Gill believed there was nothing incongruous in symbolizing mankind in such a way, down on one knee before the Tree of Life. After all, animals have been depicted in churches - Roman, Byzantine and Gothic - throughout history. Indeed the International Society of Sacred Art protested at the removal of the monkey, pointing out that a dangerous precedent was being established by changing the work of an eminent artist after his death. Animals are also often shown with saints. St Jerome is frequently seen accompanied by a lion, St Patrick with snakes, and St Francis, who was not above praying with animals, is portrayed with a wide variety, including a wolf. More wrote to Erasmus that he dreamed of being a Franciscan and the order claims him as a Tertiary. Would he have objected to the monkey?

There is a third possible reason for the inclusion. Animals were often used for symbolic purposes in the Renaissance. A monkey, or ape, was symbolic of the baser instincts of man. More would have known this and, almost certainly, so did Gill. But even if the monkey was intended to have such symbolism, and Gill gave no clear indication of this, in the altarpiece St Thomas More's complete attention is devoted to Our Lord on the Cross. The monkey, down on one knee and reaching upwards, is disregarded. If the animal was to be seen as a distraction, then it is being very obviously ignored.

A work of art cannot be altered without loss of integrity and impact. The altarpiece has lost an important feature and appears unbalanced. Nothing but a few faint traces of the monkey remains. As for Cardinal Griffin, rightly or wrongly he has gone down as the man who didn't like animals (particularly monkeys). But perhaps the final word should come from one of those who wrote to *The Catholic Herald* in February and March 1947. Such a one was Revd Martindale SJ. He wrote: 'Imagine how intrigued children would have been by that monkey! How 'real' it would have made St Thomas seem to us! Goodbye lost opportunity!'

The altarpiece today - without the monkey.

With thanks to John Skelton, Eric Gill's nephew, who, before his death in 1999, allowed access to a pencil and ink drawing by Gill of the altarpiece and monkey dated 29 July 1939. Other pencil drawings by Gill of the altarpiece, numbered UCLA EG 312-314 and dated 20-26 July 1939, are held by the William Andrews Clark Memorial Library of the University of California, Los Angeles.

2. From Lions to Ladybirds

Although of no great historical significance, it is perhaps worth pointing out the remarkable number and variety of animals portrayed in Westminster Cathedral - almost six hundred of them - carved in stone and marble, inlaid in wood, cast in bronze and made up of glittering mosaic tesserae. They range from lions to ladybirds and dolphins to doves.

Mammals

Starting with the king of beasts first, a winged lion is the emblem of St Mark the Evangelist and it appears at the top of the great 30 foot high crucifix which hangs between the nave and the sanctuary, also on the left of the blue sanctuary arch mosaic and finally at the foot of the figure of St Mark on the side of the pulpit. Another lion is on the inner wall of St Paul's Chapel, but this relates to the riddle of Samson 'Out of the strong came forth sweetness' (Judges 14:14) and refers to the conversion of St Paul. In the Vaughan Chantry there are four lion's heads at the corners of Cardinal Vaughan's sarcophagus, and in St Peter's Crypt four more crown one of the great red granite columns. The old Irish regimental badges in St Patrick's Chapel also contain lions - a male for the 8th King's Royal Irish Hussars, while the Royal Munster Fusiliers have a Bengalese tiger and the Royal Dublin Fusiliers have a tiger and an elephant.

St Luke, another Evangelist, has a winged ox as his emblem so this also appears on the great crucifix, in the blue sanctuary arch mosaic, and on the pulpit. It is St Luke's gospel that recounts most about Our Lady and so, in the Lady Chapel at the end of the mosaic pictures which portray her life, St Luke is shown writing, with an ox above him. On the other side, and further up, is another ox in the scene of the Nativity. This includes shepherds and three wise men who have clearly just arrived by camel, two of which are behind them. With the ox is, of course, a donkey (ass) and it appears again further on, carrying Jesus and Mary away on their flight to Egypt. A reliable donkey this, totally unperturbed by the pagan idols shattering as the Holy Family passes by.

Moving to St Andrew's Chapel, roe deer are to be found either side of the Saint on the west wall, with sheep above the altar opposite. There are also twelve marble ram's heads below the cornice in the Lady Chapel and twenty-eight more above the little columns in St Patrick's Chapel. From sheep to lambs, and one is shown on the front of the pulpit representing Christ, the Lamb of God. The same symbol

A roe deer.
The west wall of
St Andrew's Chapel.

appears on the floor of St Joseph's Chapel and in the centre of the vault in the Blessed Sacrament Chapel. Just inside this chapel's entrance arch, guarded by two archangels, Noah is shown on the right about to offer up a lamb after the flood, while Abel on the left is preparing to do the same. Further on, Abraham appears with a ram caught in a thicket which he will also subsequently sacrifice.

Two griffons are portrayed inlaid in the wooden panelling in the sanctuary, though it seems debatable whether such winged, mythical creatures can be classified as mammals. The most recent mammal to arrive in the Cathedral is a bear. It is shown on the shield of one of the assassins of St Thomas Becket on the west wall of the Chapel of St Thomas of Canterbury, also known as the Vaughan Chantry. Across the nave in the Lady Chapel, high up to the right of the entrance, is a mosaic rabbit standing bolt upright and clutching a fir cone. Almost directly opposite on the left of the chapel is a red squirrel, with

Two griffons. The sanctuary wood panelling.

another amongst the foliage in a window arch half way along on the right. Two more squirrels feature in the gilt bronze triptych above the altar in St Joseph's Chapel.

Birds

There are more birds portrayed in the Cathedral than any other animal. Many of these have symbolic meanings or carry a message. To start with there is the eagle, symbol of St John the Evangelist, the youngest of the apostles. This appears at top right in the blue sanctuary arch mosaic, also at the base of the 30 foot high crucifix at the end of the nave, and in marble at the foot of the figure of St John on the pulpit. Another eagle can be found in St Patrick's Chapel - in the badge of the Royal Irish Fusiliers.

A phoenix (symbol of resurrection). The approach to the Blessed Sacrament Chapel.

The Blessed Sacrament Chapel contains a variety of symbolic birds. In a niche on the right in the approach to the entrance is a phoenix, said to rise from its own ashes and the symbol of resurrection. Opposite is a peacock, symbolising immortality and the all-seeing eyes of God. There is another peacock on the floor of St Joseph's Chapel, four more beside the altar in St Paul's Chapel, one in the Lady Chapel and eight at the top of one of the little columns supporting the pulpit. Returning to the Blessed Sacrament Chapel, the next bird is a pelican with three young, in gilt bronze at the top of the entrance arch. It is the symbol of sacrifice since the bird was said to feed its offspring with blood from its own breast. The origin of this was probably the staining of the pelican's feathers with regurgitated fish as it fed its young. Another pelican is at the top of the tabernacle on the altar, and at the other end of the Cathedral are two more, looking very well-fed, in flight above the entrance to the tower.

Probably the most commonly portrayed bird in churches is the dove, since it carries so many messages. Two doves (representing Christians) are shown drinking from a chalice (everlasting life) in the oak panelling on the right of the sanctuary. In the apse above the altar of the Blessed Sacrament Chapel it symbolises the Holy Spirit. On the arch dividing the apse from the nave in this chapel twelve doves symbolise the twelve apostles, while on the right just after the entrance is Noah's dove (looking very similar to a wood pigeon), carrying an olive branch and symbolising peace between God and mankind.

Near the Cathedral entrance at the end of the north aisle is a mosaic of St Francis of Assisi in a niche above a holy water stoup. Surrounding St Francis are some of the birds to which he is said to have preached. The fifty-seven birds to be seen include a hoopoe, a sparrowhawk, two types of owl, kingfishers, bee eaters, storks, a grey heron with two red fish in its bill, and a cuckoo. The mosaic of St Francis is on the side of a great, marble-clad, brick pier facing one of the entrances. On the other side of this pier, in the early years of the Cathedral when there was no marble covering the bricks, there was an almost perfect representation of a small bird on the surface of one of the bricks behind

Noah's dove. The Blessed Sacrament Chapel.

the statue of St Peter. This curiosity was pointed out to visitors by the 'Green Man' - Sgt Crooke who was the Cathedral commissionaire and wore a green uniform. However Mgr Johnson, who was the Diocesan Treasurer and Archbishop Bourne's secretary at the time, strongly disapproved of this and ordered that the bird be removed.

Across the nave in the Chapel of St Gregory and St Augustine, St Gregory is portrayed with his own personal dove - the Holy Spirit of course - whispering into his ear. It is said that his secretary once pulled back a curtain to reveal him being given divine inspiration in this way. The doves next door in St Patrick's Chapel are rather more worldly, twenty-

A magpie on the Tree of Life. The Lady Chapel.

eight of them at the top of the columns below the windows. Nearby in St Andrew's Chapel thirty-three birds are shown in mosaic on the underside of its arches, including three kingfishers, two jays, a moorhen, a green woodpecker and, of course, a dove. Another dove, of the collared variety, is in the foliage above one of the confessionals in the south transept.

On the left of the Lady Chapel is an alert robin above the flower-studded garland which is really a rosary. Then a diving swallow and a blackbird feeding three nestlings. A lark flies in the arch to the left of Our Lady of Perpetual Succour, with two bluetits to her right. Another swallow is above St Dominic with his rosary while below, in the scene of the Annunciation, the dove of the Holy Spirit is again shown above the archangel Gabriel. Two more doves are below the Pieta and further along a chaffinch perches high up above St John.

Above the altar in the Lady Chapel the Tree of Life rises above the living water from which a shelduck is about to drink. In the tree are a magpie, a blackbird, another black bird with a pink head, and a dove. To the right, the window arch below St Agnes contains two more doves, that below St Lucy has four bluetits with a pair of jackdaws underneath, while just one bluetit appears in the arch below St Justina. In the rosary above the windows are first a swallow, then a wagtail and finally a magpie, while over the passage to the sacristy is a very grand peacock. Finally the coronation of Our Lady on the entrance arch is surmounted by a dove.

Insects

Starting with bees, there are six of them on the inner wall of St Paul's Chapel relating (like the lion) to the riddle of Samson and referring to St Paul's conversion. Moving down to the Lady Chapel there are three more bees around a beehive high on the left just inside. The Tree of Life in the Lady Chapel contains within its branches an amazing variety of insects. Five butterflies are to be found, together with a grasshopper, a stag beetle, a dragonfly, a caterpillar, four ladybirds and three other unidentified flying insects. Gilbert Pownall, who designed this mosaic in the 1920s, filled his notebooks with pictures of English insects and birds. The results are to be seen here.

A variety of insects on the Tree of Life. The Lady Chapel.

Two to three feet above and to the right of the head of Christ on the Tree of Life is a bird with a black body and pink head. After completion in 1932 dust, dirt and candle smoke caused the pink head to blend in with the surrounding gold mosaic. As a result all that could be seen was a small black form closely resembling a slug, described by one priest (Canon Francis Bartlett) to visitors as 'surely the least attractive of God's creatures'. Only periodic cleaning of the mosaic revealed the slug to be in fact a bird.

Cardinal Wiseman's dragon. St Peter's Crypt.

Reptiles

From insects to reptiles and down in St Peter's Crypt is the first dragon - a very small and wingless one at the foot of the effigy of Cardinal Wiseman, first Archbishop of Westminster, with his crozier thrust firmly into its mouth. But in the Cathedral above, in the Shrine of the Sacred Heart and St Michael, the archangel can be seen vanquishing a fully grown and savage adult dragon. There is another green dragon on the underside of the Cathedral's great sanctuary arch.

From dragons to serpents and snakes, all of which normally symbolise evil, though on the right of the Blessed Sacrament Chapel is a brazen serpent employed by Moses for healing purposes. On the inner wall of the Chapel of the Holy Souls is the serpent in the Garden of Eden coiled around Adam, with the skull of death in its jaws. Opposite, the same serpent is crushed underfoot by Christ. Crossing the nave to St Patrick's Chapel there are eight snakes decorating the altar and forty-eight more at the top of the pink marble columns below the windows - thirty-two of them with gaping jaws and sharp teeth. Tradition has it that St Patrick expelled the snakes (and thus evil) from Ireland. The mosaic of St Patrick on the left of the entrance of the chapel shows him standing on one.

A crab set in Iona Green marble. St Andrew's Chapel.

Fish

The most unusual fish in the Cathedral are shown in mosaic in the Lady Chapel where the vines around the rosary are emerging from the mouths of eleven fishlike creatures which are all mouths and ears and very little else. Similar creatures appear in the apse mosaic of San Clemente Church in Rome. Across the Cathedral sanctuary, in the apse of the Blessed Sacrament Chapel, two fish are shown on a plate at the feeding of the five thousand while under the three windows on the left are two more fish with the Greek word for fish (IXOYC) between them. This word is made up of the initial letters of the phrase 'Jesus Christ, Son of God, Saviour'. So a fish was a symbol of Christ. There are two more fish (possibly red mullet) in a grey heron's bill among the birds surrounding St Francis of Assisi near the main entrance, while two others appear on St John Fisher's mitre in the altarpiece of St George's Chapel.

Some of St Anthony's congregation. The narthex.

Four dolphins decorate the wooden surround to the Archbishop's throne in the sanctuary, with two more and a swordfish in mosaic in St Peter's Crypt, while a fish also appears on the floor of St Joseph's Chapel and another is shown leaping in a pool in the mosaic at the entrance to St George's Chapel. But it is in St Andrew's Chapel across the nave that fish really hold sway. St Andrew, like his brother St Peter, was of course a fisherman and there are twenty-nine fish and other marine creatures set in Iona Green marble amidst the waves on the floor, including another swordfish, cod, skate, sole, plaice, salmon, rays, eels, a lobster and two crabs, a starfish, anemone, whelk and scallop.

And finally to St Anthony of Padua, whose shrine is in the narthex near the Baptistry. He appears both in the form of a wooden statue carved from a tree trunk, and in mosaic surrounded by the fish to which he is said to have preached. Not just fish because his congregation here includes sea anemones, sea urchins, starfish and tube worms, as well as three jelly-fish which appear at the top. One of the fish carries a gold ring in its mouth - a reference to St Anthony finding things that are lost.

A fish (symbol of Christ). The floor of St Joseph's Chapel.

Adding them all together there are 45 insects, 73 reptiles and 153 fish and other marine creatures in the Cathedral. There are also 83 mammals and 229 birds, altogether making up a total of 583 living creatures, surely more than in any other church in the country.

PART VIII

SOURCES

A view from the top of the tower looking south.

Sources

Part I. Before the Cathedral

I.1. Tothill Fields

John Stow, *A Survey of London written in the year 1598*, Sutton Publishing; Henry Mayhew and John Binney, *Criminal Prisons of London*, Griffin, Bohn & Co 1862; *Westminster Cathedral Chronicle*, 12.1909, 8.10, 9.10; Winefride de l'Hôpital, *Westminster Cathedral and its Architect*, Hutchinson 1919; George Cunningham, *London*, Dent & Sons 1927; Wilfrid Scott-Giles, *The History of Emanuel School*, Old Emanuel Association 1977; Peter Cunningham, *A Handbook of London*, E P Publishing 1978; *The Blewcoat School*, National Trust 1988; Vera Burrell, *Lessons from the Past: A History of the Grey Coat Hospital 1698-1998*, Gresham Books 1998; Simon Bradley and Nikolaus Pevsner, *The Buildings of England: Westminster*, Yale University Press 2003; Liza Goddard, *Victorian London*, Weidenfeld & Nicolson 2005; Peter Whitfield, *London: A life In Maps*, British Library 2006; *Oremus*, 7/8.2007; Weinreb, Hibbert and Keay, *The London Encyclopaedia*, MacMillan 2008; Maps of London by Rocque 1746, Horwood 1792-99 and 1819, Chelsea Water Works (plan) 1815; Cruchley 1829, Stanford 1862, Cassell 1863, Ordnance Survey 1869 and 1913, Bacon 1883; Information from the City of Westminster Archive Centre.

I.2. The House of Correction

Henry Mayhew, *London Labour and the London Poor*, Griffin, Bohn & Co 1861-62; Henry Mayhew and John Binney, *Criminal Prisons of London*, Griffin, Bohn & Co 1862; *Westminster Cathedral Chronicle,* 12.1909, 8.10, 9.10; Winefride de 1'Hôpital, *Westminster Cathedral and its Architect*, Hutchinson 1919; Weinreb, Hibbert and Keay, *The London Encyclopaedia*, Macmillan 2008; Information from the City of Westminster Archive Centre.

I.3. We might have been Gothic!

J G Snead-Cox, *The Life of Cardinal Vaughan*, Burns & Oates 1910; Winefride de l'Hôpital, *Westminster Cathedral and its Architect*, Hutchinson 1919; J Fairfax Blakeborough, *Sykes of Sledmere*, London 1929; Shane Leslie, *Letters of Herbert Cardinal Vaughan to Lady Herbert of Lea*, Burns & Oates 1942; Norbert Wibiral and Nikolaus Pevsner, *A Westminster Cathedral Episode* in *Architectural History* 20, 1977; C S Sykes, *The Visitors Book*, Weidenfeld & Nicholson 1978; Penelope Hunting, *From Gothic to Red Brick* in *Country Life* 28.2.1980; Christopher Simon Sykes, *The Big House*, Harper Collins 2004; *The Oxford Dictionary of National Biography*.

I.4. But is it Byzantine?

W R Lethaby and Harold Swainson, *The Church of Sancta Sophia Constantinople: A Study of Byzantine Building*, Macmillan 1894; Letter from J F Bentley to Charles Hadfield dated 5.7.1895 in P Howell (Ed), *Architectural History* 25, 1982; *The Tablet*, 6.7.1895, 21.3.1903; *Westminster Cathedral Record*, 1.1896, 4.96, 7.96, 10.96; Winefride de 1'Hôpital, *Westminster Cathedral and its Architect*, Hutchinson 1919; Richard Krautheimer, *Early Christian and Byzantine Architecture*, Pelican History of Art 1965; S G A Luff, *The Christian's Guide to Rome*, Burns & Oates 1967; Michael Maclagan, *The City of Istanbul*, Thames & Hudson 1968; Jane Taylor, *Imperial Istanbul*, Weidenfeld & Nicholson 1989; Giuseppe Bovini, *Ravenna Art and History*, A Longo Editori 1991; Fatih Cimok, *Hagia Sophia*, Yayinlari, Istanbul 1995; Kenneth Powell, *A Hymn to Byzantium* in *The Architects Journal* 22.6.1995; F Matthews, *The Art of Byzantium*, Weidenfeld & Nicholson 1998; E Vio, *The Basilica of St Mark in Venice*, Scala 1999; David Watkin, *A History of Western Architecture*, Laurence King 2000; E Vio, St Mark's: *The Art and Architecture of Church and State in Venice*, Riverside Book Co, New York 2003; *Byzantium 330-1453*, Royal Academy of Arts 2009.

I.5. Beginnings

Letters from J F Bentley to Charles Hadfield dated 5.7.1895, 16.1.99, 4.2.99, 13.1.1902, 28.2.02 in Peter Howell (Ed), *Architectural History* 25, 1982; *The Tablet*, 6.7.1895, 13.5.99, 17.6.99, 29.12.1900, 7.6.02; *Westminster Cathedral Record*, 1.1896, 4.96, 7.96, 10.96, 2.97, 12.97, 2.99; *The Architectural Review*, 5.1902, 7.02, 3.03; Charles Hadfield, *Westminster Cathedral*, Paper read before the Royal Institute of British Architects, 16.3.1903; J A Marshall, Paper read before the Architectural Association 12.4.1907 and summarised in *The Builder*, 20.4.1907; J G Snead-Cox, *The Life of Cardinal Vaughan*, Burns & Oates 1910; Winefride de l 'Hôpital, *Westminster Cathedral and its Architect*, Hutchinson 1919; *Westminster Cathedral Chronicle*, 6.1955; A S G Butler, *John Francis Bentley*, Burns & Oates 1961; Peter Doyle, *Westminster Cathedral 1895-1995*, Geoffrey Chapman 1995; Kenneth Powell, *A Hymn to Byzantium* in *The Architects Journal* 22.6.1995.

I.6. A Cathedral in Miniature

Letter from J F Bentley to Charles Hadfield dated 16.1.1899 in P Howell (Ed), *Architectural History* 25, 1982; *Westminster Cathedral Record*, 2.1899; *The Tablet*, 17.6.1899; Census Record for West Square, Southwark, 1901; J A Marshall, Paper read before the Architectural Association 12.4.1907 and summarised in *The Builder*, 20.4.1907; *Westminster Cathedral Chronicle*, 10.1919; Winefride de l'Hôpital, *Westminster Cathedral and its Architect*, Hutchinson 1919; Letters from Farmer & Brindley to Mgr A Jackman at Westminster Cathedral dated 10.10.1921, 23.12.21; *Oremus*, 5.2010, 7/8.2011.

Part II. Liturgy and Music

II.1. The Choir that never was

The Tablet, 6.7.1895, 13.5.99, 29.12.1900, 7.6.02, 21.3.03; *Westminster Cathedral Record*, 2.1899; J G Snead-Cox, *The Life of Cardinal Vaughan*, Burns & Oates 1910; Richard Terry, *Westminster Cathedral Music* in the *Book of the Consecration of Westminster Cathedral* 1910; Winefride de l'Hôpital, *Westminster Cathedral and its Architect*, Hutchinson 1919; *Westminster Cathedral Chronicle*, 5.1925, 8.43, 7.55; Shane Leslie, *Letters of Herbert Cardinal Vaughan to Lady Herbert of Lea*, Burns & Oates 1942; A S G Butler, *John Francis Bentley*, Burns & Oates 1961; A Mill Hill Father, *Remembered in Blessing: The Courtfield Story*, London 1969; Rene Kollar, *Westminster Cathedral: From Dream to Reality*, Faith and Life Publications 1987; Rene Kollar, *The Return of the Benedictines to London*, Burns & Oates 1989; Peter Doyle, *Westminster Cathedral 1895-1995*, Geoffrey Chapman 1995; *Oremus*, 6.2007.

II.2. The First Cathedral Parish

Kelly's London Post Office Directory (Streets) for Horseferry Road and Medway Street, 1855; *The Universe*, 14.2.1903, 21.3.03; *The Catholic Herald*, 20.2.1903, 27.3.03; *The Tablet*, 21.3.1903, 11.4.03, 18.4.03, 6.6.03, 18.7.03; *Westminster Cathedral Chronicle*, 2.1907, 8.10, 9.10, 9.24, 10.24, 8.43, 9.43, 7.55; J G Snead-Cox, *The Life of Cardinal Vaughan*, Burns & Oates 1910; Winefride de l'Hôpital, *Westminster Cathedral and its Architect*, Hutchinson 1919; Shane Leslie, *Letters of Herbert Cardinal Vaughan to Lady Herbert of Lea*, Burns & Oates 1942; *Oremus*, 3.2003, 9.03.

II.3. Death of a Cardinal

The Tablet, 6.7.1895, 21.3.1903, 2.5.03, 13.6.03, 27.6.03, 19.12.03, 26.12.03, 2.1.04; *The Catholic Herald*, 25.4.1902, 16.5.02, 18.7.02, 15.8.02, 20.2.03, 20.3.03, 27.3.03, 1.5.03, 15.5.03, 12.6.03, 1.1.04; *The Universe*, 14.2.1903, 21.3.03; *The Illustrated London News*, 27.6.1903, 2.1.04; J G Snead-Cox, *The Life of Cardinal Vaughan*, Burns & Oates 1910; Winefride de l'Hôpital, *Westminster Cathedral and its Architect*, Hutchinson 1919; Shane

Leslie, *Letters of Herbert Cardinal Vaughan to Lady Herbert of Lea*, Burns & Oates 1942; *Westminster Cathedral Chronicle*, 8.1943, 9.43, 10.43, 11.43; John Cleary, *Westminster Cathedral: The First 70 Years*, London 1973; Peter Doyle, *Westminster Cathedral 1895-1995*, Geoffrey Chapman 1995; *Oremus*, 6.2003, 6.07; Michael J Walsh, *The Westminster Cardinals*, Burns & Oates 2008.

II.4. A Sequence of Organs

Guide to Westminster Cathedral, Burns & Oates 1902; *The Tablet*, 21.3.1903, 31.3.03, 26.12.03; *Westminster Cathedral Chronicle*, 3.1907, 7.07, 5.13, 10.21, 1.22, 4.22, 6.22, 7.22, 7.23, 6.24, 8.25, 1.27, 6.27, 1.32, 2.32, 4.32, 8.55, 10.55, 3.56, 4.56; Richard Terry, *Westminster Cathedral Music* in the *Book of the Consecration of Westminster Cathedral* 1910; Winefride de 1'Hôpital, *Westminster Cathedral and its Architect*, Hutchinson 1919; Henry Willis, *Westminster Cathedral: Grand and Apse Organs*, 1927; Harrison & Harrison, *Westminster Cathedral: The Organs*, 1984; *Westminster Cathedral Bulletin*, 2.1994, 2.96; James O'Donnell, *Music at Westminster Cathedral*, 1995; Peter Doyle, Westminster Cathedral 1885-1995, Geoffrey Chapman 1995; *Oremus*, 9.2000, 11.02.

Part III. Creation and Survival

III.1. St Edward's Tower

Westminster Cathedral Record, 1.1896, 7.96; *The Tablet*, 7.6.1902, 10.1.03, 31.3.03, 17.10.03; Guide to Westminster Cathedral, Burns & Oates 1902; *The Catholic Herald*, 20.2.1903; Winefride de 1'Hôpital, *Westminster Cathedral and its Architect*, Hutchinson, 1919; Westminster Cathedral Chronicle, 2.1929, 7.55; *The Daily Telegraph*, 1.8.1929; *The Times*, 1.8.1929; *The Daily Chronicle*, 13.9.1929; Catholic Truth Society Guidebook, 1939; Shane Leslie, *Letters of Herbert Cardinal Vaughan to Lady Herbert of Lea*, Burns & Oates 1942; Photos of religious services held during construction of the tower (The Beckenham ladies) 9.11.1956.

III.2. Let There be Light

W R Lethaby and Harold Swainson, *The Church of Sancta Sophia, Constantinople: A Study of Byzantine Building*, Macmillan 1894; *The Tablet*, 6.7.1895, 29.12.1900; *Westminster Cathedral Record*, 1.1896, 7.96, 10.96; *The Catholic Herald*, 20.2.1903; *Westminster Cathedral Chronicle*, 12.1910; Winefride de l'Hôpital, *Westminster Cathedral and its Architect*, Hutchinson 1919; A S G Butler, *John Francis Bentley*, Burns & Oates 1961; Gavin Stamp, *Robert Weir Schultz, Architect, and his Work for the Marquesses of Bute*, Mount Stuart 1981; Teresa Sladen, *Byzantium in the Chancel: Surface Decoration and the Church Interior*, in *Churches 1870-1914*, The Victorian Society, London 2011.

III.3. The Great Rood

Westminster Cathedral Record, 1.1896; *The Tablet*, 7.6.1902, 19.12.03; Letters between Cardinal Vaughan and W C Symons dated 17.1.1903, 22.2.03, 10.3.03, 3.4.03, 29.12.03; Letters from W C Symons to Bentley, Son & Marshall dated 24.1.1903, 24.4.03; *The Catholic Herald*, 20.2.1903, 29.5.03, 14.8.03, 28.8.03; Letters from W C Symons to Canon Johnson dated 18.6.1903, 13.7.03; *The Illustrated London News*, 19.12.1903; Letter from Revd Herbert Lucas to W C Symons dated 10.1.1904; *The Builder*, 21.1.1904; Winefride de 1'Hôpital, *Westminster Cathedral and its Architect*, Hutchinson 1919; *Westminster Cathedral Chronicle*, 1.1934, 1.35, 2.37; Ernest Oldmeadow, *Francis Cardinal Bourne*, Burns, Oates & Washbourne 1944; John Browne and Tim Dean, *Westminster Cathedral: Building of Faith*, Booth-Clibborn 1995; Peter Doyle, *Westminster Cathedral 1895-1995*, Geoffrey Chapman 1995; Letter from Nigel Leaney re carving of the rood in Bruges dated 8.12.2005; Cathedral architectural drawings numbered A-8, B-22, B-23, B-24, B-25, B-26, B-34, F-84.

III.4. The Baldacchino

The Tablet, 7.6.1902; Letter from Revd Herbert Lucas in *The Tablet*, 19.9.1903; Letter from Bernard Whelan in *The Tablet*, 22.12.1906; *The Graphic,* 5.1.1907; Guide to Westminster Cathedral, 1913; *Westminster Cathedral Chronicle*, 4.1914, 11.55; Winefride de 1'Hôpital, *Westminster Cathedral and its Architect*, Hutchinson 1919; Shane Leslie, *Letters of Herbert Cardinal Vaughan to Lady Herbert of Lea*, Burns & Oates 1942; *Oremus*, 12.2006; Cathedral architectural drawings numbered B-21, B-22, B-23, B-24, B-25, B-26, B-27, B-28, B-29, B-30, B-31, B-32, B-33, B-34, B-35, B-36, B-38, B-40.

III.5. A Tale of Five Pulpits

Westminster Cathedral Record, 1.1896, 4.86; *The Tablet*, 7.6.1902; *The Catholic Herald*, 12.6.1903; *Westminster Cathedral Chronicle*, 5.1914, 6.29, 1.34, 9.34, 10.34, 11.55; Winefride de l'Hôpital, *Westminster Cathedral and its Architect*, Hutchinson 1919; *The Times*, 16.8.1934; Ernest Oldmeadow, *Francis Cardinal Bourne*, Burns, Oates & Washbourne 1944; Letter from Ditta Paolo Medici & Figlio, Rome, dated 14.6.1988; John Browne and Tim Dean, *Westminster Cathedral: Building of Faith*, Booth-Clibborn 1995; Peter Doyle, *Westminster Cathedral 1895-1995*, Geoffrey Chapman 1995; Cathedral architectural drawings numbered H-34, H-37, 13696.

III.6. Cathedral Bronzes

The Tablet, 3.6.1899, 10.6.99, 7.6.1902; *The Catholic Herald*, 15.8.1902, 20.2.03; *Westminster Cathedral Chronicle*, 10.1909, 2.10, 12.10, 3.12, 5.12, 6.12, 11.13, 9.17, 7.23, 4.44, 9.47, 11.49, 4.50, 5.58, 7.58, 6.60, 3.61, 10.67; Letter from J A Marshall to Mgr A Jackman dated 6.8.1919; Winefride de l'Hôpital, *Westminster Cathedral and its Architect*, Hutchinson 1919; Cathedral Art and Architecture Committee Minutes, 24.1.1956; Letter from Arthur Pollen to Mgr Gordon Wheeler dated 3.4.1960; Robert Maillard, *A Dictionary of Modern Sculpture*, Methuen 1962; *Westminster Cathedral News Sheet*, 3.1969, 6.69, 7.69; *Westminster Cathedral Journal*, 6.1972; *The Friends of Westminster Cathedral Newsletter*, Spring 1984; *Westminster Cathedral Bulletin*, 11.1993; John Browne and Tim Dean, *Westminster Cathedral: Building of Faith*, Booth-Clibborn 1995; Joan Cerrito, *Contemporary Artists*, St James 1996; *Oremus*, 7/8.1998, 11.98, 7/8.99, 10.99, 11.99.

III.7. The Stations of the Cross

Westminster Cathedral Chronicle, 3.1909, 10.13, 12.15, 9.16, 2.18, 3.18, 4.18; Eric Gill drawings numbered 1920-12-11-1 dated Spring (April) 1914, the British Museum, Department of Prints and Drawings; *The Universe*, letters 30.7.1915 - 5.11.15; *The Observer*, articles 3.10.1915, 17.10.15, letters 10.10.1915 - 28.11.15; *The Builder*, 5.11.1915; *The New Witness*, 4.11.1915; Winefride de 1'Hôpital, *Westminster Cathedral and its Architect*, Hutchinson 1919; Eric Gill, *Autobiography*, Jonathan Cape 1940; Walter Shewring (Ed), *Letters of Eric Gill*, Jonathan Cape 1947; Robert Speaight, *The Life of Eric Gill*, Methuen 1966; Donald Attwater, *A Cell of Good Living*, Geoffrey Chapman 1969; Malcolm Yorke, *Eric Gill, Man of Flesh and Spirit*, Constable 1981; *The Friends of Westminster Cathedral Newsletters*, Autumn 1985, Spring 1986; Fiona MacCarthy, *Eric Gill*, Faber & Faber 1989; Judith Collins, *Eric Gill: The Sculpture*, Herbert Press 1998; Eric Gill sketches for the Stations of the Cross, Victoria and Albert Museum, Department of Prints and Drawings; Cathedral architectural drawings, folder numbered C-5 (George Daniels sketches) and Eric Gill sketches (unnumbered).

III.8. The Russian in the Crypt

The Tablet, 16.12.1916, 23.12.16, 20.1.17, 27.1.17, 7.4.17; *The Times*, 12.1.1917, 13.1.17, 15.1.17, 16.1.17, 23.1.17; *The Westminster Gazette*, 15.1.1917, 22.1.17; *Westminster Cathedral Chronicle*, 2.1917, 3.40; *Westminster Cathedral Bulletin*, 7/8.1993; Sheila Fitzpatrick, *The Russian Revolution*, OUP 1994; Information from Mrs Humphrey Brooke (Count Alexander Benckendorff's grand-daughter), Sir Adam Ridley, and Count Constantine Benckendorff (Count Alexander Benckendorff's great-grandsons), 30.5.2005 - 24.5.2007.

III.9. The Parish Priest of Westminster

Bernard Ward, *History of St Edmund's College, Old Hall*, Kegan Paul, Trench, Trubner & Co 1893; Albert B Purdie, *The Life of Blessed John Southworth, Priest and Martyr*, Burns, Oates & Washbourne 1930; *Westminster Cathedral Chronicle*, 5.1930, 6.30, 7.30, 8.30, 2.34, 1.55; Geoffrey Anstruther O.P, *A Hundred Homeless Years*, Blackfriars 1958; Geoffrey Anstruther O.P, *St John Southworth, Priest and Martyr*, CTS 1981; *Oremus*, 6.1999, 7/8.99, 6.2002, 6.04; Michael Archer, *St John Southworth*, CTS 2010; Nicholas Schofield and Gerard Skinner, *St John Southworth, The Parish Priest of Westminster*, St Pauls 2012; *British Catholics in Douai*, Musée de la Chartreuse, Douai, France; *Douai, Ville d'Art*, Office de Tourisme, Douai, France; *The Oxford Dictionary of National Biography*; Information from Arundel Castle, West Sussex.

III.10. Our Lady of Westminster

Philip Nelson, *The Archaeological Journal*, 1925; A Rostand, *Les Albâtres Anglais du XVe Siècle en Basse-Normandie*, 1928; W L Hildburgh, *Antiquaries Journal*, 1937; W L Hildburgh in *The Burlington Magazine*, 1946, 1955; *The Connoisseur*, June 1955; *The Tablet*, 10.12.1955; *Westminster Cathedral Chronicle*, 12.1955; H M Gillett, *Shrines of Our Lady in England and Wales*, Samuel Walker 1957; Francis Cheetham, *Medieval English Alabaster Carvings*, Nottingham 1973; Musée d'Aquitaine, *Sculpture Médiévale de Bordeaux et du Bordelais*, 1976; Colin Platt, *Parish Churches of Medieval England*, Secker & Warburg 1981; Francis Cheetham, *English Medieval Alabasters*, Oxford 1984; Leigh and Podmore, *Outstanding Churches in Craven*, 1985; *Westminster Cathedral Bulletin*, 11.1995; *Sculptures d'Albâtre du Moyen Age*, Rouen 1998; *Les Sculptures Anglaises d'Albâtre*, Cluney Museum, Paris 1998; Letter from Brimo de Laroussilhe, Paris, dated 28.5.1999; *Guide to All Saints Church* (undated), Broughton-in-Craven.

III.11. The Cathedral in Wartime

Westminster Cathedral Chronicle, 10.1914, 2.15, 6.15, 4.16, 9.16, 10.16, 7.17, 8.17, 10.17, 2.18, 9.39, 10.39, 6.40, 10.40, 11.40, 5.41, 1.42, 9.42, 9.43, 9.44, 12.44, 9.45, 11.45 (L H Shattock, *The Cathedral and the Blitz*), 6.46, 5.49; Letter from J A Marshall to Fr Coote dated 27.12.1918; Minutes of the Advisory Committee on the Decoration of Westminster Cathedral, 2.3.1939 - 18.8.1942; Letter from G L Smith to Archbishop Hinsley dated 15.11.1939; Letter from L H Shattock to G L Smith dated 22.11.1940; Letter from H S Goodhart-Rendel to G L Smith dated 19.12.1940; Letter from G L Smith to Mgr Elwes dated 12.1.1941; Letter from Mgr Elwes to G L Smith dated 16.1.1941; *The Catholic Times*, 24.12.1943; *Westminster Cathedral News Sheet*, 12.1968; *Westminster Cathedral Bulletin*, 5.1992, 12.93; John Travers Clarke, *More Backward Glances*.

Part IV. The Cathedral Marbles

IV.1. A Tour of the Marbles

The Tablet, 29.12.1900; *Westminster Cathedral Chronicle*, 1907-1967; John Watson, *British and Foreign Marbles and Other Ornamental Stones*, Cambridge 1916; Winefride de l'Hôpital, *Westminster Cathedral and its Architect*, Hutchinson, 1919; Mgr Canon Francis Bartlett, Annotated Photographs of the Cathedral, 1954-56; Mgr Canon Francis Bartlett, *The Friends of Westminster Cathedral Newsletters*, Spring and Autumn 1989; J B Ward-Perkins, *Marble in Antiquity*, British School at Rome 1992; *Westminster Cathedral Bulletin*, 5.1995, 6.95; *Oremus*, 11.2000; Cathedral architectural drawings; Information from Gerald Culliford of Gerald Culliford Ltd, Ian Macdonald of McMarmilloyd Ltd, Henry Buckley and Dave Smith of the Natural History Museum in London, Monica Price of Oxford University Museum of Natural History and Tom Heldal of Norway's Geological Survey, Trondheim.

IV.2. Identifying the Marbles

G H Blagrove, *Marble Decoration and the Terminology of British and Foreign Marbles*, London 1888; *Westminster Cathedral Record*, 1896-1902; *The Tablet*, 29.12.1900; *Westminster Cathedral Chronicle*, 1907-67; W G Renwick, *Marble and Marble Working*, London, 1909; *The Builder*, 10.12.1915; John Watson, *British and Foreign Marbles and Other Ornamental Stones*, Cambridge 1916; Winefride de l'Hôpital, *Westminster Cathedral and its Architect*, Hutchinson 1919; Mario Catello, *Il Piemonte Marmifero*, Turin 1929; G M Davies, *The Geology of London and South-East England*, Chapter 16, Thomas Murby 1939; M Grant, *The Marbles and Granites of the World*, London 1955; Mgr Canon Francis Bartlett, Annotated Photographs of the Cathedral, 1954-56; Letters between Mary Winearls Porter and Mgr Canon Francis Bartlett dated 13.1.1965, 21.1.65, 2.2.65; Mgr Canon Francis Bartlett, *The Friends of Westminster Cathedral Newsletters*, Spring and Autumn 1989; Cathedral architectural plans and drawings; Royal Commission on Historic Monuments, Vol 17 *County Hall*, Athlone Press 1991; *TRE Annual Lapidei* 1996, 1997, Conegliano, Italy; International Italmarmi SRL, Massa, Carrara, Italy; Information from: Mrs Pia Bruno Allasio, Mondovi, Cuneo, Italy, 1996-2000; Prof Vanni Badino, Turin University Mining Department, Piedmont, Italy, 2000; Aelred Bartlett, 2000-2; Jacques Dubarry de Lassale, *Identifying Marble*, Editions H Vial, Paris 2000; Monica T Price, *Decorative Stone: The Complete Sourcebook*, Thames & Hudson 2007; Information from: Department of Mineralogy, Natural History Museum, London; Oxford University Museum of Natural History; Sedgwick Museum of Geology, Cambridge; Trinity College Museum, Dublin; Office of Public Works, 51 St Stephen's Green, Dublin; Gerald Culliford, Gerald Culliford Ltd, Kingston, Surrey; Ian Macdonald, McMarmilloyd Ltd, Great Bedwyn, Wiltshire.

IV.3. The Lost Columns

John Ruskin, *The Stones of Venice*, Dent 1851; W R Lethaby and Harold Swainson, *The Church of Sancta Sophia, Constantinople: A Study of Byzantine Building*, Macmillan 1894; *Westminster Cathedral Record*, 2.1899; *The Tablet*, 13.5.1899, 29.12.1900, 7.6.02; Winefride de l'Hôpital, *Westminster Cathedral and its Architect*, Hutchinson 1919; Henry Tristram, *Cardinal Newman and the Church of Birmingham Oratory*, Birmingham 1934; Shane Leslie, *Letters of Herbert Cardinal Vaughan to Lady Herbert of Lea*, Burns & Oates 1942; Westminster Cathedral Guidebook, 1913; *Westminster Cathedral Chronicle*, 4.1914, 5.49; Paul Chavasse, *The Birmingham Oratory Church*; Cathedral architectural drawing numbered F-65.

IV.4. A Pavement Like the Sea

W R Lethaby, *Architecture, Mysticism and Myth*, London 1891; *Westminster Cathedral Record*, 2.1899; Letter from J F Bentley to Charles Hadfield dated 29.12.1901 in Peter Howell (Ed), *Architectural History* 25, 1982; Norwich Union Insurance Company Minutes for 1901; *The Tablet*, 7.6.1902; *The Catholic Herald*, 14.8.1903; *The Architectural Review*, 1.1908; W G Renwick, *Marble and Marble Working*, London 1909; Winefride de l'Hôpital, *Westminster Cathedral and its Architect*, Hutchinson 1919; Shane Leslie, *Letters of Herbert Cardinal Vaughan to Lady Herbert of Lea*, Burns & Oates 1942; *Westminster Cathedral Chronicle*, 9.1943, 7.55; Edward Skipper, *Celebrating Skipper 1880-1990* (undated pamphlet); Stefan Muthesius, *The Marble Hall: G J Skipper and the Norwich Union* (undated pamphlet); Norwich Union brochures *Surrey House, Inside Surrey House, The Surrey House Marble*; Corporation of London, *Guide to the Old Bailey*, 1992; Cathedral architectural drawings numbered F-52, F-86, F-87.

Part V. Cathedral Mosaics

V.1. Mosaics and Methods

Pliny the Elder, *Natural History* Book 36; W R Lethaby and H Swainson, *The Church of Sancta Sophia, Constantinople: A Study of Byzantine Building*, Macmillan 1894; Giuseppe Bovini, *Ravenna Mosaics*, George Rainbird 1957; Giorgio Vasari, *Vasari on Technique*, Dover 1960; W Oakeshott, *Mosaics of Rome*, Thames and Hudson 1967; S G A Luff, *The Christian's Guide to Rome*, Burns and Oates 1967; John Beckwith, *Early Christian and Byzantine Art*, Penguin Books 1970; Dr Ante Sonje, *Porec Eufrasian Basilica*, Porec Pazin 1987; Giuseppe Bovini, *Ravenna Art and History*, A Longo Editori 1991; Giuseppe Schiro, *Monreale - City of the Golden Temple*, Edizioni Mistretta, Palermo 1992; M Farneti, *Glossorio Tecnico-Storico del Mosaico*, A Longo Editori, Ravenna 1993; Fatih Cimok, *Hagia Sophia*, Yayinlari, Istanbul 1995; *St Saviour in Chora*, Yayinlari, Istanbul 1995; *I Colori della Luce - Angelo Orsoni e l'Arte del Mosaico*, Marsilio Editori 1996; F Matthews, *The Art of Byzantium*, Weidenfeld and Nicholson 1998; P Ling, *Ancient Mosaics*, British Museum Press 1998; Giuseppe Schiro, *The Palatine Chapel*, Casa Editrice Mistretta 1999; E Vio, T*he Basilica of St Mark in Venice*, Scala 1999; E Goodwin, *The Art of Decorative Mosaics*, Crowood Press 1999; E Vio, St Mark's - *The Art and Architecture of Church and State in Venice*, Riverside Book Co, New York 2003.

V.2. The First Mosaics

Letters from J F Bentley to C Hadfield dated 17.2.1899, 22.2.99, 1.3.99 in P Howell (Ed), *Architectural History* 25, 1982; *Westminster Cathedral Record*, 18.2.1899, 13.5.99, 17.6.99; Letters between J F Bentley and W C Symons dated 6.3.1899 - 20.10.1901; *The Tablet*, 13.5.1899, 1.6.1901, 28.12.01, 14.11.03; G Bridge in *The Builders Journal and Architectural Record*, 27.9.1899, 18.10.99, 13.12.99; Kellys London Post Office Directories (Commercial and Trades), entries for Clayton & Bell, Salviati & Co, Venice & Murano Glass and Mosaic Co 1900-05; James Powell & Sons, Window Glass Order Book entries for 3.1901, 6.01, 8.01, Cash Book entries for 5.01, 7.01, 11.01; Horniman Museum Annual Report 1901-02; Letters from W C Symons to Cardinal Vaughan dated 17.1.1903, 7.5.03; Letters from Bentley, Son & Marshall to W C Symons dated 22.1.1903 - 5.12.1910; *The Universe*, 25.4.1903; *Westminster Gazette*, 29.4.03; Letter from G Bridge to W C Symons dated 30.4.1903; Letters between H Lucas and W C Symons dated 16.11.1903 - 22.11.05; Letter from W C Symons to Cardinal Bourne dated 29.12.1903; *The Catholic Times*, 20.10.1905, 27.10.05, 10.11.05; *Westminster Cathedral Chronicle*, 3.1909, 6.10, 9.10, 1.11, 4.11, 10.11, 11.11, 2.12, 9.16, 7.28, 3.32; Letters from J A Marshall to Mgr Jackman dated 7.8.1913, 31.5.16, 22.1.18; *The Observer*, 3.10.1915, 12.10.15, 28.11.15; James Powell & Sons, Window Glass Order and Cash Books entries 4092 of 27.11.1915 and 5.8.16; Winefride de l'Hôpital, *Westminster Cathedral and its Architect*, Hutchinson 1919; Wendy Evans et al, *James Powell & Sons of London*, Museum of London 1995; *William Christian Symons 1845-1911*, Rye Art Gallery 1999; Letter from Robin Imray (Ethel Linfield's grandson) dated 18.l0.1999; J Cram and A Coldwells, *The Albert Chapel, the Frogmore Mausoleum*, Jarrold 1999; Sheldon Barr, *Venetian Glass Mosaics 1860-1817*, Antique Collectors Club 2008; Letters from Paul Bentley dated 21.11.2008, 11.4.09, 18.10.10; Nikolaus Pevsner et al, *The Buildings of England* series.

V.3. The Arts and Crafts Men

W R Lethaby, *Architecture, Mysticism and Myth*, London 1891;*Westminster Cathedral Record*, October 1896, 29.1.1900; R W Schultz, *Byzantine Art* in *The Architectural Review* 1897; C Harrison Townsend, *The Art of Pictorial Mosaic*, RIBA Journal 23.3.1901; R Anning Bell, *Notes on the Practice of Pictorial Mosaic*, RIBA Journal 23.11.1901; The Horniman Museum Annual Report 1901-02; *Westminster Cathedral Chronicle*, 3.1907, 3.10, 4.10, 1.13, 2.13, 4.13, 10.13, 1.14, 8.14, 12.15, 3.16, 4.16, 7.16, 9.16, 1.22, 9.28, 2.29, 1.34; Letters from J H Marshall to W C Symons dated 1.4.1910, 24.4.10; Letters from J H Marshall to Mgr A Jackman dated 12.4.1912, 7.8.13, 11.4.14; Letter from R Anning Bell to J H Marshall dated 14.6.1912, to Mgr A Jackman dated 20.9.1913; Undated (1913) note by J H Marshall listing the designers of the Cathedral Stations of the Cross; James Powell & Sons, Window Glass Order Book entry for 6.10.1914, Cash Book entries for 6.10.14, 12.10.14, 13.4.15, 5.8.16; Henry Holiday, *Reminiscences of My Life*, Heinemann 1914; *The Times*, 7.1.1915, 28.11.33. 29.2.52; *The Scotsman*, 29.11.1915; *The Building News and Architectural Review*, 1.12.1915; *The Builder*, 10.12.1915, 3.3.16; *Country Life*, 8.1.1916; *The Observer*, 23.1.16, 6.2.16; W Curtis Green, *Recent Decoration at the Roman Catholic Cathedral, Westminster* in *The Architectural Review*, 7.1916: Winefride de l'Hôpital, *Westminster Cathedral and its Architect*, Hutchinson 1919; Letter from M Josey to E Hutton dated 8.12.1933; Robert W S Weir, *William Richard Lethaby*, Central School of Arts and Crafts, 1938; David Ottewill, *Robert Weir Schultz (1860-1951): An Arts and Crafts Architect* in *Architectural History* 22, 1979; Gavin Stamp, *Robert Weir Schultz, Architect, and his Work for the Marquesses of Bute*, Mount Stuart 1981; A S Gray, *Edwardian Architecture*, Duckworth 1985; A Carruthers and M Greensted, *The Arts and Crafts Collection at Cheltenham*, Cheltenham Art Gallery and Museums 1994; *Dictionary of Scottish Architects, Robert Weir Schultz.*

V.4. A Dream and a Petition

Westminster Cathedral Record, 29.1.1899, 18.2.99; Letter from J F Bentley to C Hadfield dated 17.2.1899 in P Howell (Ed), *Architectural History* 25, 1982; *The Catholic Times*, 20.10.1905, 27.10.05, 10.11.05, 17.11.05, 5.2.32, 26.2.32 10.8.34, 6.12.35; Letters between W C Symons and Revd H Lucas dated 21.11.1905, 22.11.05; W de l'Hôpital, *Westminster Cathedral and its Architect*, Hutchinson 1919; *Westminster Cathedral Chronicle*, 8.1923, 3.26, 5.26, 1.27, 5.27, 6.27, 7.27, 1.28, 1.30, 4.30, 5.30, 9.30, 1.31, 1.32, 3.32, 10.33, 1.34, 2.34, 8.34, 10.34, 1.35,7.35; Letter from G Pownall to his daughter dated 13.8.1926; Letters between G Pownall and L H Shattock dated 16.11.1926, 19.11.26, 27.10.27, 9.11.27, 6.5.30, 16.5.30; *The Evening News*, 5.1.1928; *The Daily Chronicle*, 18.3.1930; *The Times*, 22.9.30, 2.2.32, 28.11.33, 3.12.35; Ernest Oldmeadow, *The Mosaics in the Lady Chapel of Westminster Cathedral*, March 1932; Letter from *The Burlington Magazine* to E Hutton dated 5.1.1933; *The Daily Telegraph*, 7.12.1933, 9.1.34, 6.8.34, 18.8.34, 4.12.35, 17.12.35; *The Universe*, 5.1.1934, 6.12.35; *The Burlington Magazine*, 2.1934; Letters between Cardinal Hinsley and E Hutton dated 14.8.1935, 4.9.35, 30.10.35, 31.10.35, 2.12.35, 3.12.35; Letter from Cardinal Hinsley to Bishop Myers dated 2.12.1935; *The Manchester Guardian*, 3.12.1935; *The Evening Standard*, 3.12.1935; *The Observer*, 8.12.1935; Letter from H F Graham (Pownall's solicitors) to Charles Russell & Co (Hinsley's solicitors) dated 15.4.1936; Letter from Charles Russell & Co to Cardinal Hinsley dated 10.7.1936; Edward Hutton's Notes and Papers at the British Institute in Florence; Information from Jane Buxton (Pownall's daughter) 1995-96; Information from Christine Mariutto re Fillipo Mariutto 10.5.2000; Information from Charlotte Moore-Maddelena re Gian Battista Maddelena and from Pia Gambardella re Carlo di Spirt 11.5.2005.

V.5. Russian and Roman

W de l'Hôpital, *Westminster Cathedral and its Architect*, Hutchinson 1919; *Westminster Cathedral Chronicle*, 8.1924, 9.52. 1.54, 3.56, 5.56, 6.57, 1.59, 4.59, 5.59, 6.59, 7.59, 9.59, 10.59, 1.60, 5.60, 6.60, 10.60, 12.60, 4.61, 6.61, 8.61, 1.62, 2.62, 8.62, 4.63, 5.63, 7.63, 8.63, 11.63, 12.63, 3.64, 4.64, 7.64, 2.65; *The Times*, 17.11.1953, 18.11.53, 3.8.56; Letter from Cardinal Griffin to Mgr Collingwood dated 18.12.1953; Letter from H S Goodhart-Rendel to Boris Anrep dated 25.10.1954; Letter from Mgr Gordon Wheeler to H S Goodhart-Rendel dated 5.11.1954; Letters from Boris Anrep to Mgr Gordon Wheeler dated 14.2.1955, 9.5.55, 19.10.59; Note by H S Goodhart-Rendel dated 23.3.1955; Minutes of the Westminster Cathedral Art Committee, 17.5.1955, 25.4.56, 13.11.57; Letters from H S Goodhart-Rendel to Arthur Pollen dated 24.4.1956, 11.5.56; Letter from Mgr Gordon Wheeler to Arthur Pollen dated 28.5.56. *The Pimlico News*, 31.5.1957; Letters between Mgr Gordon Wheeler and Sir John Rothenstein dated 3.1.1961, 10.5.61, 12.5.61; Letter from Mgr Gordon Wheeler to Prof Bodkin dated 7.3.1961; Letter from Mgr Gordon Wheeler to the Westminster Cathedral Art Committee dated 20.6.1961; Camilla Grey, *The Blessed Sacrament Chapel - The Anrep Mosaics*, 1962; Mgr Gordon Wheeler, *Westminster Cathedral*

- *The Blessed Sacrament Chapel Mosaics*, 1962 (Revised by Mgr George Stack, 1998); *A Tribute to Boris Anrep, Westminster Cathedral News Sheet*, 7.1969; J Vulliamy, *Boris Anrep 1883-1969*, Harvane Gallery, Chelsea (exhibition pamphlet), 11.1972; *The Church of the Holy Wisdom of God - Aghia Sophia in London*, 1978; J Vulliamy, *Some Reflections on Mosaic Decoration* in *The Friends of Westminster Cathedral Newsletter*, Autumn 1987; Peter Doyle *Westminster Cathedral 1895-1995*, Geoffrey Chapman 1995; T Dean and J Browne, *Westminster Cathedral: Building of Faith*, Booth-Clibborne 1995; *I Colori della Luce - Angelo Orsoni e l'Arte del Mosaico, Marsilio* Editori 1996; Paul Bentley, *New Mosaics in Westminster Cathedral* in *The Catholic Herald*, 13.6.2003; *Oremus*, 3.2004, 2.05, 9.05; Lois Oliver, *Boris Anrep - The National Gallery Mosaics*, National Gallery, London 2004; John Keyworth, *A Short Tour of the Bank of England, Tablets*, Spring 2008; *The Oxford Dictionary of National Biography*; H S Goodhart-Rendel papers in folders G-ReH/12/1 in V & A Prints Department Library; Information from Aelred Bartlett 2000-2; Information from Paul Bentley 2005; Letter from Paul Bentley dated 11.4.2009.

V.6. Recent Mosaics

Raphael Brown, *The Little Flowers of St Francis*, Doubleday 1958; *Westminster Cathedral Chronicle*, 7.1964, 1.65, 2.65, 11.65, 12.65, 3.69, 6.69; *The Friends of Westminster Cathedral Newsletters*, Spring 1987, Autumn 2004, Spring 2005, Spring 2007, Autumn 2007; Meeting of the Catholic Record Society, 19.11.1988; *Mosaic Matters*, Summer 1992; Peter Doyle, *Westminster Cathedral 1895-1995*, Geoffrey Chapman 1995; *The Times*, 13.6.1997; *Oremus*, 7/8 1997, 7/8.98, 3.99, 4.99, 6.2001, 7/8.01, 3.03, 4.05, 3.06, 11.06, 4.07, 10.08, 12.08, 10.10, 3.11, 4.11, 5.11, 6.11; Correspondence of Christopher Hobbs with Tessa Hunkin and Mosaic Workshop, Westminster Cathedral, and the Cathedral Art and Architecture Committee June 1999-June 2006; Paul Bentley, *New Mosaics in Westminster Cathedral* in *The Catholic Herald*, 13.6.2003: Tessa Hunkin, *Modern Mosaic - Inspiration from the 20th Century*, Quintet Publishing 2003; Information from Walter Bernadin 2003-10; Emma Biggs and Tessa Hunkin, *Mosaic Patterns*, New Holland Publishers 2006; *The Word Made Mosaic - Tom Phillips talks to Ruth Guilding, Apollo Magazine*, 1.2008; *Catholic Record,* 9.2008; *Catholic Life,* 10.2008; *The Tablet,* 8.8.2009; Information from Tessa Hunkin of Mosaic Workshop 2009-10; Information from Leonard McComb RA 9.3.2010; Information from Ivor Davies 2010-11.

Part VI. Makers of the Cathedral

VI.1. John Francis Bentley

Letters from J F Bentley to Charles Hadfield dated 5.7.1895, 16.1.99, 4.2.99, 13.1.1902, 28.2.02 in Peter Howell (Ed), *Architectural History* 25, 1982; *The Tablet*, 6.7.1895, 13.5.99, 17.6.99, 29.12.1900, 8.3.02, 7.6.02, 21.3.03; *The RIBA Journal*, 8.2.1902, 8.3.02, 26.7.02; Death Certificate of J F Bentley 3.3.1902; *The Architectural Review*, 5.1902, 7.02, 3.03; Architectural Association Notes, Jan 1903; Charles Hadfield, *Westminster Cathedral*, Paper read before the Royal Institute of British Architects, 16.3.1903; J A Marshall, Paper read before the Architectural Association 12.4.1907 and summarised in *The Builder*, 20.4. 1907; J G Snead Cox, *The Life of Cardinal Vaughan*, Burns & Oates 1910; Winefride de l'Hôpital, *Westminster Cathedral and its Architect*, Hutchinson 1919; Shane Leslie, *Letters of Herbert Cardinal Vaughan to Lady Herbert of Lea*, Burns and Oates 1942; A S G Butler, *John Francis Bentley*, Burns & Oates 1961; Helen E Smith, *J F Bentley: An Introduction to his Life and Work*, Exhibition Catalogue May 1976; R Bennett and J E Wright, *The Church of Holy Rood, Watford*, Watford 1989; *Westminster Cathedral Bulletin*, 2.1994, 3.94, 4.94; Kenneth Powell, *A Hymn to Byzantium* in *The Architects Journal*, 20.6.1995; *Oremus*, 4.2002.

VI.2. William Brindley

Kelly's London Post Office Directories (Streets, Commercial and Trades), entries for Farmer & Brindley dated 1863, 65, 68, 81, 83, 85, 87, 88, 96, 99, 1908, 24, 29; *The Builder*, 16.8.1873, 12.11.87, 12.5.88, 20.9.90, 14.3.1919 (obituary); William Brindley in *RIBA Transactions* 1887, 88; *The Building News*, 11.4.1890, 19.9.90; W P Lethaby and Harold Swainson, *The Church of Sancta Sophia Constantinople: A Study of Byzantine Building*, Macmillan 1894; William Brindley in *The RIBA Journal*, 1895, 96, 1902-3, 1905, 1907; *Westminster Cathedral Record*, 2.1899; William Brindley, *The Ancient Marble Quarries of Greek Cipollino* in *Stone Magazine* Vol XVIII No 2 1899; *The Quarry and Builders Merchant*, Vol 44 1899; *The Catholic Herald*, 20.2.1903; Mary Winearls Porter, *What Rome was built with*, London 1907; W G Renwick, *Marble and Marble Working*, London 1909; Will of William Brindley, 2.6.1919; *Westminster Cathedral Chronicle*, 10.1919, 1.22, 3.24, 9.28, 9.30; Winefride de l'Hôpital, *Westminster Cathedral and its Architect*, Hutchinson 1919; *Quarterly Journal of the Geological Society*, 1920 (obituary); *Survey of London* Vol XXXVIII, London 1975; Stephen Bayley, *The Albert Memorial*, Scolar Press 1981; Benedict Read, *Victorian Sculpture*, Yale University Press 1982; Royal Commission on Historic Monuments, Vol 17 *County Hall*, Athlone Press 1991; Emma Hardy, *Farmer & Brindley: Craftsmen Sculptors 1850-1930*, in *Victorian Society Annual* 1993; Farmer & Brindley references in Nikolaus Pevsner et al, *The Buildings of England* series; Farmer & Brindley Company Records; Cathedral architectural drawings numbered B-23, B-25, B-28, B-31, B-40, C-8, C-11, C-50, C-52, C-55, D-5, D-9, D-16, D-68, D-83, D-88, F-65, H-4, H-15.

VI.3. Sir Richard Runciman Terry

A Mill Hill Father, *Remembered in Blessing; The Courtfield Story*, London 1869; Letter from Cardinal Herbert Vaughan to Richard Terry dated 22.3.1902; *The Tablet*, 7.6.1902; *Westminster Cathedral Chronicle* (Church Music notes), 2-5.1907, 8.10, 4.13, 6.13, 8.13, 9.16, 8.17, 10-12.17, 2-4.18, 6-12.18, 1-12.19, 1-6.20, 8-12.20, 1-8.21, 10-12.21, 1-4.22, 10-12.22, 1-8.23, 5-7.24; Richard Terry, *Westminster Cathedral Music* in the *Book of the Consecration of Westminster Cathedral* 1910; J G Snead-Cox, *The Life of Cardinal Vaughan*, Burns & Oates 1910; Letter from Cardinal Francis Bourne to Richard Terry dated 10.10.1911; Winefride de l'Hôpital, *Westminster Cathedral and its Architect*, Hutchinson 1919; *The Times*, 19.4.1938; *Westminster Cathedral Chronicle*, 5.1938, 8.55, 10.55; Shane Leslie, *Letters of Herbert Cardinal Vaughan to Lady Herbert of Lea*, Burns & Oates 1942; Hilda Andrews, *Westminster Retrospect: A Memoir of Sir Richard Terry*, OUP 1948; Timothy Day, *A Discography of Tudor Church Music*, British Library National Sound Archives 1989; Peter Doyle, *Westminster Cathedral 1895-1995*, Geoffrey Chapman 1995; *The Oxford Dictionary of National Biography*.

VI.4. John Arthur Marshall

Kelly's London Post Office Directories (Streets and Trades), entries for the Bentley firm 1902-16; *Westminster Cathedral Chronicle*, 3.1907, 1.09, 5.10, 8.10, 12.10, 6.11, 2.12, 3.12, 1.13, 2.13, 4.13, 2.14, 5.14, 12.15, 4.16, 7.16, 9.17, 1.22, 6.22, 7.23, 6.24, 8.25, 9.26, 1.27 (obituary), 1.34; J A Marshall, Paper read before the Architectural Association 12.4.1907 and summarised in *The Builder* 20.4.1907; Letters from J A Marshall to Mgr A Jackman dated 1.12.1912, 1.4.14, and 6.8.19 (enclosing designs for the decoration of Patrick's Chapel); *The Observer*, 17.10.1915; *The Builder*, 5.11.1915; Winefride de l'Hôpital, *Westminster Cathedral and its Architect*, Hutchinson 1919; Letter from J A Marshall to L H Shattock dated 26.10.1926; Death Certificate of J A Marshall 3.1.1927; Eric Gill, *Autobigraphy*, Jonathan Cape 1940; Walter Shewring (Ed), *Letters of Eric Gill*, Jonathan Cape 1947; Robert Speaight, *The Life of Eric Gill*, Methuen 1966; Cathedral architectural drawings B-73, D-1 (folder), D-65, E-5 (folder), F-11 (folder), F-99, F-100, H-8, H-35, H-37.

VI.5. The Bartletts

Westminster Cathedral Chronicle, 3.1956, 6.57, 1.59, 4.59, 6.59, 7.59, 9.59, 10.59, 1.60, 5.60, 6.60, 7.60, 10.60, 12.60, 4.61, 6.61, 8.61, 3.62, 8.62, 1.63, 4.63, 5.63, 7.63, 8.63, 11.63, 12.63, 7.64, 2.65, 2.71; *The Westminster and Pimlico News*, 31.5.1957; Correspondence between Sir John Rothenstein and Mgr Gordon Wheeler dated 12.12.1960, 3.1.61, 10.5.61, 12.5.61; Letter from Mgr Gordon Wheeler to the Westminster Cathedral Art Committee dated 20.1.1961; *The Catholic Herald*, 14.2.1992; *The Tablet*, 14.2.1992; *The Times*, 21.2.1992, 16.11.2000, 7.5.04; *The Independent*, 7.3.1992; *Westminster Cathedral Bulletin*, 4.1992, 5.95, 6.95, 11.95; *The Friends of Westminster Cathedral Newsletter*, Autumn 1992; Letter from Aelred Bartlett to Mgr George Stack dated 25.7.1994; *The Sunday Telegraph*, 15.1.1995; *Oremus*, 7/8.1997, 12.1999, 1.2000, 12.00, 6.04, 7.10; *The Daily Telegraph*, 24.4.2004; Information from Aelred Bartlett 2000-2002.

Part VII. Animals in the Cathedral

VII.1. Thomas More's Monkey

Minutes of the Advisory Committee for the Decoration of Westminster Cathedral, 2.3.1939 - 18.8.1942; *Westminster Cathedral Chronicle*, 7.1940, 2.47, 3.48; *The Catholic Times*, 24.12.1943; Correspondence between Mary Gill and L H Shattock dated 10-11.1946; *The Catholic Herald* (letters), 7.2.1947, 14.2.47, 7.3.47, 14.3.47, 21.3.47; Walter Shewring (Ed), *Letters of Eric Gill*, Jonathan Cape 1947; Robert Speaight, *The Life of Eric Gill*, Methuen 1966; Malcolm Yorke, *Eric Gill, Man of Flesh and Spirit*, Constable 1981; Fiona MacCarthy, *Eric Gill*, Faber & Faber 1989; Graham Greene, *Yours etc, Letters to the Press 1945-1989*, Penguin Books 1991; *Westminster Cathedral Bulletin*, 6.1992, 11.95; Judith Collins, *Eric Gill: The Sculpture*, Herbert Press 1998; John Guy, *Thomas More*, Edward Arnold 2000; Drawing of altarpiece, with monkey, reference UCLA EG 312-314, dated 20-26.7.39, held by the William Andrews Clark Memorial Library, University of California, Los Angeles (UCLA), USA; Drawing of altarpiece, with monkey, inscribed Westminster Cath. St George's Chapel, reredos (revised dr.) 1/8 full size E G 29.7.39, held by John Skelton (Eric Gill's nephew) until his death in 1999.

VII.2. From Lions to Ladybirds

Mgr Canon Joseph Collings, *Westminster Memories* in *Westminster Cathedral Chronicle*, 11.1955; Mgr Canon Francis Bartlett, *Notes for Westminster Cathedral Children's Tours* (undated); E Cobham Brewer, *The Dictionary of Phrase and Fable*, Avenel Books, New York, 1978.

Our Lady of Westminster on arrival in the Cathedral in 1955.

Index